BLACK SCANDAL

Black Scandal

America and the Liberian Labor Crisis, 1929–1936

I. K. Sundiata

ISHI *A Publication of the*
Institute for the Study of Human Issues
Philadelphia

Manufactured in the United States of America

Library of Congress Cataloging in Publication Data:

Sundiata, I K
    Black scandal: America and the Liberian labor crisis, 1929–1936.

    Bibliography: p.
    Includes index.
    1. Liberia—Politics and government—1871–1944. 2. Labor and laboring classes—
Liberia. 3. Slave-trade—Liberia. 4. Liberia—Foreign relations—United States. 5. United
States—Foreign relations—Liberia. 6. Afro-Americans—Politics and suffrage. 7. League
of Nations—Liberia. I. Institute for the Study of Human Issues. II. Title.
DT635.S9   327.666'2'073   79-25601
ISBN 0-915980-96-7

Credits for photo section (between pages 50 and 51)—King: Institute for Liberian Studies,
Philadelphia; Firestone: Free Library of Philadelphia; Moffat: Library of Congress; Detzer:
Women's International League for Peace and Freedom; DuBois: Library of Congress;
Azikiwe: Langston Hughes Memorial Library, Lincoln University.

For information, write:

Director of Publications
ISHI
3401 Science Center
Philadelphia, Pennsylvania 19104
U.S.A.

Contents

A section of photographs appears between pages 50 and 51.

Acknowledgments

This study is the outgrowth of research done between 1969 and 1978 with funds provided partially by a Fulbright-Hays grant, the Northwestern University Program of African Studies, and the Northwestern University Faculty Research Committee. Most information was acquired from archival sources. In Great Britain this involved the Public Record Office, the John Holt Papers, the Methodist Missionary Society, the Baptist Missionary Society, the Church Missionary Society, the Anti-Slavery and Aborigines Protection Society, and Rhodes House, Oxford University. The library of the British Museum was also useful.

In the United States a great body of material was found in the National Archives, the Library of Congress, the New York Public Library, and the Northwestern University Library. The last was particularly helpful, providing me with United States National Archives microfilm relating to Liberia, and with the Grimes, Porte, and Cassell collections of Liberian papers. The Houghton Library of Harvard University, the Phelps-Stokes Archives in New York, the Chicago Historical Society, and the Fisk University Library in Nashville, Tennessee supplied excellent information from the private papers of various persons involved in Liberian affairs.

In Liberia the National Archives furnished invaluable insights into the Liberian perception of the scandal of 1929. Indeed, without the records of the Liberian government, any account of the Black Republic's affairs runs the risk of disregarding the strategies and dilemmas faced by its rulers, thus ignoring one of the central issues of this study—the Liberian response to external pressure.

Research was also done in Spain. Though that country's relationship to the Liberian scandal has hitherto been largely overlooked, the use of Liberian labor in Spanish Guinea must form an important part of any attempt to see Liberian labor migration in this period in its totality. Secondary material was found in the Dirección General de Promoción de Sahara (whose primary documents are unfortunately unavailable for use by scholars) and in the Biblioteca Nacional. I was also given access to the library of the Colegio Mayor Universitario Nuestra Señora de Africa, and on Fernando Po itself (now part of Equatorial Guinea) I obtained limited access to the collection of journals kept by Los Hijos del Immaculado Corazón de María. I also interviewed several prominent residents of Santa Isabel (now Malabo).

I wish to give special thanks to those persons who aided me in my trip to Liberia in the summer of 1978. Dr. Joseph Guannu of the Ministry of Foreign Affairs provided very useful insights into the running of the Liberian National Archives. My friends and colleagues at the University of Liberia, Dr. Zamba Liberty and Dr. Amos Sawyer, were most kind in offering to read my draft manuscript. I greatly appreciated Dr. J. P. Chaudhuri's allowing me to read his dissertation on Anglo-Liberian relations, and I benefited from my conversations, however brief, with Dr. Jane Martin, who has extensively researched settler-indigene relations in Maryland County. Thanks must also go to Ms. Linda Thomas, a fellow researcher during the summer of 1978, and to Mr. Augustine Jallah, the Archivist of the Liberian National Archives. I am grateful to Mr. John Singler, who made my short trip to Robertsport possible.

In the course of this study's very slow evolution, I was especially fortunate to be able to communicate with some of the scholars who have already researched aspects of Liberian history and ethnography. Elizabeth Tonkin and Mary Jo Sullivan were very useful correspondents. Dr. George Brooks and Dr. J. Gus Liebenow, both of Indiana University, and Dr. Frank Chalk pointed out works that I might otherwise have overlooked, and I thank them. More than appreciation is due Dr. Arnold Taylor of Howard University, who lent me photocopies of the J. P. Moffat Papers. Dr. La Ray Denzer very helpfully lent me photocopies of *The Negro Worker*.

The conception of this research project would have been impossible without the help of my fellow Africanists at Northwestern University. I wish to thank Mrs. Margaret Priestley Bax (now at the University of Ghana), who saw the original proposal formulated, Drs. John Rowe and Ivor Wilks, who often provided needed liaison with the Program of African Studies while research was in progress, and Dr. Ibrahim Abu-Lughod, who read a draft and evaluated its worth. I also wish to acknowledge the assistance offered by the two men who have previously done research on Equatorial Guinea, M. René Pelissier of Paris and Dr. Donald Wiedner of Temple University.

I am obliged to those persons who aided my research on the Fernando Po terminus of the Liberian labor traffic. Señora María Asunción de Val of the Dirección General de Promoción de Sahara assisted me greatly in using the Dirección's library and extended very generous photocopying privileges. Gratitude must also be expressed to my oral informants in the Republic of Equatorial Guinea, who patiently answered my questions under the most adverse conditions. Although the amount of material obtained in those interviews was small, it was extremely important in fleshing out the character of the leaders of early twentieth-century Fernando Po. Among those who helped were Mr. Edward Barleycorn, Mrs. Abigail Mehile, Mr. Seraphim Dougan, Mr. Alfredo Jones, and Mr. Stephen Vivour. I also appreciated the help of Mr. Roland Subert, an employee of the United Trading Company on Fernando Po in the nineteen-thirties whom I interviewed in London. Finally, great credit must be given Ms. Carla Lerman, Mr. Bruce Mertes, and Ms. Gail Wright, without whose aid, moral and editorial, this project would never have come to fruition.

Introduction

In June of 1929 the U.S. State Department informed the Liberian government that there had come to its attention disturbing reports about "the so-called 'export' of labor from Liberia to Fernando Po" (then a Spanish island). The reports indicated that the labor system in question was "hardly distinguishable from organized slave trade, and that in the enforcement of this system the services of the Liberian Frontier Force, and the services and influences of certain high Government officials, are constantly and systematically used."[1] So began a scandal that would have worldwide repercussions.

An investigation of Liberia by the League of Nations in 1930 soon revealed that indigenous Liberian workers, mostly from the Kru and Grebo peoples, were being crudely exploited by the Americo-Liberian elite, heirs of the American freedmen who had "founded" Liberia in the nineteenth century. In some quarters it was argued that descendants of slaves were themselves virtually enslaving others, a sign that Liberia— sometimes lauded as a model of black self-government—had "failed" as a nation. Racists equated this "failure" with black incapacity; their attacks, in turn, prompted an outpouring of apologetic literature. The investigation thus became part of a larger debate on the fitness of blacks (particularly Westernized blacks) for self-determination.

Various suggestions were made—some well-intentioned, others not—for protecting the Kru and Grebo by giving foreign nations certain controls over the Liberian government. If these plans had succeeded, Liberian sovereignty would have been diminished, a possibility that infuriated many Afro-Americans. In part their anger was directed at the American government, which intervened in Liberia ostensibly to protect the human rights of black Africans. But the suspicions of Afro-Americans and anti-imperialists were also directed at the Firestone Rubber Company, owner since 1926 of extensive plantation land in the Liberian countryside. They saw Firestone, a representative of American capital, as the prime mover in an effort to tamper with the independence of Africa's lone Black Republic. United States diplomatic intervention thus raised the issues of "dollar diplomacy," the appropriate role of the United States in Africa, and the effect of American capital on what is now called a "developing" nation.

The findings of the League of Nations' Commission of Inquiry had serious repercussions both within and without Liberia. The vice-president and president of Liberia were forced to resign, and for a while it appeared that the hegemony of Liberia's dominant political party, the True Whig Party, would be broken. From 1931 to 1934 the League attempted to formulate and implement a plan to reform the Liberian administration and alleviate those abuses which had sparked the investigation of 1930. The U.S. State Department and the Firestone Rubber Company, as parties with definite interests in Liberia, also sought to pressure the Liberians to make the needed "reforms." To many outside observers the need was underlined by the outbreak of a revolt among the Kru people of the southern Liberian coast and by the international circulation of reports that the Liberian government had a calculated policy of genocide against the Kru. It was not until 1936 that the crisis of the Liberian administration definitely passed. In that year Liberia renegotiated the terms of a 1926 loan agreement with Firestone and thereby, according to critics of U.S. capital, removed one of the most persistent reasons for calls for American intervention. Kru resistance to the government was quelled in the same year and control over the disaffected areas reasserted.

During this crisis of Liberian independence, it was widely charged that since its very birth Liberia had failed egregiously; to understand this reaction we need to look briefly at the history of the Black Republic. Afro-American settlement was sponsored by the American Colonization Society, which sought to transport free or recently manumitted blacks back to Africa in a professed effort to improve their condition. Monrovia, the capital of Liberia, was founded in 1822. The Maryland State Colonization Society established a colony at Cape Palmas (Harper) in 1833, the Louisiana and Mississippi Colonization Societies a settlement at Sinoe (Greenville) in 1837. In the 1840s the colonization society collected funds in the United States for extensive land purchases along the coast. By 1850 the littoral between the Gallinas and San Pedro Rivers (with one small exception) was claimed by Liberia or by the independent settlement known as Maryland. In 1837 all the colonization society settlements except Maryland had joined to form a commonwealth. Ten years later they proclaimed their independence as a sovereign republic.

A decade after that the Maryland settlement was formally incorporated into the new state.

Even early in its history Liberia was seen either as a symbol of black achievement or as a black failure. Because the American Colonization Society included slaveholders among its directors, many Afro-Americans suspected that the society wanted nothing more than to transport unwanted free blacks out of the United States. Others championed the cause of Liberia, basing much of their support on the acknowledged racial subordination of blacks in the United States and the impossibility of blacks ever achieving equality in American society. To many of its champions, such as West Indian born Edward Blyden (1832–1912) or Bishop Henry McNeal Turner (1834–1915) of the African Methodist Episcopal Church, Liberia represented the true unfolding of a racial destiny. In the Black Republic the oppressed former slaves of the New World would at last achieve true manhood. In West Africa they would also greatly further the work of "African redemption." Carriers of Western technology and skills (as well as religion), the emigrants would be the catalyst which would begin to transform indigenous African societies. The despised of one continent would become the saviors of another. Blyden also viewed the process as reciprocal; American blacks, degraded by the experience of slavery, would be reinvigorated by contact with the virile and uncontaminated culture of certain African peoples.

But those blacks who urged Afro-American emigration were opposed by the majority of black leaders, many of whom suspected the aims of the sponsors of Liberia and pointed to the contributions blacks had made to American society as reason for them not to abandon the land of their birth. Frederick Douglass (1817–1895) saw in emigration an evasion of the questions of slavery and racial subordination in America. Martin Delany (1812–1885), who favored emigration to other parts of West Africa, attacked Liberia as a "poor miserable mockery—a burlesque on a government . . . a mere dependency of Southern slaveholders."[2] Throughout the nineteenth century, critics of Liberia pointed to the country's mortiferous climate and its government's dubious dealings with indigenous peoples as reasons for Afro-Americans to remain at home. And most did, apparently wanting advancement within the context of American society. Emigrationist sentiment, rising and ebbing with the fortunes and prospects of blacks in the United States, swelled somewhat in the period immediately preceding the Civil War and again in the post-Reconstruction period of the late nineteenth century. But by 1900 only 15,000 black emigrants (at most) from the United States and little over 300 from the West Indies had emigrated to the Republic of Liberia.[3]

As further evidence of Liberia's failure, critics often cited the settlers' inability to establish a viable economy or fulfill their mission to "redeem" the indigenous peoples. An emigrationist propagandist like Bishop Turner might call Liberia "the place to make money by the bushels if you can raise a little to start with," but most settlers found it hard to sustain themselves.[4] Many found the climate unhealthy, in spite of the American Colonization Society's expressed belief that Afro-Americans could quickly adjust to the West African environment. Moreover, the emigration of Afro-Americans to the West African coast could not help but raise questions about the relationship between settler and indigene. Propagandists for Liberian settlement tended to gloss over the conflicts bound to arise when the newcomers requested land and then labor. Indeed, from the early days of the Liberian experiment armed conflict was a feature of settler-indigene relations. Critics of the Black Republic claimed that emigrants impinged on indigenous lands without taking due account of preexisting land rights. Far from melding with the indigenes, they maintained, the Americo-Liberian community self-consciously went about creating barriers between the "civilized" and the "uncivilized." Visitors remarked on the use of indigenous children in Americo-Liberian households and often compared this system of "apprenticeship" to domestic slavery.

The Liberian scandal originated partly in this creation of a settler community with a fairly precarious means of support. In the early days many of the settlers took to commerce rather than agriculture, developing a good trade in fish and rice between indigenous villages and Americo-Liberian settlements. Cloth, rum, and tobacco were also exchanged for camwood, cane sugar, palm kernels, rice, and some ivory, but the settlers failed to exploit this trade on a large scale.[5] Although a prominent emigrant argued that "civilized men could, with but little difficulty, increase the cultivation of these articles [palm oil, maize, sugar cane, cotton] among the natives, and ship them to traders to their own advantage,"[6] these ventures gained little headway. The same was true for agriculture among the settlers themselves. It has been said that "clearly no attempt at large-scale farming . . . achieved sustained success [in Liberia] in the nineteenth century."[7] There were attempts. In 1835 black Quakers established farms near the mouth of the St. John River. Three years later an agricultural settlement was founded at the mouth of the Sinoe River by freedmen sent out by the Mississippi Colonization Society. In the same year Lewis Sheridan, a North Carolina freedman, was granted a long lease on six hundred acres. Visitors to Liberia in the 1830s often remarked on the extension of farming, and at the end of the next decade an official of the colonization society noted "substantial farmhouses surrounded by well-cleared and cultivated plantations of from ten to thirty to fifty or seventy acres."[8]

But in spite of this early start, agriculture experienced impediments. Local food crops were not attractive to the settlers and the market for cash crops appeared limited. A visitor was told, "Little more is done than to supply ourselves with the necessaries and a few of the conveniences of life."[9] After 1850, however, the possibility of marketing indigenous coffee presented itself. In 1855 Liberia produced under 5,000 lbs. of coffee. After 1869 export rose significantly, partially as a result of the spread of the Ceylon coffee-leaf disease in Asia. In 1892 the country produced over 1,800,000 lbs. and a missionary could comment, "There are at present few male citizens who do not own and operate a coffee plantation."[10] The coffee boom did not last. Liberian producers suffered from competition with Indonesian and Brazilian producers and from failure to rationalize marketing organization. World prices for coffee declined from approximately twenty cents a pound to as low as five cents and the African state's export returned to a level of under 500,000 lbs.[11]

Liberia's economic problems led some critics to conclude that the Western education (sometimes minimal) of the emigrant blacks inhibited their industriousness and self-reliance. The emigrants' life-style and aspirations seemed to militate against an interest in the soil, giving them an effete disdain of agriculture Europeans frequently criticized. Yet the backward state of Liberian agriculture cannot be blamed solely on the mercantile inclinations of the Americo-Liberians. Dearth of labor, laterite soils, and competition in international markets all helped retard the development of export-oriented agriculture. Added to this were obstacles to the employment of African labor—a sparse population, unevenly distributed, socially conservative, and with no demand for cash income.[12]

We may also speculate that the nineteenth-century failure of settler agriculture was related to a lack of military force. Since the settlers were not generally attracted to yeoman farming, some instead sought to replicate the labor-intensive methods of the Old South, but the use of such methods was impeded by the settlers' inability to attract or coerce sufficient labor from the indigenous population. The labor that could sometimes be obtained—such as Africans (Congos) recaptured from slavers and landed at Monrovia—was often expensive. The Americo-Liberians were, until the present century, confined to a coastal strip thirty to forty miles wide. Even here their presence was contested. Not until the early decades of this century, it can be argued, did the balance of force tip decidedly in favor of the settlers, who were then able to "open" the country to wider labor exploitation. In that sense the failure of small groups of settler blacks to prosper at the growing of cash crops may have been due to the lack of coercive means possessed by other settler regimes; the disdain for agriculture may very well relate to the early lack of the Maxim gun and other paraphernalia of "pacification."

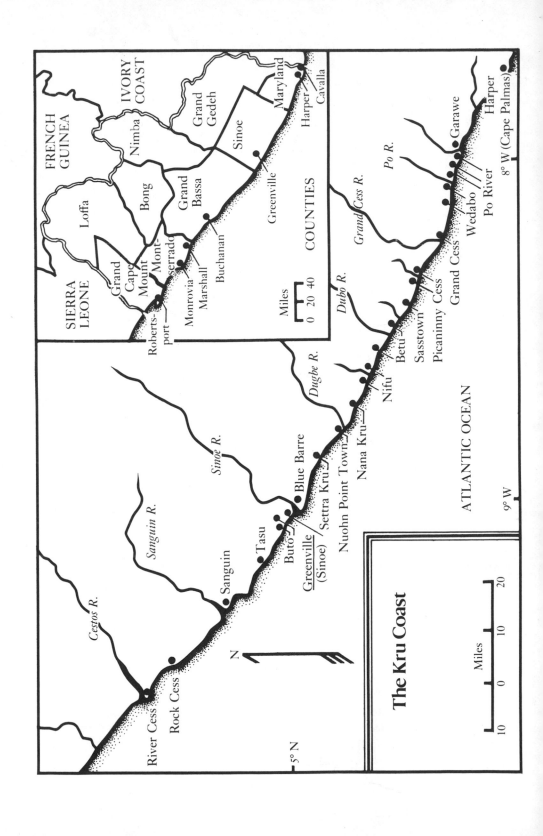

The Kru Coast

Inset map (Counties):

FRENCH GUINEA

IVORY COAST

SIERRA LEONE

Loffa

Bong

Nimba

Grand Gedeh

Grand Cape Mount

Mont-serrado

Grand Bassa

Sinoe

Maryland

Roberts-port

Monrovia

Marshall

Buchanan

Greenville

Harper

Cavalla

COUNTIES

Miles
0 20 40

Main map:

ATLANTIC OCEAN

Cestos R.

River Cess

Rock Cess

Sanguin R.

Sanguin

Tasu

Buto

Blue Barre

Sinoe R.

Greenville (Sinoe)

Settra Kru

Nuohn Point Town

Nana Kru

Dugbe R.

Nifu

Dubo R.

Betu

Sasstown

Picaninny Cess

Grand Cess R.

Grand Cess

Wedabo

Po River

Po R.

Garawe

Harper

8° W (Cape Palmas)

9° W

5° N

N

Miles
10   0   10   20

Despite indigenous resistance, the Afro-American emigrants (Americo-Liberians) organized their settlements into a republic. The coastal settlements were grouped into five counties (Grand Cape Mount, Montserrado, Grand Bassa, Sinoe, and Maryland) with administrative centers at Robertsport, Monrovia, Buchanan, Greenville (Sinoe), and Harper (Cape Palmas). In each of these counties several prominent and interrelated families came to predominate: the Shermans and Watsons in Grand Cape Mount; the Barclays, Colemans, Coopers, Dennises, Grimeses, Howards, Kings, Johnsons, and Morrises in Montserrado; the Harmons and Horaces in Grand Bassa; the Grisbys and Rosses in Sinoe; the Dossens, Gibsons, and Tubmans in Maryland County. The constitution of Liberia was modeled on that of the United States and provided for an executive president and a vice-president who presided over the Senate. The cabinet consisted of seven secretaries: state, treasury, justice, war, interior, public instruction, and postmaster general. Ten senators and twenty-one representatives constituted the legislature at the time of the League of Nations investigation in 1930. The judiciary was made up of a supreme court, with three judges, and four provisional courts. There was also an attorney general and a solicitor-general. Each county had a monthly court and judge, in addition to a justice of the peace. Within the counties the most significant officers—the county superintendent, customs collector, and subtreasurer—were appointed by the president.[13] "Civilized" towns (those largely inhabited by Americo-Liberians) came to be administered by township commissioners (or municipal commissioners, or mayors), appointed by the president, usually, though not always, with the approval of the local citizenry.[14]

In 1930 Liberia's Americo-Liberian population was, perhaps exaggeratedly, estimated at between 10,000 and 12,000. The indigenous population was estimated at between 1,500,000 and 2,000,000 and consisted of at least sixteen ethnic groups.[15] These included the Kpelle, Gola, Loma, Mano, Gio, and Kissi of the Liberian "Hinterland," as well as the Vai, Bassa, Kru, and Grebo of the coast. On the coast, county administration constituted a species of dyarchy. Indigenous communities probably accounted for at least half the total population of the five counties and were ruled by traditional office holders operating under the purview of Liberian authorities. For the most part, the existing pattern of communal land tenure was not changed, although the amounts of land held and the traditional patterns of land use were subject to stresses and strains (including the demand in certain communities for the granting of individual land titles). Traditional officials were vested with authority by the president of the republic, who could intervene in their selection.

The bulk of the indigenous population lived outside the five coastal counties, in the Hinterland. Here a system of Indirect Rule was installed

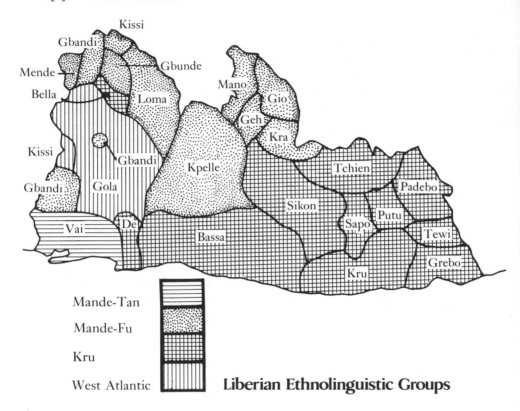

Mande-Tan

Mande-Fu

Kru

West Atlantic

Liberian Ethnolinguistic Groups

in the early twentieth century. In 1911 President Arthur Barclay reminded the legislature that it had never provided bills for the Hinterland's organization and local government. He proposed that the African towns be grouped together into districts similar to the already established counties. The leading families of each indigenous group would govern in their traditional fashion and one chief would be appointed as paramount tribal authority in that area. The use of African customary law would be permitted in indigenous courts. District Commissioners' Courts would hear appeals from the Native Chiefs' Courts and further appeals were to be sent to a County Court of Quarter Session. The adoption of Barclay's plan was an important step in the implementation of Indirect Rule. In 1912 the indigenous leadership was bound together in a Council of Chiefs with the secretary of interior as its presiding official. As time passed, the structure of Indirect Rule became elaborated by the appointment of special commissioners, tax assessors, and station masters.

Barclay created district commissioners to administer the Hinterland districts. Their official function was to maintain law and order, to instill respect for the laws of the republic, to protect chiefs against exploitation by traders and other outsiders, and to encourage farming. It was stipulated that chiefs were to supply the district commissioner with 125 sacks, hampers, or bags of rice and two tins of palm oil each month. "Natives" were to provide labor for the construction of roads, rest homes, barracks, and district commissioners' quarters. They were also to work on "government" farms (holdings which were sometimes indistinguishable from the private farms of the commissioners and other government officials).[16]

"Uncivilized" Africans eventually had to pay hut, poll, and education taxes collected by a chief under the supervision of a district commissioner; the chief, however, was supposed to retain ten percent of all taxes. When called upon to participate in a road-building project in the Hinterland, residents sometimes contributed as much as nine months' *corvée* labor per year, furnishing their own tools and equipment. Moreover, the district commissioners and their aides were in large part inadequately trained and insufficiently and irregularly paid, and this encouraged them to transform their areas into arenas of extortion.

Monrovia's control of the Hinterland was maintained by the Liberian Frontier Force, whose creation was in part a response to British and French encroachment on Liberian borders. In 1907 the legislature passed a bill creating the force, charging it with enforcing the law, guarding boundaries, and aiding surveying expeditions. The Frontier Force's abuse of Indirect Rule was often flagrant, and revolts by Liberia's indigenous peoples marked the early years of the century: Grebo (1910), Kru (1915), Gola (1918), Joquelle Kpelle (1920). Illegal requisitions and the destruction of property, along with forced concubinage of Hinterland women, were frequently reported. By the 1920s the Frontier Force was also active in the forced recruitment of Liberian labor for shipment abroad.

The 1930 investigation of the Black Republic did much to harm its already tarnished reputation. Could blacks in Africa govern themselves? This was the initial and most obvious question. Thus, the fate of Liberia was an important issue for many blacks in the Diaspora, especially for the Pan-Africanists, who campaigned against racial discrimination in Africa and abroad and sought the eventual termination of colonial rule in Africa. Once again, as it had been in the nineteenth century, the Black Republic was the center of a heated debate, a test case of black capabilities. To many, acknowledgment that the Liberian administration could not run its own affairs would have been an admission that African countries, especially West Africans, could never hope to gain independence as sovereign states on the Western model. The attack on Liberia, both diplomatic and journalistic, assumed implications far beyond the fate of the republic itself.

For the historian as well, the Liberian scandal raises important questions. What exactly was the role of Liberia in Pan-Africanist thought in the early 1930s? How did Liberia's position as the one independent African republic affect the attitudes of millions of overseas blacks? Within Liberia itself, how was the ruling group able to weather the challenge presented by the slavery allegations? What changes, if any, did the events of the early 1930s bring to the internal order in Liberia, and to the relationship between the indigenous peoples and the Westernized elite?

The diplomatic intervention of the United States in Liberia was the one notable foray of that power into Africa in the colonial period. American intervention ostensibly was concerned with human rights—an issue with a contemporary ring that seems especially significant in light of the United States' failure to intervene against labor abuse elsewhere in Africa during the colonial period. The question of other motives naturally arises. The Firestone Company's involvement raises the issue of economic imperialism: was this, as many have thought, a major influence on the U.S. government's actions? The lobbying of various groups within the United States poses as another problem the impact of pressure groups on America's African policy.

The tripartite relationship between the United States government, Liberia, and New World blacks is our major focus. It is also hoped that this study will help delineate the nature of American economic penetration into Africa in the twentieth century. As we shall see, any image of American noninvolvement in Africa before the advent of the Cold War is invalid. In its dealings with Liberia the United States displayed the lineaments of neocolonialism well before the invention of the term.

This involvement gives the scandal of 1929 great relevance to the contemporary situation. It is significant that a government which today avoids direct diplomatic intervention in South African labor affairs found it necessary to intervene in Africa's Black Republic forty years ago. It can only be hoped that those who consistently defend the United States' concern with human rights in the Liberian affair will, with the same consistency, urge its extension in contemporary Africa. The precedent exists.

1· The Labor Scandal

Liberia . . . has a treaty with Spain whereby she provides Spain with black labor for Spanish cocoa plantations in Fernando Po at the rate of twenty-five dollars a head. Slavery? Oh dear no! All these laborers are free citizens of a free republic. . . . [Salvador de Madariaga, Spanish delegate to the League of Nations Liberia Committee, in *Americans*, 1930]

As the United States hoped when it sent its note of protest in 1929, Liberia, under pressure, agreed to a League of Nations inquiry into labor conditions. The American member of the commission of inquiry was Charles S. Johnson of Fisk University, a black sociologist and expert on race relations.[1] The man finally chosen as League member and chairman of the commission was an Englishman, Dr. Cuthbert Christy, a medical officer with extensive colonial experience in West, Central, and East Africa.[2] The Liberian member of the commission was former President Arthur Barclay, who, because of his age and infirmity, did not accompany the commission on many of its travels. The Christy-Johnson commission met in Monrovia on April 8, 1930.[3] The labor traffic to the cocoa-producing island of Fernando Po was investigated, the conditions of labor employed in road building and porterage were probed, and evidence was taken on the practice of pawning (an arrangement in which an individual was left as human collateral in return for payment).

The commission's report was completed in September of 1930. It concluded that Postmaster General Samuel Ross, Vice-President Allen Yancy, and others had connived at the forcible export of labor, although the actual presence of "slavery" (i.e., organized slave markets) was not found. The report noted the persistence of the practice of pawning in the

Liberian Hinterland. It characterized Liberia's road-building projects as not well thought out and stated that they were wasteful of labor and demoralizing to the indigenous population. The commission recommended that Liberia (1) abandon its policy of the "closed door" (the discouragement of foreign investment); (2) reestablish the authority of the chiefs; (3) appoint Americans to administrative positions in the government (commissioners, district officers, etc.); (4) declare domestic slavery and pawning illegal; (5) cease the shipment of laborers to Fernando Po and other foreign places; (6) increase discipline over military forces; and (7) encourage Afro-American immigration.[4]

The commission of inquiry was especially censorious of Postmaster General Samuel Ross's forced recruitment of Liberian labor for the Spanish Island of Fernando Po. The investigation of 1930 found that Ross had accepted head monies from European shippers for each worker he delivered to the coast. Ross's political base was Sinoe County, and by the late 1920s his export of labor had involved local political subordinates as well as a clique of prominent Americo-Liberians. In 1928 he negotiated a labor recruiting contract which was signed by two of his sons-in-law (Thomas Pelham and Robert Draper), as well as by E. G. W. King, the brother of C. D. B. King, the president of the republic. It is also known that David Ross, an adopted son of the Sinoe political boss, operated as a labor recruiter.

Ross, who long served in the national legislature, employed the Liberian Frontier Force and the taxation system to coerce labor, even in situations where the indigenous economy clearly could not support such demands. Because public and private interests overlapped, labor procurement often bore the stamp of semilegality. The 1930 commission, for instance, found that in August or September of 1927, Edward Blackett, a quartermaster for the commissioner of Liberian District Number Four in the Hinterland of Sinoe County, was ordered by his superior to procure and deliver to Ross a large number of workers from the towns under Blackett's jurisdiction. Each man was to carry, in addition to his own food, a hamper of rice to be sold. It appears from the commission's findings that both Blackett and the district commissioner were Ross's confederates. The quartermaster arrived with 300 laborers, who were confined in a barracoon in Greenville awaiting shipment to Fernando Po the following day. According to commission testimony the laborers had been observed "en route to the compound of Ross under the escort of soldiers, two soldiers after ten boys." An employee of Ross, Jacob Dennis, testified that, despite the vigilance of the shippers, ten of the "boys" escaped during the night.[5]

In September of 1927 Ross's recruitment methods created an incident which attracted national attention. On September 21, 1927, Blackett was ordered by his district commissioner to take soldiers and capture up to 250 men for delivery to Greenville. In the Sinoe interior, Blackett, according to the testimony of a chief, flogged and bound all who refused to accompany him. On October 5 the quartermaster and his labor contingent arrived on the coast. By chance Blackett's arrival coincided with that of Reginald Sherman, then postmaster general of Liberia, who had come south to inspect the local postal service. Ross requested that Sherman forward a radiogram for him asking permission to send workers by a German steamer instead of the usual Spanish vessel. The message was transmitted, but Sherman, even in the face of a proffered bribe, refused to countenance the forced shipment of men. After inspecting the compound where the workers were kept he sent an indignant radiogram to the attorney general in Monrovia. Ross, for his part, radiogramed the secretary of state, then acting president:

> Sorry P.M.G. [i.e., Postmaster General] visited compound without even Superintendent['s] knowledge and alleges an insult was offered him by one Blackett[,] District Quartermaster, who accompanied boys down. Will have each boy over this morning before Superintendent and P.M.G. and let each boy express his willingness, or not to go to Fernandipo [sic]. Boys all agree to go to Fernandipo rather than return to bush. Local prejudice led by Rev. Cooper Claudius Major and few others are trying to create disturbances. All satisfaction will be given P.M.G. Revoke decision and let boys go. Ross.[6]

The central government ordered the release of all workers who did not agree to go to Fernando Po, but the "Sinoe Incident" betrayed the ambivalence of the Liberian ruling circle on the export of labor. The incident's outcome followed an existing pattern: abuses when exposed were verbally condemned but their perpetrators remained in government service. Sherman's denunciation of the Sinoe labor shipments did result in a court action by certain residents of Greenville, and the subsequent investigation did reveal forced recruitment. Quartermaster Blackett also testified that the rice taken to the coast was sold and the proceeds given to his superior, District Commissioner Watson, who, it was revealed, shared part of the payment for the "boys" with Ross. These disclosures, however, did not lead to Ross's indictment; indeed, the 1930 investigation surmised that Ross had powerful friends in Monrovia and that interference in his recruiting activities would have been politically unwise.[7] An attempt was made to indict Blackett, but a grand jury refused unless the same was done to Ross. In 1928, with the case still pending, Ross was appointed postmaster general to succeed Sherman, the complainant. The county attorney who investigated the case was deprived of office, while the district commissioner involved remained at a post in the Hinterland administration.

Ross's activities demonstrated the control Americo-Liberian politicians had come to exercise over labor migration from the Kru Coast (the southern coast of Liberia) by the early twentieth century. The forced export of manpower, however, had begun as a voluntary flow of migrants; the scandal of 1929 thus had its origins in patterns of African labor migration dating back to the last decades of the eighteenth century.

The people who came to be defined as "Kru" had, since at least the 1780s or 1790s, been employed as paid seamen on European vessels. Although the Kru maintained that they were never slaves and never kept slaves, they were, at various points in the eighteenth and nineteenth centuries, involved in the slave trade as intermediaries, pilots, and interpreters. Many also served on the vessels of the British antislaving squadrons or worked as stevedores in ports such as Freetown in Sierra Leone. Later Kru were employed in a variety of onshore tasks: mining, lumbering, porterage, and plantation agriculture. Laborers from the Kru Coast were with David Livingstone in his trek across central Africa, with the British Niger Expedition of 1841, and with Ferdinand de Lesseps in both his Suez and Panama Canal projects.[8] By the end of the nineteenth century Kru had been employed as far away as the Congo Basin, Namibia, and South Africa. A few had even labored for wages in the Americas.

Several reasons have been given for the outward movement of laborers from the Kru Coast. It has been hypothesized, for example, that demography played a very important role. The presence of a fairly large population on the coast could be related to the red and red-brown tropical soils that increased the agricultural productivity of immigrants to the coast. As the coastal population grew in density and intensified its use of local resources, the peoples of the area may have turned to work beyond the shore. In this sense, the introduction of rice cultivation and an increased number of towns may have been the preconditions for the rise of overseas labor migration.[9] It has also been argued that littoral peoples may have used their numbers and economic position to advantage in establishing links with interior peoples. Trade in fish to protein-deficient interior areas may have strengthened the shore-living communities. By the nineteenth century economic and kinship ties between interior and coastal peoples appear to have been manipulated so as to facilitate the recruitment of laborers from the interior for work on the coast.

Demography may have interacted with the ebb and flow of coastal commerce to produce migration. Beginning in the fifteenth century, the trade in Malaguetta pepper drew some European traders to the coast, and in the eighteenth and nineteenth centuries some ivory was exported. The decline of this commerce in the eighteenth century—especially the trade in pepper—may have stimulated seafaring elements to seek work on other parts of the coast. Some may have turned to employment in the slave trade, which appears to have increased on the Grain and Ivory Coasts in the eighteenth century.[10] The disruption of this trade during the post-1793 Anglo-French wars may have led some male inhabitants of the coast to seek employment in the British antislaving establishment at Freetown.[11]

Beginning in the 1840s Americo-Liberians steadily destroyed the indigenous domination of coastal trade. The settlers, through regulation of labor recruitment and taxation of returning migrants, sought to turn the preexisting pattern of labor migration to their own benefit. As early as the "Fish War" of 1838 between the Americo-Liberians settled at the mouth of the St. John River and local Kru, it had been obvious that settler claims to the coast would not be uncontested.[12] But the settlers had another advantage; indigenous groups migrating to the coast were aware that the aid of the Liberian government could be obtained against recalcitrant coastal inhabitants. Where such alliances were successful, the coastal groups were frequently driven into the interior and their lands given to the government's "native allies."

An 1865 Port of Entry law limited labor export and trade to six Americo-Liberian settlements: Robertsport (Cape Mount), Monrovia, Marshall, Buchanan, Greenville (Sinoe), and Harper (Cape Palmas). The Kru and Grebo, the main groups migrating from the coast, protested that these settler attempts to derive economic benefit from traditional patterns of employment imposed heavy burdens.[13] For their part, the Liberian government charged that embarkation and disembarkation of migrant workers was "the cloak for a gigantic system of wholesale smuggling" and ordered vessels to deal with laborers at the designated ports only. This arrangement was to the disadvantage of the Kru and Grebo, many of whom were forced to walk coastwise some distance from their homes. The Americo-Liberian attempt to regulate trade, along with the land hunger of the settlers, was a constant irritant. In 1875 war broke out between the Monrovia government and the Cape Palmas and Cavalla River Grebo peoples. The confrontation produced an abortive attempt at unity among the Grebo; groups from Grand Cess to the San Pedro River (in the Ivory Coast) formed themselves into the Gebebo Re-United Kingdom, a political union influenced by the example of the Fanti confederation in the Gold Coast. United States military support enabled the Liberian government to put down the "revolt," but the restitution of peace did not bring any significant lessening of tension. In 1893 the Americo-Liberians, this time with the aid of the Cape Palmas Grebo, declared war on the Cavalla Grebo groups on the pretext that customs laws were being violated. In 1910, however, Cape Palmas Grebo again collided with the Monrovia government, in part over land policies and dislocations resulting from previous wars.

In 1908 President Arthur Barclay had tried to allay some of these tensions by creating a commission to investigate and deal with complaints of Grebo migrants on the payment of customs. It decided that certain goods brought in by returnees should be duty free. As a further concession, an educated Grebo was appointed to assist in assessing duties in Harper (Cape Palmas).[14] The 1908–09 session of the Liberian legislature reduced the tax on exported labor from $5.00 per person to $4.00 "because the natives of Maryland County who form the majority of labourers usually shipped from the country have made known to the Government that the taxation of five dollars per head on each labourer shipped, together with the increased duty of their various articles brought home is a grievance and a burden on them."[15] Unfortunately, this act was ignored by Maryland officials, and Grebo migrants continued to pay both the old tax and duties on all goods brought into the country, calculated on the basis of usually higher local prices—altogether, a large percentage of their foreign earnings. Customs officials reportedly also charged excessive duties on desirable articles, keeping them for themselves when workers were unable to pay. Workers' belongings, ordered left overnight on wharves, reportedly were pilfered by customs inspectors. Despite Barclay's attempted reforms, in 1910 Paramount Chief Zula Gyude wrote the United States government and the American Colonization Society complaining that the Cape Palmas Grebos remained targets of unjust exactions.[16] Not content with manipulation of customs regulations, the Liberian administration also taxed the foreign users of Kru labor, collecting head monies from European shipping firms before the laborers left Liberia.

The expropriation of workers' profits continued into the 1920s and beyond. Many laborers were recruited in Monrovia, where a "Krutown" had emerged. In 1928 it was reported:

> On his return from a boat, the Kru boy pays one shilling into a municipal fund, used by the Krutown Governor to construct public works, including an "Executive Mansion" to house himself. The Governor also imposes a sanitary tax of three and a half shillings. The Central Government collects light and poll taxes, so that together with the exactions of the boat headman and "gifts" made to the Governor, the Kru boy is lucky if he escapes with half of his earnings.[17]

In 1931 the people of Sasstown on the Kru Coast complained: "To be sure the average duty levied on the value of each Kroo box [containing the laborer's earnings] is estimated at over £6. No consideration is made of the allowances laid down in the Customs Regulations."[18]

In the nineteenth century two of Liberia's most important exports had been coffee and labor. By the 1920s coffee had become relatively unimportant, but the export of manpower had burgeoned into a major source of revenue for the Liberian government and for individual politicians. Part of the impetus behind the labor shipments, as far as the government itself was concerned, was the country's chronic need of funds, a situation that international loans in 1871 and 1906 had not remedied. A new loan, negotiated in 1912, had made the republic subject to an international receivership responsible for managing its revenue. The First World War injured the German-dominated Liberian economy, and attempts to reach financial agreement with the Bank of British West Africa and the American government produced no permanent results.[19] By 1922 Liberia was faced with the prospect of bankruptcy. Labor was one of the few available sources of revenue for a government apparently plunging toward its financial nadir. Thus, the Liberian policy on the Kru Coast did not seek to make the indigene a wage laborer in the national economy so much as simply to make a profit from the export of his services. Since the settler population could not, in any event, afford to hire many laborers, it followed the same policy as parts of Portuguese Africa—the use of unpaid labor within the country combined with the export of labor as a principal source of income.

In this economic climate, Samuel Ross's labor recruiting activities had flourished long before the 1930 investigation. Most of Liberia's labor migrants came from Sinoe and Maryland counties (after the mid-nineteenth century they were often indiscriminately referred to as "Kroo-men," "Crew-men," or "Kru-boys" regardless of whether they were Bassa, Kru, or Grebo). Sinoe, Ross's base, encompassed most of the Kru Coast and was also the county with the sparsest settler population. By the opening of the twentieth century it was already evident that certain local politicians viewed the county as a satrapy, geographically and politically removed from close supervision by Monrovia. Samuel Alford Ross was the son of Georgia-born J. J. Ross, the county's dominant political figure in the late nineteenth century, a man who, on several occasions, felt confident enough to challenge the national executive. The elder Ross served as a judge, county superintendent (thrice), senator, and vice-president of the republic from 1896 to 1899.[20] He died in the latter year, but Samuel continued the political tradition of his father. Charles Johnson of the League of Nations commission described the younger Ross as the "huge, black and genial political boss in Sinoe County" who had "at various times . . . been lawyer, preacher, and merchant and at all times a shrewd politician. . . ."[21] Ross sought not only to derive profit from the preexisting flow of labor, but also to use the police power at his command to coerce an increasingly reluctant labor force to migrate. Ross's policies, and those of his southern colleagues in Maryland County, were not always consonant with national policy. At times when politicians in the northern counties attempted to prohibit the egress of "native" manpower on the grounds that it was needed for internal development, Ross doggedly persisted in attempts to maximize the outflow of labor from the area under his control.

As early as 1896, Ross, already a prominent member of the Americo-Liberian community in Sinoe, attempted to use an interethnic dispute on the Kru Coast to coerce money and belongings from a group near Blue Barre.[22] His "Native Policy" often encountered resistance, resistance which the Sinoe politician ruthlessly suppressed. In 1911 he lynched a Kru chief for supposedly aiding rebels, then hanged five other local officials without trial. An underlying source of tension between the administrator and the local people was a 1905 order from Monrovia making the town of Settra Kru a Port of Entry. The superintendent, apparently fearing that expansion of local trade options would divert part of the labor traffic and the produce trade from his control, blocked the central government's decision. Liberian officials on their way to Settra Kru were detained in Greenville when they arrived, and no further effort was made to open that town to trade. The residents were enraged and engaged in acts of defiance. In response, in 1910, Ross, now a senator, fined Settra Kru some three thousand dollars. Because the people were unable to pay, a detachment of the Frontier Force sacked the town, taking payment in the forms of produce, cattle, and women.

In order to obtain redress for a number of grievances, the Kru sent a long petition to the United States government in 1912. The Kru of Settra Kru asked the United States to intervene on their behalf to put an end to Ross's imposed trade embargo. In November of 1912 disturbances broke out at River Cess, also in Sinoe County. A year later the American minister in Monrovia warned: "The Krus have profound contempt for Liberian Officers and know of their lack of skill and military stamina. . . . The Kru Coast is destined to give the Liberian Government a great deal of trouble in the near future."[23] Two years later the minister said, "The natives despise the Americo-Liberians and feel fully capable of defeating the armed forces of the government if American . . . support is withheld. They keep well informed of the conditions of the government at all times."[24] In 1915 sporadic fighting was reported on the Kru Coast: in June the towns of Grand Cess and Picaninny Cess fought each other, in September Kru from River Cess to Betu rose in revolt. Their grievances included resentment against the exactions of Liberian officials and the imposition of a hut tax at a time of trade depression (the

World War); but the immediate cause of the rebellion, according to Kru interviewed by American commissioners, was Ross's decision to enlarge the labor pool.[25]

The Kru hoped the British would aid them in their struggle against Americo-Liberian rule, but the British consulate tersely discouraged this idea: "You have been told by me before," said the consul, "to live peacefully and do your duty to the Liberian Government whose subjects you are. . . . I have told you that when trouble or misunderstanding came you should come to Monrovia quietly and respectfully and ask the Liberian Government to put things right for you. . . ." The rebels were told that they should expect no aid from the British government and that the consulate would receive no more letters from them.[26] (Nevertheless, in early 1916 the American minister accused the British, despite denials, of landing ammunition on the Kru Coast.)

Without modern arms the Kru proved no match for the Frontier Force, backed as it was by an American war vessel. The Kru were defeated, the chiefs of the warring tribes hanged, a number of prisoners killed. The government then tried and sentenced at least sixty-two Kru leaders to death for treason. President Howard commuted forty-seven of the sentences, but his clemency (life imprisonment) did not become known in Greenville until all but twenty of the men had been executed. A Kru later testified that all "natives" who were on the coast at the time of the revolt were suspect: "In the land of the Kru chiefs the principal question was 'where were you—were you in Sierra Leone, or Lagos, or where?' That was the principal question. If he said, 'yes, I was in Liberia', then he was pretty guilty. . . ."[27] In Sinoe County the reprisals caused considerable alarm. The people appealed to Colonel James F. Cooper for leniency. President D. E. Howard supposedly was dissuaded from such a course by Secretary of State C. D. B. King, who advised, "Bad sore requires hard medicine."[28]

The punishment of the Kru was completed by disarming them, a regulation later extended to all tribes within the republic. At the end of 1916, the American minister observed that "the [Kru] coast is now in the hands of and under the control of the [Liberian] Government for the first time since its existence."[29] This breaking of Kru resistance marked the last major outbreak of violence before Ross's death in 1929. But the end of the Kru War of 1915 did not bring any lessening of exactions; on the contrary, it paved the way for the increase of exactions that eventually contributed to the scandal of 1929.

Another labor exporter named in the League's investigative report was Allen Yancy, superintendent of Maryland County from 1920 to 1928. Yancy was born in Cape Palmas (Harper) in 1881, the son of a Georgia preacher. As a resourceful son of immigrant parents, he had a variegated career that was a study in upward mobility. His political life began in 1905 when he was appointed justice of the peace. In the 1910 war between the Americo-Liberians and a section of the Cape Palmas Grebo, Yancy chose to be neutral, even though he was a captain in the Liberian Guard, a stance which allowed him to repair guns for the Grebo (he had married a Grebo woman in 1902) and make a healthy profit. He was later persuaded to take up his duties as an officer, but expressed an unwillingness to participate in warfare; his company mutinied and fled in the face of a Grebo attack. Finding himself opposed by both his fellow Americo-Liberians and the Grebo, he reportedly attempted to leave the country for the Gold Coast, and narrowly missed execution.

Yancy then devoted himself to business, managing a store for the English trading firm Woodin and Company. He became a good friend of future President Edwin Barclay and in 1918, with Barclay's aid, was appointed county attorney of Maryland. Two years afterwards he became superintendent of Maryland; seven years later he was elected vice-president. The year of the League investigation the British consulate in Monrovia sanguinely analyzed Yancy's prospects: "Said to be active, intelligent and fairly honest in his commercial transactions. . . . Will probably run for President at the next election as the official candidate of the True Whig party."[30]

During his superintendency of Maryland County, Yancy behaved much like his northern counterpart, Ross. Head monies were collected from European shippers for his benefit and that of his colleagues. By 1929 he reportedly had spread the profits of his activities to several prominent citizens: County Superintendent Brooks, Senator William Tubman, Senator Dossen, and three members of the House of Representatives (Dunham, Macborough, and D. B. Cooper). The district commissioner of District Five in the Maryland Hinterland also benefited from Yancy's export of labor.[31]

In the years preceding the labor scandal Yancy exploited disputes between indigenous groups to his own advantage in the labor trade. The 1924 incident of the Wedabo people is a case in point. Early in the century the Wedabo became involved in a disagreement with the Po River people, a small group, of Kru origin, living between the Garawe people and a shore-living section of the Wedabo.[32] After the turn of the century the Po River and Wedabo peoples had agreed on a *modus vivendi* which provided the Wedabo, most of whom lived inland, with access to the sea and to the seaport of Harper (Cape Palmas). In 1908 this accord received the legal sanction of the "civilized" courts, as well as traditional reconfirmation. However, the pact was not always observed; between 1908 and 1923 seven Wedabo were killed while en route to or from the sea. The Wedabo appealed to Yancy, but received little satisfaction; supposedly they were told: "You Wedabo people are damn fools. When you see people are killing you why don't you do something to them instead of always complaining?"[33]

When three Po River people were killed in a 1923 dispute, the Wedabo took their first step toward entanglement in Yancy's web of labor recruitment. A district commissioner summoned Wedabo Paramount Chief Tuweley Jeh. Sixty subchiefs were detained while Chief Jeh was sent home to collect £100. After Chief Jeh's payment to the district commissioner, Superintendent Yancy heard of the affair and ordered the matter referred to him. Jeh was told he needed legal counsel and three lawyers were recommended, among them Senator, and later President, William Tubman. The superintendent reportedly told Jeh to "go back and bring [the] lawyers' £100."[34] However, when the matter reached court Yancy allegedly said the sum already delivered (£100) would not cover the fees. Again the paramount chief returned home, and it was resolved to borrow the required funds from a European trading firm. Three hundred pounds sterling were so borrowed and turned over to Yancy. Jeh was then informed he had won his case. However Yancy demanded and got a further £60 for his good offices.

But the Wedabo matter was not concluded. The Po River people were dissatisfied and sent a delegation to President C. D. B. King, who ordered Jeh to Monrovia. To defray his travel expenses he was authorized by his people to approach the Woodin Company for a £100 loan. Yancy intervened to negotiate the loan. The Chief received only £20; among other things, £40 had been given to Senator Tubman for his legal services, and £25 had been paid to an Americo-Liberian interpreter. In Monrovia, Chief Jeh was subject to further exactions. The president of the republic demanded the payment of a fine of £300, plus the surrender of the murderers of the Po River people. To insure payment, the Wedabo paramount was retained as a hostage. Again Yancy intervened, offering to advance the money if the Wedabo would produce men for shipment to Fernando Po. A council of chiefs balked at the suggestion, but was forced to comply by Yancy's threat to saddle the group with still another fine. A consignment of 500 men was demanded and a Spanish ship sent to Wedabo Beach. Unfortunately, the men were not present on its arrival, and Yancy threatened to burn two towns if they were not produced. Townspeople were taken as hostages, and by daybreak 316 men presented themselves for shipment. Later, after the Wedabo had supplied the full complement, Jeh's ransom was paid and he was permitted to return home with the proviso that those guilty of clashing with the Po River people be bound over to Yancy.[35] His return coincided with a new demand for 200 workers. The Wedabo leader demurred and Yancy dispatched a force to take the men and discipline the chief. The League's commission of inquiry heard evidence that the Liberian Frontier Force attacked the town of Julucan, where they seized twelve old men, flogged and tied them, slaughtered animals, and demanded a payment of £10. The elders were marched to a neighboring town and then delivered to Yancy in Harper, where they were held pending the delivery of 200 laborers. Afterwards they were taken to the superintendent's farm, where they were set to work cleaning coffee and cassava, carrying sticks, and making lines for rubber trees. The hostages remained on Yancy's estate for approximately two months, by which time a full labor contingent had surrendered.

Labor recruitment under the auspices of Yancy and his subordinates had a marked effect on the Wedabo people. Of 700 Wedabo men shipped in 1924–25, the League of Nations' 1930 report said that many died and others returned with very little money. In 1930 in Soloken, the major Wedabo town, there were thirty percent more females than males in a population of 651.[36] Of the families remaining ninety-one had members who either had died on Fernando Po or for some reason had failed to communicate with or return to their homeland. Of the returnees, two were ill and one was insane. Notably, in spite of the reduced population, the hut tax assessment on the village was not lessened.[37]

Yancy and Ross and their confederates controlled only one terminus of the Liberian labor traffic. On the workers' destinations—for most of them, Fernando Po; for a few in the later years, French Gabon—the League's 1930 report had little to say. But in the aftermath of the "slavery" revelations many asked whether the Spaniards, and to a lesser degree the French, had clean hands in the matter of labor export. An American journal noted that "the Liberians do not export slaves without inducement, and in this case the inducement apparently comes from Spaniards at Fernando Po."[38] An Associated Negro Press news release pointedly questioned the silence on the role of Spain and France in the labor traffic and said that "when the League delegates learned that France and Spain were the nations to be censured, the matter was dropped—there was not even a suggestion that Paris and Madrid be asked to explain."[39] An article in The Crisis, the journal of the National Association for the Advancement of Colored People, echoed these sentiments, saying that Spain and France deserved "quite as much censure as the Liberian Government. After all it was they who demanded the enslaved labor which was supplied." If these countries were not also judged, the whole proceeding would be "a piece of smug hypocrisy."[40] The Nigerian nationalist Benjamin Nnamdi Azikiwe marveled at "the irony of it all." He found it strange that the "so-called commentators on

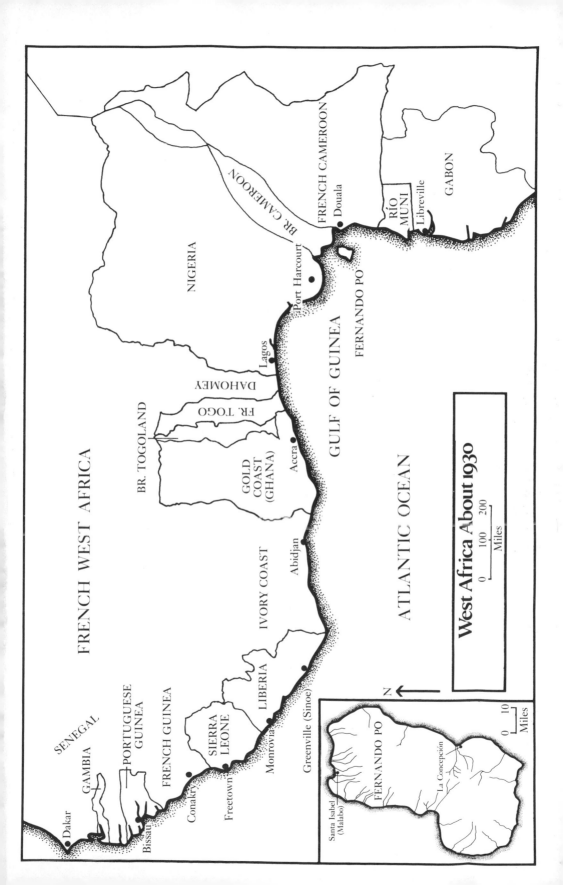

West Africa About 1930

Liberian affairs have failed to drag Spain, in unequivocal terms without mincing their words, into this international debacle." On the contrary, he acerbically noted, they had "docilely made Liberia the scapegoat and whitewashed Spain, thereby strengthening my conviction that a flea will always make a skating rink out of a bald man's head!"[41]

Indeed, the voracious demand for Liberian labor abroad (especially on Fernando Po) encouraged the ruthless labor recruitment policies followed in Sinoe and Maryland counties. Liberia's lack of an important export crop also fostered the export of manpower itself. Attempting to maintain a place for its coffee in the international market, the Liberian government could not avoid an awareness that the colonial powers valued Liberia's labor far more than the declining product of its soil. That the government sought to benefit from both is evident in these observations of a Britisher shortly after World War I:

> The Government have . . . without giving any notice, pounced upon the tribal Chiefs for hut and other taxes; they having had no time to prepare payment for these claims in kind, the officials sent up, under escort of a detachment of the Liberian Frontier Force, not only confiscated their cattle, grain, etc., but brought down as hostages numbers of their boys who were relegated to work, for no payment, on the Liberian Coffee Estates for some time, then shipped to Fernando Po, for which the Liberian Government received £5 per head head-money from the Spanish Government.[42]

In 1914, with Liberia pressed as always for revenue, President D. E. Howard had signed an intergovernmental labor agreement with the governor-general of Spanish Guinea, which included the cocoa-producing island of Fernando Po. The accord offered the Liberian government head monies for laborers shipped to the cocoa plantations and promised as well to safeguard the workers' well-being. The agreement with Spain provided that there should be a Liberian consul in Santa Isabel, the capital of the island. It authorized labor recruitment in selected Liberian ports by agents under the supervision of the Spanish consul in Monrovia.[43] Liberia would select four recruiting agents and planters from Fernando Po who could go to Monrovia to make arrangements with the Liberian authorities. Copies of the labor contracts would be given to the Liberian customs, the Liberian secretary of state, and the Liberian consul-general on Fernando Po. Each statement would contain the name, county, town, district, tribe, chief, and period of contracted labor of the worker. The statement was to be presented to the labor agent in Liberia three days before the transportation of the laborers to Fernando Po. The maximum period of a contract was two years and the minimum was one year; workers were to be refused to employers not approved by the governor of Fernando Po and the Liberian authorities. Labor was to be refused to insolvent farmers; contracts would not be subject to extension and wages were to be paid in English money, one half on Fernando Po and one half through the Spanish consul upon the worker's return to Liberia. The labor agreement itself was subject to termination by either country on six months' notice.

For the agriculturists of Fernando Po the agreement was economically burdensome, but as long as it delivered labor, the island's black and white planters stood to gain. Thousands of laborers were shipped under the 1914 convention; between 1919 and 1926 a known 4,268 were recruited and employed on the island. The 1930 Christy-Johnson commission calculated that, averaging 600 a year, the total number from 1914 to 1927 was at least 7,268 (a calculation which seems to fall well below the number one would expect).[44]

Imported labor was dear, especially for the smaller producers: in 1915 the Primitive Methodist Mission on Fernando Po reported that economic conditions were acute, and that "the cost of each worker has increased alarmingly during the recent years both in Government demands and standard of wage, together with increase in rations."[45] Moreover, the exigencies of the First World War endangered the shipment of laborers from Liberian ports. A decree of July 15, 1918 authorized the reengagement for two years of workers who had completed their contracts.[46] But early the next year Liberia proposed to terminate the agreement entirely after six months—according to the American minister in Monrovia because of reports of labor abuse on Fernando Po. He noted "a well defined feeling among Liberian officials that most of the complaints of the laborers have some foundation in fact."[47] There was another defect in the working of the convention—the unwillingness of Spanish ships to land laborers at any place other than Monrovia. The agreement was also looked upon as depriving Liberian planters and "tribal farms" of labor. The minister observed:

> There is a great deal that might be said both for and against this agreement. Whether its advantages outweigh its disadvantages or vice versa is a matter which could perhaps only be determined with any degree of accuracy after a very careful investigation. If the agreement is terminated the Republic will lose, I am advised, about $10,000 per year as head money revenue. It may be that the Spanish government will make some substantial concessions to Liberia in order to keep the agreement alive, as it appears that it is of vital interest to Spanish planters to have a source of labor supply outside the colony of Fernando Po.[48]

In any event, the Hispano-Liberian labor convention continued beyond 1919 and so did stories of labor abuse. In 1920 the British consul on Fernando Po noted that "the law is carried out in a very slack way. . . ."[49] Criminal offenses were supposedly punished with excessive cruelty and police brutality allegedly was rampant. In 1921 Britain launched an investigation of these conditions when a Sierra Leonean, Kaba-Limba, was severely flogged after being accused of robbing the house of the widow of a prominent planter.[50] The flogging caused the acting British vice-consul to lodge a protest and the affair eventually reached the ambassadorial level; in August of 1921, a protest was made in Madrid. In 1922 another case arose when Tommy Timini, a Sierra Leonean recruited in Liberia, was not paid and complained to the Liberian vice-consul on Fernando Po. Timini was an employee of the black planter Joseph Dougan and the British vice-consul noted that he "was surprised to hear from the Curador [Spanish labor officer] himself that Mr. Dougan is anything but the gentlest of masters. He is at the present 'under going' a fine for ill-treatment to boys."[51]

In 1921 an act of the Liberian legislature directed the Liberian president to give six months' notice that shipment of laborers from Montserrado County and the territories of Grand Cape Mount and Marshall would be prohibited.[52] Though next year full-scale labor traffic to Fernando Po was renewed, the supply of labor continued to be sporadically interdicted. An upswing in the Liberian economy in the latter part of 1923 made it possible, perhaps, for Monrovia to adopt a more critical attitude to the labor convention. Tariff revenues were up and the import-export balance began to shift in the republic's favor, although government customs revenues did not reach their prewar level.[53]

In 1925 the Liberian legislature prohibited the shipment of laborers from the county of Grand Bassa, but Fernando Po planters, with the consent of certain Liberian politicians, continued to cajole labor from other areas of Liberia. In February of 1925, this symbiotic and exploitative relationship was ruptured when the Liberian consul on Fernando Po was arrested after a minor altercation; the labor trade came to a halt. In response to the detention of its consul, Liberia demanded £500 sterling, one half of which was to be paid by July 18, 1925. The island's planters themselves collected the indemnity and gave it to their government for transmission to Liberia. The affair played havoc with the island's precarious economy; no laborers were sent to Fernando Po in 1925 and only forty were sent in the first six months of 1926.[54]

In June of 1926, the governor-general of Spanish Guinea ordered the military subgovernors in Río Muni (the miniscule Spanish colony north of Gabon) to intensify the recruitment of workers for service on Fernando Po.[55] Employed for a period of two years, they averted agricultural disaster; their labor was urgently needed if lands already in cultivation were to be maintained, and if expansion, even on a limited scale, was to continue. In 1927 only 80,000 of Fernando Po's 2,500,000 hectares were under cultivation and it was estimated that 40,000 workers from Río Muni would be needed to put the maximum amount of land into cocoa production.[56] In 1928 the majority of the workers on Fernando Po were from Río Muni, but this supply of labor was not assured.[57] It was threatened supposedly by a declining birth-rate occasioned by the absence of men from home and by an increased demand for labor within Río Muni itself.

Liberian labor, then, was still desperately needed on Fernando Po, and pronouncements from Monrovia gave little indication of willingness to cooperate in the old way. Rumblings were already evident in the Liberian press in February of 1925. The *Agricultural World*, commenting on the visit to Liberia of the governor-general of Spanish Guinea, said, "We would drop this hint just here . . . that unless we see more of our boys returning home when the time for which they [were] shipped is out, . . . certain steps will be taken to put an end to the labor shipping contract, if this part of the Agreement is not satisfied. . . ."[58] A year later the *Liberian News* both assured and threatened the planters of Fernando Po that the labor demands of the American Firestone Company would have no effect on the shipment of workers as long as "our boys are treated more humanly [*sic*] than heretofore by the authorities at Fernando Po."[59] In March of 1926 the president of Liberia visited the island and explained to its planters' association that Liberia was about to embark on a vast program of internal development, a message amplified in an address to the Liberian legislature the following October. The president's statements implied a future termination of the labor traffic; again the island faced the prospect of uncollected cocoa harvests and financial ruin. This prospect seemed real when in late 1927 the Liberian secretary of state terminated the labor agreement of 1914 without six months' notice.[60]

This rupture, like its predecessors, caused consternation in Spanish Guinea. Liberia apparently had Fernando Po at its mercy, and before agreeing to a new convention, it sought a preferential tariff for its coffee and other produce. The Spanish colonial regime, for its part, attempted to escape from its predicament by attracting permanent Liberian settlement. Liberian Secretary of State Edwin Barclay heard of this maneuver and commented to the Liberian consul on Fernando Po, "It would seem to me to argue a very low estimate of the Liberian Government's intelligence if the Spanish Government have the slightest idea that they could put such a [worker settlement] scheme over."[61] He correctly noted that the island was at the mercy of Monrovia's labor policies.

In defense of their interests the planters of Fernando Po hung on tenaciously. Two representatives, one black and one white (Edward Barleycorn and Emanuel Gonezrosa), were sent to Monrovia to arrange for the continuance of some sort of labor flow.[62] At first the prospects for a private agreement did not appear bright. The Liberian secretary of state took the position that he "could not negotiate with a private organization on a question of this nature unless there existed a general treaty of amity between the two States which would guarantee the rights of our citizens laboring in the Spanish possession."[63] But the Fernando Po interests were desperate for labor and willing to pay well, a fact appreciated by Senator Ross. A private agreement was soon entered into between a group calling itself the Sindicato Agrícola de Guinea and a group of Liberian citizens headed by Ross.[64] The Liberian group included the brother of President C. D. B. King (E. G. W. King), as well as two of Ross's sons-in-law.[65] The Sindicato promised to pay the Liberian recruiting agents for 3,000 laborers at £9 each. It also promised to provide transportation and a bonus of £1,000 for each 1,500 laborers shipped. A Spanish ship would call at Greenville and Harper to pick up laborers. Ross and his associates were to use the £9 to pay various imposts (head monies, taxes, etc.).[66] The agreement went into effect April 12, 1928, and it was as fraught with difficulties as was the previous accord of 1914.[67] The Spanish consul complained that Ross demanded the payment of £900 for the transportation of certain workers from Monrovia to Greenville, since such transport was prohibited from Montserrado County. Ross, for his part, maintained that he previously had paid out of his own pocket for the transshipment of workers and threatened that no more workers would be forthcoming unless the Spaniards made payment.[68]

Ross paid $2.50 per head into the Liberian treasury,[69] which gave the national government an interest in the Greenville labor operation at a time when it was experiencing great difficulty in controlling and profiting from the migration of laborers. In March of 1928 the secretary of the interior had attempted to regulate recruitment in Monrovia and the attempt had backfired. By then almost all headmen for ships and most Kru ship laborers were recruited in Monrovia or Freetown. In an effort to ward off a threatened strike over wages, working conditions, and dishonest headmen, the secretary told the agents of steamship lines that they must supply lists of headmen they were willing to employ. From this list the Liberian government would solicit those who would be allowed to work. The government also offered to blacklist any headman who might foment a strike. But the proposal met with opposition from the shippers, who jealously guarded their right to choose headmen who would not question company policies and rates of pay. The Holland Line, the American West African Line, and the Elder Dempster Line all agreed to recruit their headmen in Freetown. The German Woermann Line, the largest employer of Liberian ship labor, joined the boycott in May.[70] The shippers' boycott encouraged the national government to look to Ross's activities as a source of compensatory revenue, a step which was soon to have severe international repercussions.

Samuel Ross was not alone in the 1928 labor shipments; Allen Yancy became a subcontractor. The two men, their associates, and their subordinates were in their heyday in the years immediately preceding the 1930 investigation. The lucrativeness of the labor export created some jostling between them; in 1929 the American minister in Liberia reported: "I have to admit that Ross and Yancy don't get on well together. . . . Ross has tried to corner the market. The Spanish consul has told me he does not like Ross, but thinks Yancy a gentleman."[71] Yancy widened his labor-exporting activities by sending laborers to French Gabon. Charles Johnson, the American member of the League commission, reported, "It is understood that a group of French men offered more than Fernando Po to Yancy and many of the men who, on the Ross agreement should have gone to Fernando Po, were sent to Libreville [Gabon]."[72] Evidently, shipments from Harper were very much in progress in 1929. In June, Washington was informed that, according to the Monrovia representative of the Barber Line, that company's agent at Harper was booking 100 Liberians as deck passengers for Libreville. The American minister told the Liberian government of this proposed shipment and threatened criminal proceedings against the steamship company.[73] On October 24, 1929, some twenty-four laborers were placed in a surf boat at Monrovia to be carried first to Harper and then to Fernando Po. Secretary of State Edwin Barclay intervened and asked the laborers whether or not they wanted to go. Some did and some did not. Nonetheless, a few days later a full contingent of laborers was shipped.[74]

The League investigation hastened the termination of the labor traffic and it probably also hastened Ross's death in November of 1929. As the time of the inquiry approached, the labor exporter decided to visit Germany. His departure embarrassed the regime and he was persuaded to return and write a letter absolving President King of complicity in the traffic. While in Monrovia, Ross died mysteriously. His body was then sent to Greenville by launch; the craft capsized, the body disappeared, and Ross's young son drowned.[75]

Between them Ross and Yancy, along with associates and subordinates, had managed to ship over 2,000 workers to Fernando Po.[76] Between the autumn of 1928 and December 31, 1929, 2,431 workers were sent to the island, 1,005 from Harper and 1,426 from Greenville.[77] In 1930, with the practice under international attack in the League of Nations, shipments from Maryland County were still in progress.[78]

The League investigation paid scant attention to the issue of labor abuse on Fernando Po, even though testimony before the commission of

inquiry indicated that labor conditions in the European colony left much
to be desired. Chief Hoto of Manohlu testified:

> Now after I got too close to Cape Palmas, Mr. Yancy called me and said
> why did my boys object to go to Fernando Po, and that Fernando Po was
> an altogether good place, they were not fighting war down there. To satisfy
> myself, he suggested that he pay my passage and I go down and see what
> the work the boys were doing was like. It was not my will and pleasure to
> do this. I went down there through the same process of forcing. I went
> down there, and was not at all satisfied with the conditions of the boys at
> Fernando Po. The Spanish people would not allow us to see the boys. On
> that occasion we were two chiefs sent down by Mr. Yancy to see our boys.
> Only Doblah happened to see two of his accidentally one day, and when
> they were asked about the treatment, his tale was that of woe. He stopped
> with a Liberian down there. The name of the Liberian Consul at this time
> was one Mr. Johns. He did not give us any help.
>
> On my return I told Mr. Yancy that I did not like the idea of my boys
> going to Fernando Po because they were not being treated at all good down
> there, but he would not listen to me. When I came back, he gave me £2.
> But I was not satisfied and still I am not satisfied with the whole Fernando
> Po business.[79]

Rather amazingly in light of its silence on labor abuse in Spanish Guinea, the League report itself concluded that "the interests of the boys
cannot be effectively safeguarded in the island to which they are sent."[80]
Several years before the commission's investigation, Liberian Consul
Johns had himself protested deductions from the workers' pay which
amounted to almost six months' salary.[81] (In October of 1927 he also
wrote disapprovingly of the landing of approximately two hundred
forced laborers shipped from Greenville with the mistaken impression
that they were going to Monrovia.)[82]

Some of the information collected by the 1930 commission begged
for further investigation. The wage paid on Fernando Po was £1.10.0 per
month and a food ration. One half the worker's salary was paid to him
on the island in Spanish currency, the other half supposedly paid to him
on his return to Liberia. Many returned workers complained that they
received insufficient payment or none at all.[83] The workers were usually
illiterate and rarely retained payment slips; only in one case was the
commission able to see such a slip: the laborer had been on Fernando Po
for fourteen months and the slip called for the paltry sum of £1.12.13.
The commission also noted that when workers changed employers on
the island they were paid only by the last employer and only for the time
they were employed by him. The commission reported the testimony of
Samuel Togba, appearing as a representative of the Sasstown chief, who

"complained that of the 500 or more boys who had been sent away through the agency of one Robert Bro, a Recruiting Agent for the Maryland County Recruiting Company [Yancy's group], those who returned had little to show for their two years of service and to demonstrate gave the particular case of his brother, who spent his entire amount received on his return in the purchase of 20 heads of tobacco and one cloth."[84]

The report of the much-heralded Christy-Johnson commission did not immediately stop the labor traffic. The government of Liberia formally prohibited labor export in October of 1930, but it itself inadvertently mentioned a case of robbery perpetrated on a worker returned from Fernando Po in 1931.[85] Visiting Liberia in that year, George Schuyler, an Afro-American journalist, reported: "The Spanish steamships do not call at Liberian ports with the frequency that they did before the slave scandal broke, but I note that they do call at Monrovia once a month. Whether they call at other Liberian ports I cannot say. Certainly, it is no more difficult now to crowd a score of 'boys' into a Kru surf boat and carry them out to a waiting steamer than it was before the traffic was outlawed."[86] The journalist interviewed Liberian laborers and found evidence of abuse at the Fernando Po terminus of the traffic:

> In addition to the weekly rice-and-fish ration, they received also a kilo of coffee and a cup of palm oil. They revealed that on Fernando Po they were put to work at 6 a.m., worked until 11 a.m., went to work again at 1 p.m. and quit at 6. . . . They lived in warehouses, fifty "boys" being packed close together on beds of cocoa staves and banana leaves. Women were difficult to get and those available were diseased. If the "boys" contracted sleeping sickness, venereal disease or any of the other numerous maladies to be caught there the Spanish sent them to the hospital, but they received no pay during their illness, whether or not they were at fault. These conditions prevail in Fernando Po today.[87]

In 1929 the United States managed to drag Liberia before the bar of world opinion for shipments of labor to French and Spanish colonies. Shouldn't these colonial powers be included in that indictment? The Liberians themselves, attempting to exculpate their actions with regard to this "slave trade," pointed out that at various times Liberia had sought to interdict the outflow of labor. In his annual message of 1929, President C. D. B. King declared, "It has never been understood nor admitted by the Liberian Government that any compulsion could or should be employed to induce laborers to emigrate." He maintained that, "on the contrary, it has been publicly announced that in view of the increasing economic need of the country, there is a definite limit to the number of laborers who could with the consent of the Administration be permitted to contract for protracted over-seas service."[88] Liberia had acted, according to King, to protect workers against abuse in the territories of the European colonial powers.[89]

King was justified in one respect. The investigation of 1930 proved a finely honed instrument, bypassing Fernando Po and falling with full impact on Liberia. If humanitarian concern sparked the examination of labor conditions, this concern obviously did not extend to the continuing abuse of labor in Spanish Guinea. This omission calls for an examination of the motives which impelled the United States to level its charges at the little Black Republic.

2· Investment and Investigation

If the Government of the United States wants to establish control over a foreign country, it has no business accomplishing this control through the medium of Wall Street banks or rubber manufacturers; it should do it openly, and with the authorization of Congress. [Raymond Leslie Buell, political scientist, in the *Virginia Quarterly*, 1931]

How did the United States come to involve itself in the affairs of Messrs. Ross and Yancy? In 1928 one observer could say: "From the standpoint of international affairs Liberia's outlook was never better than it is today. She has always shown a desire to meet her responsibilities and as soon as funds became available paid up her obligations to the United States and to other groups."[1] A year later this rather sanguine view of the Liberian scene would appear totally false. The United States, Liberia's "best friend," was breathing heavily down the neck of the small republic and a British magazine was noting: "No one who follows the question would be surprised if . . . the United States were invited to take a more definite administrative interest in Liberia. It is thought that America may be prepared to enter upon an extension of a colonial policy in West Africa."[2]

Indeed, with its note of protest of June 8, 1929 the United States thrust itself directly into West African politics. Many since have seen American interest as part of a series of machinations designed to promote an American protectorate. At the time of the scandal, several black writers penned ringing denunciations of the American government's role. The Nigerian B. N. Azikiwe wrote:

One wonders at the hypocrisy of the United States which, after failing to curb forced labor for private purposes within her territory, as was pointed out by the International Labor Conference, yet had the audacity to sign the Slavery Convention with reservation on Article V, Section 2, which [imposes] sanctions [on] the very practices indulged [in] by the United States. If peonage is slavery and forced labor is slavery, the United States has no right to charge Liberia with slavery because the United States itself is a slave state.[3]

Another black writer, George Padmore, made a similar attack:

When one remembers the part played by Washington in establishing a stranglehold over Liberia through the machinations of Firestone on the one hand, and the fact, that within the very borders of the United States—"the land of the free and the home of the brave"—twelve million Negroes are held enslaved under the most vicious and brutal system of peonage and Jim Crowism, segregation and Mob [Rule]—when hundreds of thousands of Negro workers are [reduced] to virtual slavery on the cotton and tobacco plantations and Turpentine Camps in the Southern states; when on the very day that [Secretary of State] Stimson [handed] his note to the Liberian Minister in Washington one of the most bestial lynchings occurred, this gesture of the Yankee slave masters in the role of "champions" of human rights, is enough to make the proverbial cat laugh.[4]

The Spanish, for their part, dismissed the international outcry as an attempt to sabotage the development of Fernando Po and pointed to international silence on abuses elsewhere. Still others have claimed that United States concern arose from purely humanitarian considerations. The question has never been adequately answered: why did the United States intervene diplomatically in Liberia?

Those who have seen this intervention as economically motivated have pointed to the heavy investment of American capital by the Firestone Rubber Company. The company's interest in West Africa arose out of the United States' need for some alternative to British and Dutch control of the major sources of natural rubber. In 1922, when Great Britain's colonies were producing 75 percent of the world's rubber and Americans were using 70 percent, the British enacted the Stevenson Act restricting the production of their Asian rubber plantations. This situation created concern in the American Congress and a bill was unanimously passed assigning $500,000 for an investigation of rubber resources. Harvey Firestone commenced an independent world-wide search and in late 1923 sent an expert to Liberia to explore the possibility of rubber exploitation. The rubber-company head was an enthusiastic proponent of aggressive American economic nationalism: "We are

trapped by a maneuver for British imperial advantage . . . we can min-
imize the immediate cost to America . . . by meeting an invading nationalism with a defending nationalism."[5] And this could best be achieved by
proving that Americans could produce their own rubber.

After study it was concluded that Liberia offered "the best natural
advantages. The labor supply is indigenous and practically inexhaust-
ible."[6] On November 18, 1926, after much negotiation, the Liberian
legislature agreed to "grant, demise, and farmlet unto the Lessee (Firestone Plantations Company, incorporated in the state of Delaware,
U.S.A., with principal offices in Akron, Ohio) for the period of ninety-
nine years . . . land . . . suitable for the production of rubber or other
agricultural products."[7] The agreement provided for a maximum lease of
a million acres. The Firestone Company agreed to pay an annual rent of
six cents an acre on land actually under development, with a proviso to
pay rent on not less than 20,000 acres in five years. Plans called for an
investment of $1 million and the employment of 350,000 Liberians.
(These grandiose expectations were not met; in 1930 only about 55,000
acres had been cleared and Firestone had not employed more than
18,000 laborers.)[8]

By the end of 1926 the Firestone Company had arranged to supple-
ment this plantation agreement with a sizable loan to the Liberian treasury. But the relationship between the company and the Liberian government was an uneasy one. Firestone soon accused the Liberians of
hindering the development of its investment and Liberia accused Firestone of attempting to dominate a sovereign nation. By 1933 relations
became so acrimonious that W. E. B. DuBois of the National Association for the Advancement of Colored People was prompted to ask
whether the company was attempting to protect its capital by urging the
United States to invade the republic: "Are we starting the United States
Army towards Liberia to guarantee the Firestone Company's profits in a
falling rubber market or smash another Haiti in the attempt?"[9]

But invasion never came. If the investigation of Liberia was
prompted by economic imperialism, how do we explain the absence of
colonial expansion? Does this rule out, as has been argued, imperialistic
motives in United States diplomatic intervention? It has been charged
that "well-meaning enemies of imperialism . . . tend to overlook the
scandalous social conditions in Liberia, the government's toleration of an
almost grotesque degree of corruption among its officials, and perhaps
most important, the lack of evidence, at least in the beginning stages of
the crisis, of other than humanitarian motives for America's diplomatic
intervention."[10] One can maintain that the American protest was only
one manifestation of the generally stricter scrutiny of African working
conditions in the 1920s. It has been said that public opinion in Europe

and America in this period had turned against forced labor, and that this found ultimate expression in the International Labor Organization's Forced Labor Convention of 1930.[11] Recently it has been argued that "The international crisis in which Liberia was involved in 1930 was essentially the result of a realization by the powers, particularly the United States of America, that given whatever length of time or opportunity, the oligarchy in Liberia would not of its own volition put its house in order and must be forced to do so by international pressure."[12]

The American note of June 1929 was not in fact unique. As we have seen, international interest in Liberian labor export had long been manifest. In 1924, for instance, the British applauded the news that Liberia planned to prohibit shipment of labor from Grand Bassa, at the same time warning that if a traffic in forced labor continued the British government would bring the matter before the League of Nations.[13]

Despite this evidence, humanitarianism alone does not explain very much in the Liberian case. While it can no doubt be a potent force in mobilizing public sentiment, nowhere is it more obvious than in the Liberian crisis that disinterested humanitarianism was not the motive force behind intervention. The U.S. State Department had long received reports of labor abuse in Liberia and paid them little attention; only when labor abuse threatened to taint American investment did the department choose to act. Nine years before the scandal broke, for example, the American minister in Monrovia had sent the State Department reports of the involvement of government officials in the purchase of human beings. In February of 1928, sixteen months before the United States' note to Liberia, the leader of the Harvard African Expedition to Liberia complained to the American president that Liberian Frontier Force troops committed "repeated and excessive abuses upon the interior tribes."[14] Also in 1928, William T. Francis, American minister to Liberia, informed the State Department of conditions surrounding the shipment of labor to Fernando Po and voiced his fear that conditions might "cause considerable trouble for Liberia and incidentally embarrass Firestone interests."[15] Response to Francis's intelligence was slow. A State Department official minuted: "Francis' letter seems rather vague, and I cannot see that the 'slavery' business concerns either us or Firestone."[16]

It would seem that labor abuse per se was not the target of American diplomatic intervention. It has been charged that those "who have dealt with the subject . . . have yielded to the temptation of seeing this episode as nothing more than a last flagrant manifestation of Dollar Diplomacy, and have painted a simplified moralistic picture of an innocent small country under attack by greedy imperialists."[17] Much Pan-Africanist and leftist writing did indeed adopt this position. While oversimplified, the approach is valid. Economic motives do appear to have been major factors.

United States attitudes and actions toward Liberia were demonstrably molded by the presence of American capital. It does not follow that the American aim was to incorporate Liberia formally in its colonial empire. In fact the United States assiduously avoided open absorption of the West African republic, not wishing to create another Haitian situation. (The United States had invaded Haiti in 1915 after the country had become indebted to American banks.) The aim of American policy was to promote the dominance of its capital behind the facade of an independent state managed by the national elite. On occasion the United States specifically backed away from direct control of Liberian affairs. At the same time it did take actions short of military intervention to foster the interests of the major American investor. Thus, the United States encouraged investment in West Africa but did not want to assume the burden of policing that investment. It was quite willing to see the Firestone Company circumscribe the independence of the Black Republic, but was unwilling to administer the *coup de grâce*. Certain members of the foreign service bureaucracy urged a forward policy of imperialism and the diminution or termination of Liberian independence, but the State Department was reluctant to make such a commitment; instead it hoped that private enterprise would be able to construct its own *imperium*.

Well before the 1920s the United States had an economic voice in Liberia. A 1912 loan agreement had granted the collection of Liberia's rubber taxes, customs revenues, and head monies to a receivership that, under the direction of a general receiver appointed by the president of the United States, included Great Britain, France, and Germany. Liberia's entrance into the First World War eliminated Germany, and in 1918 the French and British receivers were withdrawn. The United States then established a wartime credit of five million dollars for the African state and notified the other two powers that it proposed to "convert the [1912] loan and its administration into an 'all-American receivership.'" However, the armistice was proclaimed before Liberia could draw on American funds and in 1922 the American Senate refused to authorize a new disbursement.[18]

Initially, the Firestone Company agreements had contained no mention of a loan: when a company representative visited Monrovia and negotiated three draft accords in June of 1924, none mentioned lending.[19] The idea seems to have germinated among the American officials of the existing customs receivership. The general receiver, Sidney de la Rue, saw a new loan as a means of tightening United States control and increasing the amount of revenue he handled.[20] To the American official and his assistant, C. R. Bussell, the loan concept became an *idée fixe*. The latter advised Washington that the success of Firestone's venture would "ultimately necessitate either his [Firestone] obtaining a very strong voice in the Government by means of a private loan or otherwise, or the supervision of a more advanced Government over the Liberian Government until such time as the latter has become more highly developed."[21] In July of 1924 the receiver himself traveled to the United States and visited Firestone, upon whom he strongly urged the desirability of a loan—one coming under the purview of the receivership rather than that of the company.[22] Firestone did not accept the receiver's position *in toto;* indeed, Firestone's actions were largely aimed at supplanting the financial apparatus bequeathed by the loan of 1912. However, the rubber company did take up with alacrity the idea that a loan, guaranteed by governmental revenues and administered by foreigners, was necessary in light of Liberian "instability." The firm insisted that Liberia accept a loan, especially as the United States refused to revive any proposal for intergovernmental lending.[23] The company felt that liens on Liberian revenue, overseen by white officials, provided security for the Firestone investment.[24]

Initially the Liberian government, through Edwin Barclay, then secretary of state, expressed disapproval of any such arrangement. The Firestone Company then sought to circumvent Liberian scruples by establishing a subsidiary, the Finance Corportion of America, to handle the loan agreement. The corporation agreed to make a forty-year maximum loan of $5 million to refund the 1912 loan held by European and American bankers and promote internal development.[25] The basic loan agreement, as finally negotiated, dispensed with the already nominal provisions for three European receivers contained in the 1912 agreement; instead Liberia was given eight new officials, led by a financial adviser designated by the American president. Five were to manage fiscal matters and two, U.S. army officers, were to administer the Liberian Frontier Force.[26]

The U.S. State Department adopted an attitude of interested but less than aggressive solicitude toward the Firestone Company's proposals. After some procedural reservations, the assistant secretary of state advised that the department "lend appropriate support to the Company in order that it might have a fair and equal opportunity to carry out its project in Liberia."[27] Washington wanted American investment in Liberia, but was timorous about future political involvement. In December of 1924, therefore, when the rubber company allowed the State Department to examine drafts of its agreements, the department noted divergences from the tentative accords of June, 1924; the insertion of "certain allusions to protection and support in the future" caused concern that the rubber interest was attempting to gain military guarantees for its capital. The State Department, having smiled favorably on the concession, now made efforts to insure that it had issued no *carte blanche,* warning that it could offer "no different assurance in the case of Liberia than . . . in a similar case with respect to any other country." However, after some minor emendations, the department gave the "appropriate moral support" to the venture.[28] In practice, this meant that considerable pressure was to be used against the African state.

Although some American officials actively encouraged the diminution of Liberian sovereignty, others cautioned restraint. In early 1925 a U.S. Foreign Service inspector visited Liberia and reported that one of the Firestone Company's own experts did not see the necessity of a loan. The latter reportedly believed that Liberia's independence "should not now be taken away from it by a loan. . . . It would be wrongful to place [the Liberians] in such bondage as would be brought about by a loan."[29] The inspector later reported that the American receiver viewed a loan as "only necessary to give [the receivership] control of the country" and that the receiver's assistant admitted working "with the idea of making this country an American colony." The inspector was "most reluctantly compelled to conclude that [the] question of a loan has been allowed to jeopardize the [rubber] concession scheme [and that] Mr. de la Rue [the Receiver] has made [the loan] the prime and sole consideration of his activities. . . ."[30]

The official attitude toward the machinations of the General Receivership and the Firestone Company was contradictory. The State Department discouraged schemes to broaden the scope of the existing receivership while at the same time consenting to a Firestone loan which would financially hobble the Black Republic. Early in 1925 the department warned the receiver that the United States had "never taken the stand that a loan was an essential part of [the Firestone] agreement." It added that if "Liberia does not actually need a loan and if Mr. Firestone does not want to make a loan of any size, the Department could hardly urge him to do so."[31]

But Mr. Firestone did want to make a loan. The United States government thus made itself the agent of a company decision, using its influence to fasten new financial arrangements on Liberia. In May of 1925 the American secretary of state wrote the Liberians, saying that his government believed "that the successful establishment of the rubber industry in Liberia will tend to promote the country's welfare. . . . Mr. Firestone has assured the Department that as soon as the contracts are in effect there will be money available for necessary public works such as roads and ports." The secretary added that it would be "most unfortunate should a disagreement as to the exact terms of a loan prevent or delay the conclusion of a contract which will in all probability be of immense advantage to Liberia."[32] The secretary repeated his advice several times, but it was not easily taken. Throughout most of 1926 the

Liberian government and the Firestone Company engaged in heated controversy on the terms of Firestone's entry into Liberia. The legislature in Monrovia, hoping to avoid another "Haiti Affair," approved a loan agreement altered by some twenty-four amendments. Harvey Firestone would not accept such a solution and wired the State Department, "They must accept agreement without a single change if we go into Liberia."[33] Monrovia and Firestone were also at an impasse on the resolution of future disputes. Finally, in the fall of 1926, a compromise was achieved: routine disagreements were to be settled between two arbitrators, one from each side. In the event these two could not reach agreement, the American secretary of state would appoint a third arbiter, neither American nor Liberian, and the dispute would be decided by the majority.[34]

The Liberian government eventually came around, but only after American officialdom had cajoled Liberian officials on behalf of the company. The U.S. consul-general in Monrovia, for example, informed the Liberians that the State Department, "having carefully gone over the Firestone contract, felt that all that had been previously contemplated in [the] loan of 1921 might be accomplished through these Firestone Agreements."[35] After much deliberation Liberia finally ratified the loan agreement on December 7, 1926.

Even after the loan was accepted, the Firestone Company's relations with the Liberian government were not smooth. An important source of disagreement was labor. As a result of the agreements of 1926, Firestone had acquired the right to enter Liberia, but it was obvious that actual exploitation of Liberian rubber was being balked by certain government officials who found labor export a far more readily tappable source of revenue than incipient rubber plantations. The promise of future national revenue held little allure for them counterpoised against the opportunity for immediate personal gain. If Firestone was to prosper, it appeared that certain Liberians would have to be coerced into abandoning this lucrative export of labor.

At the inception of its concession, the Firestone Company had made its need for labor clear, and the Liberian government had agreed to assist in its procurement.[36] Firestone agreed not to import unskilled labor unless the local supply proved inadequate, in which case the Liberian government would have to approve the labor importation. But as Spanish and other critics of American policy later charged, the American company's demand for labor conflicted with the preexisting export of labor to Fernando Po; this then may have been one of the factors in American scrutiny of labor export to that island.[37] In 1926 the American receiver of customs noted that "with the increased demand for labor on Liberian [Firestone] plantations, those who have customarily sought employment at Fernando Po, Gold Coast, and other places have, to a large extent, stayed at home."[38] Soon reports of conflicting demands for labor were being heard from the Liberian Hinterland: "Chiefs are complaining that they have found it more difficult to find men for the roads. Likewise natives who hitherto have sought work in Fernando Po can now find employment at home [on the Firestone plantations]."[39] The vying demands of the Liberian government, the Firestone plantations, and the Fernando Po traffic became increasingly manifest. In 1927 the American legation in Monrovia reported, "Firestone is experiencing some difficulty in recruiting labor."[40] There was talk that the Liberian government, unhappy over the terms of Firestone's concession, was deliberately impeding the company's search for manpower. In October of 1928 the *Liberian Express and Agricultural World* intimated as much, only to print a retraction the following month.[41]

American interests were alive to the danger existing conditions presented to investment. A visitor noted that the Firestone holdings in the southern part of the country might be seriously threatened: "Since . . . a good proportion of the men sent into serfdom to the Fernando Po Plantations have come from Districts No. 4 and 5, the supply of labor available for the Cape Palmas Plantations will to some extent depend upon what the future policy of the Government will be towards the furnishing of workers for Fernando Po."[42] In late 1929 D. A. Ross, the young Scottish manager of the Firestone Company Plantations, personally complained to the Liberian secretary of state about the labor shortage in Maryland County.[43] Later in the same year a district commissioner informed a Firestone manager that there were 300 laborers who wanted employment with the company, but that unless he received a personal payment, he would send them to Fernando Po.[44]

The American financial adviser predicted that in the future "the rubber industry here will be in active competition with Fernando Po for a supply of labor, unless some powerful influence is brought to bear that will separate by compulsion the traffic from actual government support."[45] Commenting on a meeting of the International Labor Conference in Geneva in the spring of 1929, an American memorandum clearly touched on the dangers inherent in the Liberian situation:

> The United States Government from a political point of view and American manufacturers from an economic point of view are interested in the extent to which their competitors are using forced labor. . . . If American owners of rubber plantations and oil nut concessions in Africa, the Dutch East Indies, and other such countries are forced to compete with competitors using forced labor, the disadvantage they will suffer is obvious. . . . An instance, however, may be cited in the case of Liberia where, according to published reports of the Firestone Company, approximately 300,000 men will be

needed when the proposed rubber plantations come to fruition. The contract labor which is being shipped yearly out of the country to a Spanish concession along the coast may have serious effects upon American enterprise in limiting the available labor supply in that part of Africa unless a similar system of forced or contract labor is used by an American company.[46]

Doubtless, the U.S. State Department was aware of Firestone's labor difficulties; whether it took direct action to remove those difficulties is hard to determine. The State Department did note that the loss of labor might itself provide clear cause for complaint: "It would seem that Firestone or any other American Company doing business in Liberia and requiring considerable native labor might properly protest at the gradual reduction in the labor supply by these shipments to Fernando Po."[47] In 1930 the American chargé d'affaires blamed Liberia's parlous economic state not on the world-wide economic depression, but on the "curtailment of the Firestone operations and reduction of their expenditures due largely to the Government's labor policy and the Fernando Po traffic."[48] The interconnection between Firestone's labor needs and American action was underlined in 1931 when Harvey Firestone wrote to the secretary of state "to express my appreciation of the firm stand which our Government is taking in demanding that Liberia take effective measures to abolish enforced labor. . . . As you know [this] has seriously interfered with our obtaining free labor. . . ."[49] It seems reasonable to suppose that concern for the labor supply was at least a subsidiary motive in American intervention.

But American action was also prompted by the Firestone Company's problems in a more obvious way. Not only did the export traffic compete with Firestone for manpower, it also threatened to draw adverse criticism to American investment. In 1928 Professor Raymond Leslie Buell of Harvard maintained in his work *The Native Problem in Africa* that Firestone had already entered into arrangements with the Liberian Labor Bureau whereby the company was paying district commissioners to procure labor through chiefs: "Thus under this system, which is similar to that which has produced wholesale compulsory labor in other parts of Africa, the Firestone Plantations Company is making it financially worthwhile for the government and for the chiefs to keep the plantations supplied."[50] In Buell's eyes, the preexisting system of labor recruitment for Fernando Po was being used for the rubber plantations.

The role of such criticism in precipitating the labor inquiry has been discussed, but its importance has been dismissed:

[A] weak explanation [of United States diplomatic intervention] . . . is that the State Department's note, which after all amounted to unusual interference in the internal affairs of a sovereign nation, reflected a sudden public interest in Liberian conditions, aroused by the publication of several books and articles. . . . Of the books usually mentioned, only Reeve's *The Black Republic* appeared before June, 1929. It is difficult to see why this work, which deals with Liberian conditions only up to 1922, should suddenly be the cause for diplomatic intervention seven years later. Raymond Buell's volume, *The Native Problem in Africa*, although published in 1928, was not designed, in view of its sympathetic attitude toward Liberia, to arouse the ire of the State Department.[51]

But such dismissal of the influence of published works on American policy is an egregious error. Although State Department intervention arose from dissatisfaction with Liberian obstructionism, its immediate catalyst was in fact Buell's book. Buell, although somewhat sympathetic to Liberia, was, most importantly, highly censorious of Firestone. In 1928, in print and from the platform, Buell attacked the Firestone Company and the State Department for callous economic imperialism in Africa. In *The Native Problem in Africa*, he charged that his government had "apparently thrown its influence against the native farmer in favor of the outside capitalist."[52] Furthermore:

> The experience in other parts of Africa shows that the development of large-scale European industry inevitably outruns the local labor supply—a condition which leads employers to invoke the aid of governments in scouring the surrounding territory for men. Inevitably the system has led . . . to forms of compulsion, to the disorganization of native village life, a high death rate in labor compounds and depopulation in the villages. . . . Mr. Firestone has declared that the labor supply of Liberia is "practically inexhaustible" and that his development will require three hundred thousand or three hundred and fifty thousand men. Now the total able-bodied male population of Liberia is only between three hundred thousand and four hundred thousand and it is difficult to believe that, despite the persuasive powers of the Firestone recruiters and of the Liberian Government, Mr. Firestone will be able to place under his employ . . . the entire adult male population of the country.[53]

Buell also claimed that the United States had promised to protect Liberia from French border encroachments in return for Liberian acceptance of the Firestone agreements.[54] Liberia had thus saved itself, but at the price of sacrificing its people to exploitation by American capital. He maintained that American economic interest in Liberia would lead the United States to shield Liberia from outside questioning on the matter of labor abuse.

Buell's statements, which portrayed the United States as the fosterer of forced labor in Africa, received extraordinary attention in official American circles. In the summer of 1927 the State Department received a portion of the soon to be published manuscript of Buell's book. A memorandum from a staff member to William Castle, undersecretary of state, succinctly stated the department's fears, warning that "the Department must be prepared to meet misstatement of facts in order that the distinction may be made clear as to how much of Mr. Buell's conclusions are based on fact and how far they are to be attributed to his personal bias. . . ."[55] The following year Buell continued his attacks unabated. In May he wrote in the *Nation:* "As long as the Firestone Company makes it financially profitable for the chiefs to supply labor, the available men must work whether they like it or not. This is the system which prevails in regard to labor for the Spanish plantations in Fernando [Po]."[56]

It was obvious that at this point any revelation of abuse would redound to the detriment of American capital. In June of 1928 William Castle of the State Department wrote the American minister in Monrovia, after discussions with Sidney de la Rue, Harvey Firestone, and others, outlining the means by which United States involvement in any possible scandal could be evaded:

> I agree with you thoroughly that it would be unfortunate from many points of view if the question were to be aired at this time in the League of Nations or in other quarters, particularly in view of the critical attitude taken by Professor Buell in his recent book on the Native Problem in Africa. It is far from unlikely that any attempt may be made to shoulder Firestone and even the Department with the responsibility for undesirable conditions now existing in Liberia, both with reference to commercialized slave trading of the nature reported in your letter, but more particularly in connection with the forced labor exacted from the natives by the District Commissioners and other Liberian officials and by their friends. . . . It appears that the methods of the Liberian Labor Bureau in recruiting labor for Firestone have a tendency to result in conditions analogous to those of forced labor and are likely at some time to draw the well-merited censure of civilized opinion.
>
> When that day comes it seems highly important that the Department and the Legation may be in a position to show beyond question where the responsibility for such conditions rests and be able to show that American influence has been exerted so far as has proved possible against such conditions.
>
> As a first step it would be desirable to secure a clear and succinct statement of the present conditions and to that end I am going to ask you to prepare a strictly confidential memorandum for the use of the Department. For obvious reasons the fact that you are preparing such a memorandum must remain absolutely secret and accordingly you will have to depend almost entirely upon your general knowledge of conditions and upon such specific information as may come to your attention in the

ordinary course of conversation, correspondence, et cetera. . . . For the sake of the record the Department is sending you a formal instruction asking you to report upon the attitude of the Liberian Government toward ratifying the Slavery Convention. . . .[57]

The hypersensitivity of the State Department was no doubt due to the accuracy of Buell's indictment. He had predicted labor abuse if Harvey Firestone carried out his grandiose scheme, and even though the scheme itself did not soon come to fruition, Buell's predictions appeared correct. In the past the Liberian government had shown itself less than scrupulous in the recruitment of labor and, in the case of Firestone, it continued to make demands for labor with little regard for the details of recruitment, including whether or not coercion was used. For example, in early 1930 an aide to President King wrote to a district commissioner, "The General Manager of the Firestone Company, having represented to me that there is a shortage in their labour employ, as it is important that the Government should render such assistance as lies in its power to promote the industry of said Company, you are authorized to use your good offices in order to facilitate the recruitment within your district [of] one thousand labourers by the Representative of the above named company."[58] Recruitment for the Firestone plantations did not differ significantly from other types of labor procurement. Both the Liberian government and chiefs would receive monetary inducements to procure as much labor as possible, an arrangement which could obviously lend itself to abuse. Firestone and the Liberian Labor Bureau agreed that the company would pay one cent to the Liberian government, one half cent to the paramount chief and one half cent to the chief for each day's work. The company later claimed that recruitment through the labor bureau lasted only about four months in 1927 and accounted for only ten percent of its labor supply. Other laborers were reportedly recruited "voluntarily or through their [Firestone's] own American staff."[59] But in any case many workers complained that they had not been paid for company work. The company's explanation was that it had recontracted workers to private individuals and these had not paid the workers. Firestone also parried allegations of unpaid labor by asserting that this problem resulted from misunderstanding of the "task system" under which failure to accomplish a set task resulted in a decrease in the daily wage.[60]

In July of 1928 the American secretary of state cabled the American consul in Geneva and expressed fear that because of Buell's book Firestone's concession would be attacked by Henri de Junod of the International Society for the Protection of Natives and called to the attention of the League of Nations.[61] The consul replied that American activities in Liberia did not fall within the purview of the League.

The State Department remained uneasy, however. In August a department official warned the American legation in Monrovia that the "Department anticipates that Buell will shortly repeat his charges regarding the American loan and the Firestone concession in lectures which he is planning to deliver at the Williamstown [Massachusetts] Institute of Politics."[62] The department understood that W. D. Hines, representative of Harvey Firestone in Liberia, was discussing with President King a rebuttal to any statement Buell might make. Such a reply would be "along lines recently sent Firestone by Hines." American officials appear to have been quite willing to orchestrate a publicity campaign, with Liberians playing subsidiary roles. The American minister replied that King was absent from Monrovia, but "if publication imperative this week advise and I will find a way."[63] The State Department urged that a rebuttal to Buell's intended remarks be sent directly to the Associated Press before American papers had time for editorial comment.[64]

Buell's speech, when delivered, forcefully reiterated his previous points. He warned: "The State Department gladly accepted obligations which may sooner or later make Liberia into another Haiti or Nicaragua. It is difficult to find in the history of international relations a better example of secret diplomacy in the worst sense of the word."[65] President King dutifully replied to Buell's charges through the Associated Press after receiving two cables from the State Department. In the matter of labor abuse he strenuously defended the Firestone record; the rubber company, he insisted, was the answer to the republic's unemployment problem: "The Government has had no occasion whatever to coerce labor and reports seem to indicate that far from suffering from a dearth of laborers, the Firestone plantations are suffering from an embarrassment of riches in this respect." Portentously he added, "On this point [i.e., labor abuse] the Government of Liberia would welcome an investigation on the spot by an impartial commission."[66] The State Department itself responded to Buell's speech at a press conference, claiming the lecture contained "an enormous number of inconsistencies and untruths."[67]

Despite attempts to discredit Buell, the Firestone investment continued to arouse criticism in the United States and elsewhere. The American foreign policy apparatus wished to avoid the impression of playing "Caribbean" politics in West Africa or of conniving at labor abuse. Even before the conclusion of the Firestone agreements, a State Department official had warned, "It would be nuts for the people who are always smelling out imperialistic schemes to be able to say that we forced a loan on the Republic for the purpose of getting control."[68] In March of 1929 the department received a detailed review of the labor situation in Liberia in the form of an eighty-six page confidential memorandum from the legation in Monrovia.[69] The following month William

Castle warned of the dangers of continued inaction. He suggested that the Reverend Anson Phelps-Stokes, as one connected with missionary interests in Liberia, be briefed on the State Department's concern.[70] In early May he wrote to Dr. Robert W. Patton, bishop of the Episcopal Church, asking for a copy of a report the bishop had prepared on the Liberian situation.[71] Soon afterwards Castle told the department that if the situation in Liberia became widely known, the department might "be terribly criticized." He advised the secretary of state that now was the time for self-justification: "The telegram [to Liberia], if you decide to send it, would not be given out now. . . . But when and if the story gets out in this country and there is a row in the press, we should be able to say that we have acted and what we have done."[72]

The dominant motive behind the diplomatic note of June, 1929 was the Department of State's burning desire to distance itself and the American investor from any revelations of labor abuse. As the department had feared, the story of Liberian conditions soon reached the press. In July of 1929, Thomas J. R. Faulkner, defeated candidate for the Liberian presidency, wrote in the Baltimore *Afro-American* that the King administration was involved in forced labor practices. The American secretary of state wrote to the chargé in Monrovia that further pressure should be put on the Liberians "for it is likely that this article will be followed by other public discussion in this country."[73] A British paper printed an article ("Tyre Firm's Slave Trade Outrage") which caused consternation among State Department officials. The department nervously asked for reports on conditions in Liberia and was told by the chargé that the Firestone Company had contracted with certain Americo-Liberians (including Allen Yancy) to have lands cleared in Maryland County. Firestone's representative in Liberia, Walter Hines, fuzzily replied that he had no idea how the workers were procured.[74]

The close collaboration between the Firestone Company and the State Department, plus the latter's fear of the existence of actual labor abuse, made it imperative to disavow collusion in any such practices. The American-inspired investigation was a preemptive strike designed to ward off criticism of American officialdom and American business. In the month preceding the American note, the Monrovia legation expressed its apprehension that a scandal would break before the department could hurl its accusation at the Liberians:

It was thought by some here that the British Foreign Office would lay the matter before the League of Nations, but the Minister does not share in that belief. He thinks that the attitude of the British Government will be to keep its hands off in the hope that conditions may grow worse and thus have an adverse effect upon the Republic, interfere with the development of American Rubber Interest, and reflect on America when the stench which must sooner or later arise from this mess, reaches the nostrils of the civilized world. It is to be expected that our Government and its people having fostered and nurtured the Liberian Republic in its infancy (and in many ways after its maturity) standing between it an [sic] absorption by the British and French Governments cannot escape severe criticism for the shortcomings of its protege in a backward step into barbarism.[75]

Once the preemptive strike had been launched, Harvey Firestone enthusiastically supported it.[76] A State Department official, Henry Carter, noted, "Firestone is of course keenly interested in the whole situation and has asked that we keep him informed of all the developments which might affect his interests." He added that "this should be done by telephone or personal interview except in matters of routine, in order to keep the Department off the record."[77]

Diplomatic intervention in Liberia was aided by the generally negative attitude of both the Firestone Company and the State Department toward the Black Republic. After 1926 the Liberian government had shown a marked resistance to the demands of Firestone and its patrons in Washington. The American minister reported Liberia's attempt, through casual letters, to annul part of the loan agreement. The president of Liberia failed to answer American letters on the status of foreign fiscal officers, while the American legation continued to press rights considered to exist under the Firestone agreements.[78] By 1929 many of the unresolved issues between the Liberian elite and American business had come to a head. The Liberians complained of Firestone's reduction of the company's labor force and of attendant economic hardship. The American minister retorted that the reduction was in part attributable to the obstructionism of Monrovia.[79] Further trouble resulted from the request of President King that the receiver of customs, an American, issue permits for the shipment of eight laborers from Monrovia for overseas employment. The receiver maintained that he had no authority to do so, precipitating disagreement on the independence of the receivership.[80] In September of 1929 a Liberian, Albert Porte, complained of the highhandedness of American loan officials: "We are unofficially informed that recently when a Government Official, in conversation with one of the White employees, disagreed with the views of the latter, he [the American] intimated to him that he [the Liberian] was only an employee of the Liberian Government . . . under the dictatorship of America."[81] At the end of the year it was reported to Harvey Firestone, Jr., son of the rubber baron, "that the high executive officers of the Government of Liberia are either engaged in or acquiescing in [a] program for defeating full enforcement of the terms of the Loan Agreement by the Financial Advisor."[82] Firestone, Jr. was advised that "the bondholders should complain to the State Department, which complaint is a proper subject for their representations to the Government of the Republic of Liberia."[83]

There was also displeasure at the conduct of a Liberian customs cashier. After being dismissed by his American supervisor, the cashier appealed to the Liberian acting secretary of the treasury, who supported his stand. The American State Department accepted this as proof positive of a Liberian desire to ignore its agreements: "Not only has the Government of Liberia no desire to cooperate with the American fiscal officers but on the other hand shows positive opposition."[84] The Liberians, for the most part, viewed the American fiscal officials as attempting to subvert both the constitution and sovereignty of the Black Republic. A Liberian secretary of the treasury was later to comment:

> Messrs. Loomis, McCaskey, Fitzsimmons and Homan were all reported to have been engaged at one time in the Philippines and other smaller countries where it is believed they gave the same series of trouble[s] as regards the smooth working of [the] inhabitants. . . . It was Mr. Loomis who set forth the argument that the Fiscal Officers were not under the Treasury Department, and instilled this evil spirit into his collaborators which made them feel that they were a set of demagogues [sic], separate and distinct from the constitutionally appointed officials of the Republic.[85]

It would seem that the motives traditionally adduced for the American diplomatic intervention that prompted the Liberian inquiry do not fully fit the case. Neither positing an American scheme to yoke Liberia with formal colonial status, nor asserting that the United States was moved by abstract humanitarianism, agrees with the facts. As in parts of Latin America, the United States would have been quite content to exploit Liberia behind a facade of national sovereignty. In Liberia, however, the activities of American capital were balked by an obstreperous national elite, which threatened, moreover, to attract adverse publicity at a time when American capital was already under heavy attack. An inquiry into Liberian conditions not only provided the United States and its interests with an opportunity to disassociate themselves from embarrassment, but also promised to bludgeon the elite into a more cooperative attitude, while at the same time assuring American investment an adequate supply of labor. The Washington-inspired investigation of 1930, however, gave the United States a Pyrrhic victory. Liberia was exposed, abuses indicated; yet what should have been the end of a period of tension between the national government of the Black Republic and American investors was only the beginning of a protracted diplomatic struggle. The world asked what action would be taken in the wake of the various denunciations of Liberian conditions and the United States found itself at a loss for an answer.

C. D. B. King

Members of the Liberian Frontier Force

Harvey Firestone, Sr.

J. Pierrepont Moffat

Dorothy Detzer

W. E. B. DuBois

Benjamin Nnamdi Azikiwe

George Padmore

Didwo Twe

3· The Diplomatic Imbroglio

This incongruous diplomatic game continued for nearly three years with the scene moving between Washington, London, Geneva and Monrovia but the act remaining always the same: the magnanimous big powers, filled with concern and solicitude for the welfare of Liberia, using alternative persuasion and threats to induce the ungrateful Negro Republic to accept their disinterested assistance, and the Liberian Government constantly reiterating its gratitude but pleading that it had done nothing to deserve such generosity and preferential treatment. [Clarence Simpson, former Liberian secretary of state, in *Memoirs: The Symbol of Liberia*, 1961]

To explain the background against which black and white overseas opinion viewed the Liberian crisis, it is necessary to outline the involved and often convoluted diplomatic negotiations which followed the inquiry of 1930. Several monographs have already been written on the details of the diplomacy surrounding Liberia's struggle to maintain its independence.[1] Our purpose here is to sketch that diplomacy as prelude to a discussion of the long and often confused response it provoked in the Black Diaspora.

When in 1929 the United States decided to let the League of Nations handle the Liberian affair, it remained to be seen whether that organization would lend itself to the aims of American government and capital. The League was suspicious of American big business and Harvey Firestone was suspicious of the League as a blind for British imperialism (rubber interests particularly). The vacillation of the American government meant that no great pressure was applied consistently to either the League or the company. In this situation, Liberia maneuvered with considerable skill, playing the League off against Firestone and vice versa. Firestone's insistence on firm American control (an insistence which went well beyond the State Department) meant that Liberia could find shelter in the protective arms. of the League. When the League finally grew tired of the Liberian "problem" and threatened Liberia with expulsion and worse, Firestone's vested interest proved an excellent counterweight to the threat of a European-imposed mandate. Liberia's experience with the League has an *opéra bouffe* quality which stands in rather stark contrast to the tragic handling of the Ethiopian crisis of 1935. The Liberian affair smothered to death under the weight of its own paperwork. Committees followed commissions, which were in turn followed by other commissions. Data were accumulated and debated, and further data then collected. All of this took time, and the Liberian administration used it to play off its adversaries, who spent most of their time debating plans which never came to fruition.

The findings of the 1930 commission of inquiry greatly embarrassed the regime of President C. D. B. King, whose administration was directly implicated. In addition, the commission's recommendation that Liberia employ outside administrators was highly unpopular in the Black Republic. Caught between international censure and the demands and interests of his constituents, King attempted to satisfy both. On October 1, 1930 he issued decrees prohibiting the further export of labor and making the pawning of human beings illegal. On October 30 he submitted the League report to the legislature for action.

In December the thirteen-member House of Representatives expelled two members, P. F. Simpson and W. J. McBorrough, who were then indicted on charges of trafficking in forced labor. Former Vice-President Allen Yancy, Senator (and future President) W. V. S. Tubman, Captain J. C. Phillips of the Frontier Force, former Director of Public Works John L. Morris, and former County Superintendent D. C. Watson were all later indicted on similar charges.[2] The revelations of the Christy-Johnson commission also began the political eclipse of King himself. The president, then 57, had been in office since 1920 and previously had appeared to enjoy good political health. On the eve of his expulsion from office, the British legation felt that he had "the reputation of being relatively honest," although he was "personally interested in the organized labor traffic with Fernando Po and the French Congo, and very anxious as to the outcome of the Commission of Enquiry."[3]

But the investigation had produced a demand by King's opponents for a change of government. On June 17, 1930 a public meeting attended by about five hundred citizens adopted a resolution condemning the government for its complicity in the labor traffic and calling for the resignation and prosecution of culpable officials.[4] On September 25, after the Christy-Johnson commission's report had been made public, this group met at Clay Ashland and formed itself into a Citizens' League.

The new league thanked the commission for its inquiry and publicly accepted its report.[5]

At the beginning of October, the Citizens' League proposed installation of a provisional government until the regular elections in May of 1931. This interim government would be composed of a provisional president, the president pro tem of the Senate as vice-president, and those members of the legislature not involved in the Fernando Po scandal. If expulsion of guilty members seriously depleted either house of the legislature, the provisional president would order a plenary election immediately to avoid delaying impeachment proceedings against King. The new government would begin reforming the administration of the Hinterland forthwith, replacing the present Hinterland officials and refunding all illegal exactions made during the King regime. Domestic slavery and pawning would be suppressed. The Citizens' League's program of reforms was submitted to the legislature in October of 1930 in a petition also demanding King's resignation. Attorney General Louis Grimes had cautioned the president against taking such a step: "I invite your Excellency's most careful consideration, not only in your own interest, nor of the present administration alone, but also because of the bad precedent that might be set, and the possibility of adversely affecting the prerogative of the President of Liberia for all time."[6] But by December, the rush of events was proving too strong. The British legation reported that the president's acceptance of the recommendations of the Christy-Johnson commission "aroused opposition . . . and was highly unpopular with the masses of the people, who feared that it would bring about the complete domination of Liberia by the "white man.""[7] In the end, most of the Citizens' League proposals were lost in the convolutions of Liberian politics.

The American note had in effect signaled the abandonment of a sometime protégé. In 1926 the State Department had urged Firestone to moderate its demands since the company's "best security [lay] in a continuation of the King regime . . . to give King a chance to save face before his own people and not to hamper him by putting him in a politically indefensible position."[8] Belatedly the Liberian president reminded the United States of services rendered. The American legation wrote Washington: "The President, as previously reported, feels that the Legation's note of June 8, 1929 . . . was unnecessarily severe, and, if I remember correctly, the President intimated to the late Minister [Francis] that when Buell's charges were made the Liberian Government and the Department cooperated in refuting them."[9] King had in 1928 been the State Department's collaborator. When he stepped down in December of 1930, his successor promised to be less conciliatory. Thus, having sabotaged King, the Americans found themselves at a loss for a more pliable replacement. After his resignation, the "disgraced" president did receive some solace from the Firestone interests. The man under whose administration "slavery" had supposedly flourished became one of the company's Liberian lawyers.

The furor that preceded the resignation of President King might have been the occasion for a bloodless coup. Opponents of King's True Whig Party, centered chiefly in the People's Party headed by Thomas J. R. Faulkner, saw a chance to unseat a corrupt regime which could not be upset through electoral politics. In 1927, Faulkner, an immigrant from Baltimore, had lost what was widely considered a rigged election. The exposure of the corruption of the victorious party gave some promise of reversing that outcome. In September of 1929, Joseph Johnson, an Afro-American partisan of Faulkner's and a former American minister to Liberia, wrote the State Department saying he felt that the League's commission of inquiry "might well be empowered to look into other conditions as well, particularly conditions surrounding general elections."[10] Faulkner visited the department in 1929 and spoke of the abuses being committed under the existing regime. An official observed, "If Faulkner is clever, he can exploit politically the clamor that is sure to arise over the slavery commission, but in the meantime, I think we should continue to impress upon him in his personal conversations . . . the desirability of working for an agreement between the two parties [True Whig and People's] by direct negotiations and an agreement which will not involve a recourse to our assistance."[11]

Two months before King's fall from power, Harvey Firestone sent a message to his representative in Liberia outlining a naive *modus vivendi* for King and his foes: the president might retire the members of his cabinet and appoint in their stead Faulkner and the other principal leaders of the opposition.[12] Men like Faulkner, ex-President Daniel Howard, former Postmaster General Reginald Sherman, Chief Justice J. J. Johnson, Associate Justice Abayomi Karnga, N. H. Sie Brownell, and Doughba Carranda could participate in a new government set up on the ruins of the previous regime. But King's political eclipse did not pave the way for such a development; the president resigned, but his party continued. The opposition could rail against King, but they could not oust the party once it had decided to jettison him. The American State Department was itself cool to the idea that a change of party government in Monrovia would bring amelioration of conditions. Early in 1930 the secretary of state observed: "It is true that there exists a number of coast negroes who are in opposition to the present government and take their stand that reforms are needed. It is not believed from the character of the opposition that should they be placed in power matters would mend."[13] The opposition, therefore, remained in opposition, and at the next election history repeated itself; in May of 1931, Faulkner once again accused the True Whig Party of stuffing ballot boxes.

The continued dominance of the True Whig Party was in part due to the remarkable tenacity of its new leader, Edwin Barclay, the nephew of ex-President Arthur Barclay. The new president assumed his post with studied determination, and with each passing year arrogated more power to himself. A sedition law and, later, an expanded presidential term of eight years cemented his grasp on the reins of power.

Edwin Barclay had risen through the ranks of Liberian politics. Born in Brewerville, Liberia in 1882, in 1904 he became an attorney, and in 1911 a counselor of the Supreme Court. He also served as professor of mathematics at Liberia College. From 1910 to 1912 he was secretary of public instruction; in the latter year he became a judge of the circuit court of the First Judicial Circuit. He served as attorney general from 1916 to 1920 and secretary of state from 1920 to 1930. In that year the British consulate described him as "very touchy, hot-tempered and impulsive" and noted friction between Barclay and President King.[14] "Should he be elected in 1931," the consulate warned, "he is likely to make things very unpleasant for the foreign resident, and the British representative will have his hands full."[15]

The Americans also had misgivings. The State Department viewed Barclay (who had visited the United States in 1925) as "anti-white" and questioned the constitutionality of his accession until assured by the legation that the transfer of power had been legitimate.[16] Even so assured, both the United States and Britain refused to recognize the new regime officially (i.e., the American minister did not present his credentials).

Now that Liberia, through United States initiative, had been investigated, Washington was left with several alternatives: (1) withdraw from Liberian affairs, leaving the country alone to contend with the European colonial powers; (2) accept a League of Nations mandate over Liberia; (3) exercise camouflaged control through the Firestone Company; (4) assist Liberia in its own program of reform; (5) collaborate with the League in drafting and inaugurating a plan of reform.[17] There were conflicting tendencies within the American foreign policy apparatus. The chargé in Monrovia, Henry Carter, earnestly attempted to involve his country in full-scale intervention. In September of 1929 he observed, "It will be noted that the idea of sending a battleship has been temporarily dropped, although the telegram has been so worded as to make it possible for us to revive the idea at any time."[18] In 1930 he warned that European financial interests might gain a foothold in Liberia and argued for unilateral American intervention.

When the Liberian secretary of state hinted that American fiscal officials should help the Liberian government obtain a loan from the Bank of British West Africa, Carter advised, after a consultation with the Firestone Company's general manager in Liberia and an American fiscal official, that the United States should press for control well beyond that already exercised under the 1926 loan agreement.[19] Carter was strongly admonished by the American secretary of state, who informed the chargé, "This Government has no intention whatsoever, as you, of course, are aware, of 'intervening' in Liberia."[20] Carter was told, "The Department will instruct you; and meanwhile you will not make any commitments nor express any views on this Government's behalf in regard to important developments in the internal affairs of Liberia." Attempting to reconcile his position with the department's scruples, the chargé replied, "My intervention references envisaged a possible intensifying of American control, including a financial dictatorship, a reform of government machinery, and a reorganization by American officials of the hinterland administration. . . . The initiative for adopting such a program would have to come from the Liberian Government in the form of a request for the good offices of the United States. . . ."[21]

But the United States did not want the full "burden" of Liberia. It did want economic and political dominance. Trying to distinguish official policy from Carter's, J. P. Moffat of the State Department said, "I do not think that the word intervention as used by Mr. Carter and as we understand it in the Department, is the same." Rather fuzzily, Moffat concluded, "If by intervention is meant the use of a form of compulsion by this Government against Liberia it is quite correct to say that this Government has never intervened in the affairs of Liberia but I do not think it is entirely correct to say that this Government has never considered intervening."[22] Undersecretary of State William Castle put forward the suggestion that American dominance might be maintained behind the facade of Firestone Company rule, "a case, although the world would not know it, similar to the old East India Company."[23] The idea was advanced "as a suggestion, unsatisfactory perhaps, but with fewer inherent dangers than there would be in either turning Liberia over to the League of Nations or in accepting a mandate ourselves which would inevitably lead to military control of the country for a long time."

In December of 1930, Harvey Firestone urged the department to take an actively imperialistic role in Liberia, basing his demand on the pessimistic assumption that Liberia was headed for anarchy. Secretary of State Henry Stimson agreed with Firestone's prognosis, but told the rubber baron that the United States was loath to undertake responsibilities in Africa and was in favor of the matter being handled by the League of Nations. Stimson told Firestone that he "saw no likelihood of the

American Government being willing to assume responsibility in Liberia across the Atlantic" and that the problem of reform in Liberia "would have to be eventually handled by the League of Nations with such advice or help as [the United States] can give them, whatever that might be."[24]

A few weeks later a State Department official drafted a memorandum elucidating Stimson's policy. Control of Liberia by the American government "would inevitably lead to active and long-continued participation in Africa, which, while doubtlessly justified by many on philanthropic or racial grounds, could not fail to arouse the hostility of others as imperialism."[25] Fear was expressed that "the establishment of a virtual American colony in Africa might render the continued espousal of the Monroe Doctrine difficult to justify, and it would unquestionably arouse the suspicion of Europe and South America." Importantly, the memorandum noted that "no compensating gain, in profit or in prestige, would accrue to the United States if it took over Liberia." Soon after, Stimson reported that his president, Herbert Hoover, supported collaboration "with other nations in some form of joint international control for Liberia."[26]

In January of 1931 the British and American governments put pressure on Liberia to initiate reforms, and the African state turned back to Geneva, asking the League to investigate ways to make the general reform proposals of the 1930 commission more concrete. Liberia's appeal was considered by a special committee of the council of the League of Nations which initially included the representatives of the United Kingdom, France, Germany, Italy, Spain, Poland, Venezuela, and Liberia. The United States, although not a member of the League, sent a representative. The chairman was the United Kingdom representative (first the secretary of state for foreign affairs, who was subsequently replaced by Viscount Robert Cecil of Chelwood). As head of the Liberia Committee, Cecil adopted a paternalistic attitude toward the African republic mixed with a highly legalistic belief in the sanctity of national sovereignty.

The League noted that Liberia's financial state was parlous. In 1930 the Finance Corporation of America had declined to make further payments of the 1927 loan beyond $18,000. The Firestone-controlled corporation charged that Liberia had made nine specific violations of the 1926 loan agreement. Even before the Depression struck, Liberia had in fact accumulated a floating debt and was annually spending more than it received. The national deficit increased from $61,648 in the pre-Depression fiscal year 1927–1928 to $220,000 in 1930–1931.[27] The government's income declined from $1,276,438 in 1928 to $551,306 in 1931. The interest charges and the salaries of the American loan officials remained fixed. Monrovia estimated that, whereas these costs (interest and

American salaries) consumed only 20 percent of governmental revenue in 1928, they took up 54.9 percent in 1931.[28] The government went into default in the second half of 1931 and found it impossible to pay many of its employees.

The League was assigned the task of reforming not only economic and labor conditions, but health conditions as well. In 1929 yellow fever had made its appearance in Liberia and, in the course of the outbreak, William Francis, the American minister, and James L. Sibley, representative of the Advisory Committee on Education in Liberia, an umbrella organization of missionary and philanthropic organizations, died. Liberia reportedly was threatened by plague, an occurrence which would have endangered populations up and down the West African coast.[29] The Monrovia branch of the Bank of British West Africa closed, ostensibly in protest against the Liberian government's lack of adequate health precautions.[30]

Hoping to draw up a plan of assistance, the Liberia Committee appointed three experts to investigate all these conditions: Charles Brunot of France, administrative expert and chairman, Theodorus Ligthart of the Netherlands, financial expert, and Melville Mackenzie of Great Britain, medical expert.[31] On September 25, 1931, after a six-week mission to Liberia, they completed their report, which was not published until the following May. They found it imperative that the sanitary and financial health of the republic be improved through international assistance. To this end, they urged that a mining and agricultural survey be made and that an accurate census be taken. They called for the abolition of all compulsory labor except for communal labor on roads in tribal areas. They recommended an improved educational system, but felt no new taxes should be levied until an effective system of interior administration was operative. For this purpose, they proposed that the entire country be divided into three provinces. Most controversially, the Brunot commission recommended that Liberia hire twenty foreign technical assistants. The price of this assistance would be an estimated $398,000 per annum.[32] The question of how Liberia was to pay this sum was left open.

The Liberian reaction to the Brunot commission's report was to ask for time. In January of 1932, Monrovia said that since the report had arrived there only in November the government had not had a chance to peruse it. The Liberia Committee agreed that a final decision on the plan should be put off until April. It did decide to undertake a preliminary examination of the document, over Liberian objections. The committee then concerned itself with three points of contention in the Brunot proposals: the number and status of the foreign administrators and specialists; the issuance of a new loan; and renegotiation of the Firestone contracts. The Liberia Committee disagreed with the experts' proposal that the Firestone Company issue the second half of the 1927 loan. It reasoned that if Firestone's presence was onerous the extension of more money would make that presence all the more onerous.[33] The committee thought that reforms could be achieved with the already available resources of the Liberian government, if Firestone would cooperate, since Monrovia had its internal revenue and the unspent balance of the 1927 loan. The committee proposed a moratorium on repayment of the loan until the annual national revenues reached $650,000; after the termination of the moratorium the interest charges should be reduced and the Firestone rental on Liberian lands increased from six to approximately fifty cents an acre. In fine, the costs of assistance were to be met through economies in the Liberian national budget; the idea of a direct outside grant was not broached.

The Brunot commission sought to "strengthen" Liberian administration by injecting foreign experts into the Liberian system. The Liberia Committee advocated neither as many officials as proposed by the commission, nor as few as the Liberian government would have liked. The committee recommended that Liberia be divided into three provinces, each supervised by a provincial and a deputy commissioner. These officials would be responsible to the president of Liberia through the secretary of the interior. The League of Nations would nominate these six commissioners; Liberia would then appoint them, and their removal could be obtained only with the consent of the League. Overseeing the work of the foreign administrators would be a chief adviser. He would be responsible to and removable by the League, although, like the commissioners, he would be attached to the Liberian government. In addition to coordinating the activities of the commissioners, the adviser would be empowered to request Liberian government documents, conduct investigations, and settle disputes between the American financial adviser and the Liberian government. If the chief adviser found that certain Liberian officials were delinquent in carrying out the League's plan of assistance, he would inform the Liberian government, advising them of what steps were to be taken. Should this prove ineffective, he would make written recommendations to the Liberian government. Should this too prove ineffective, he would submit the question to the Council of the League of Nations. If Monrovia refused to carry out the council's recommendations, the council could declare its arrangement with Liberia terminated. This would void financial arrangements favorable to Liberia renegotiated with the Finance Corporation of America under the League's aegis. The council's decision on such matters would have to be unanimous, Liberia's vote not included. The president of the League Council could act on behalf of the council in urgent cases, with the proviso that he refer to the council as soon as possible. The League's plan of assistance would run for a period of five years, unless the Liberian government wanted it to continue further. The League would have the right to discontinue collaboration before the end of five years if it saw fit. In addition to administrative personnel, the Liberia Committee proposed that Liberia take on two foreign medical officers and continue to appoint the five financial officials called for under the terms of the 1926 loan contract.[34]

The United States representative at Geneva objected to the League plan on the grounds that it was "thoroughly unworkable and impractical," and that not enough authority had been given the chief adviser.[35] In May of 1932 the League Council accepted the report of its committee, noting that the Americans had reservations. Already, in January, Harvey Firestone had put forward his own plan of assistance to the Liberia Committee, proposing an American commissioner general with wide-ranging powers. The American secretary of state supported the idea, but stuck to the tack that Liberian reform should be undertaken under the "jurisdiction of the League through an international committee on which the United States would be represented."[36] Otherwise, the American government was in full agreement with Firestone. The secretary of state maintained that unless "complete executive and administrative control is granted [an American] for a period of probably ten years no genuine reforms or rehabilitation could be achieved in Liberia."

The Liberians, on the other hand, approached the matter from a completely different angle. In their view, the League's plans were altogether too heedless of Liberian sovereignty. When the Brunot report was submitted, the Liberian representatives in Geneva, Secretary of State Louis Grimes and Antoine Sottile (described by J. P. Moffat of the State Department as "the Italian Jew, who used to represent Nicaragua at the League until Liberia raised its ante and took him away from Nicaragua"[37]), maintained that Brunot and his colleagues had exceeded their investigation's terms of reference. In addition, they pointed out that any proposal for the concentration of executive and judicial authority in the same person was contrary to the Liberian constitution.[38]

On April 27, 1932, in a formal reply to the Brunot report, the Liberian government maintained that Liberia already had enough citizens who could serve as administrators. The Black Republic was willing to employ some foreign experts but "it was never contemplated by the Government that proposals would be made to substitute the native organization wholly by foreigners, nor to withdraw its native population from under direct administration of Liberians and place them entirely under the direction of an alien race. . . ."[39] "To carry out the suggestion of the Brunot Commission," the Liberian government said, "would not only rob qualified citizens of a natural right to effectively participate in the Government of the Provinces, but would destroy the fealty which the population now displays toward the Government of the Republic; and would also work against the ideal of a homogeneous people."[40] The next month (May of 1932) Monrovia submitted to the League a statement stressing that the League was not empowered to tamper with the internal political management of Liberia. The country could not "accept any assistance, plan or suggestion relating to matters other than social, health, or finance reform."[41] Liberia would not accept staff from countries which held territory adjacent to Liberia (Britain and France), nor would it accept as foreign advisers members of the Christy-Johnson or Brunot commissions.

Instead of the Brunot Plan, Liberia offered to appoint for a period of five years three provincial commissioners recommended by the League. They would be responsible to the Liberian secretary of state, but copies of their reports would be supplied to the League. No doubt the Liberians reasoned that three commissioners would cost less than six. Also, if they were subordinate to the Liberian President through a cabinet minister, there would be, in theory, less likelihood of foreign subversion of the Liberian constitution. The financial officials called for under the 1926 loan agreement would remain, unless their number could be lessened by mutual accord. In addition to these officials, a director of sanitation and a health officer would be provided for.[42]

Hoping to placate the United States' insistence on a strong presence, Barclay asked the U.S. State Department to nominate three Americans to be commissioners in the Liberian Hinterland. Although nominated by the Americans, they would operate within the purview of the Liberian government. Barclay supposedly promised that if the United States would support his proposal, future policy would "be based upon close cooperation with the United States Government and legitimate American interests established in Liberia."[43] Secretary of State Stimson did not acknowledge Barclay's maneuver. Instead, he informed Charles Mitchell, the American minister, that the Liberian administration had "brought the present difficulties upon itself by its own indifference to its responsibility to the country as such and to the native people . . . it [had] abused and exploited, and by its refusal to take advantage of the counsel of the American adviser."[44]

The American minister was instructed to put a counteroffer privately to Barclay: the Liberian President should call his legislature and request authorization for the League to appoint a commissioner general, to whom Barclay "would delegate authority and control, administrative and executive, for him to effect the re-organization and rehabilitation of the country."[45] If the Liberian president would request that the commissioner general were an American, the U.S. government would use its influence to secure favorable modifications in Liberia's contract with the Finance Corporation of America. Barclay was warned that the price for failing to take such a course would be heavy. The alternative was "a deadlock between Liberia and the League, leading to independent action toward Liberia by one or another of the powers whose interests in Africa [could] not fail to be affected by the continual disorders, social disintegration and health menace provided by Liberia in its present condition."[46] Mitchell was told to inform Barclay that Americans would probably not object to such intervention. Barclay should act at once, before it was "too late."[47]

The United States thus was overtly collaborating with the League of Nations while covertly seeking to promote the policy advocated by American business. The American minister had an "informal confidential talk" with the Liberian president and presented Secretary Stimson's plan. Barclay did not accept the suggestion, but instead presented his own compromise. According to the American minister, Barclay would accept the League of Nations plan of reform with an American chief adviser (recommended by the president of the United States, nominated by the League, and accepted by the president of Liberia). The adviser would be a minister without portfolio in the Liberian cabinet.[48] This solution was unacceptable to Stimson because it "would still further and very materially weaken the [League] plan, which was unacceptable . . . in its original form because of the basic weakness regarding the question of delegation of authority."[49]

The next month (July of 1932) the United States was pushed into a corner on the question of the nationality of the chief adviser. J. P. Moffat of the State Department wrote, "Crossing our telegram indicating that we are not going to yield without trying to have the Chief Adviser named an American, came in a telegram wherein Cecil told us that he would be pleased to support our position on nearly every other point if we would not press for an American Adviser."[50] Lord Cecil, head of the Liberia Committee, implied that the matter could be settled by the League or by the United States, but not by both in competition. Faced with this choice, Stimson backed down. On September 23, Harvey Firestone was informed that the United States government was withdrawing its strenuous insistence on an American adviser.[51] The State Department now found itself caught between the Scylla and Charybdis of Firestone and the League. Once the department had withdrawn its insistence on an American adviser, Firestone pounced, and after "the talk was over and the smoke had cleared away, the Secretary went a long way toward meeting the Firestone wishes."[52] Stimson's feeble compromise was to tell the British and the French that the State Department would not force the American company to abandon its insistence on an American adviser, though the department itself would not insist. Battered from all sides, Stimson asked the British to ponder "whether, if the situation was reversed, [they] would not find great difficulty in putting pressure on a British corporation that was the only real influence for civilization in an ill-governed tropical community to modify its contracts and advance yet further money in support of a plan until they were fully satisfied that their interests would be adequately protected."[53]

The tone in the League already inclined toward suspicion of any such argument. The Brunot commission noted that the Firestone Company's rubber contract was "very favorable to the lessee." It observed that at the end of five years the Liberian government would probably receive $40,320 from the rubber export tax and land rent, "an amount which is not sufficient even to pay the officials responsible for the service of the loan."[54] To the commissioners the financial arrangements made by Firestone appeared extremely burdensome. They reported that

> only the first instalment of [a] 5 million dollar loan was put at the Liberian Government's disposal.
>
> The second instalment, which, including a balance of 300,000 dollars due on the first instalment, was to amount to about 2,800,000 dollars, was, under the terms of the loan agreement, only to be paid out when the Customs revenue rose to almost double the present figures.
>
> Naturally, such a level can only be reached when Liberia has recovered economically, and it cannot do so without financial aid from abroad.
>
> The result is a vicious circle, from which there is no escape except by modifying the terms of the loan, in agreement with the Finance Corporation of America.[55]

The Brunot commission urged the negotiation of a new agreement between the Liberian government and the rubber company providing for a moratorium on repayment of the 1927 loan, so that the savings could be applied to Liberia's rehabilitation.[56]

Although the Christy-Johnson commission had cleared the Firestone Company of direct connivance in Liberian forced labor, Johnson reported that Christy saw the reason for Liberia's problems as "principally Firestone."[57] Suspicions concerning the company's role lingered after the submission of the 1930 report. Charles Brunot, head of the second commission, tended to be suspicious of business, since in 1924 French forestry concerns had brought about his recall as governor of the Ivory Coast because of his objection to their demands in matters of "recruitment."[58] At a session of the League's Liberia Committee, Ligthart, the Dutch financial expert, expressed the view that the Liberian concession to Firestone was "unfortunate." Because of the country's low population density "all the labor employed by the plantation represented a dead loss to native growers who had need of it."[59] It was obviously better "for the normal development of Liberia, for the Firestone Company to leave the country, but that was impossible as the contract with that company had been concluded for a period of 99 years." Ultimately, the Brunot commission decided that the large concessionaire and small native cultivation were compatible if Firestone would construct model villages surrounded by cultivable land. And it expressed the view that "dancing and the cinema attract the African negro even more than high wages."[60]

The Liberia Committee's second report to the League Council, in March of 1932, said that "in the opinion of certain members of the Committee the coexistence in Liberia of a weak State and a powerful undertaking gives rise to disadvantages."[61] Those members considered it to be "indispensable that the rate of development of the plantations . . . be adapted to the economic and social conditions of Liberia" and that the burden of the loan agreement of 1926 be reduced. One of the committee's most outspoken critics of previous policy in Liberia was the Spanish representative, Salvador de Madariaga. He questioned not only the Firestone Company's interest in Liberia, but also the initial impetus for international diplomatic concern. The Christy-Johnson report "had obviously been prepared by men of undoubted honesty and good will, but it showed a lack of perspective, and, for that reason, was to some extent wanting in objectivity."[62] Looking at the present situation, Madariaga acerbically questioned the good of obtaining money for Liberia if the Firestone Company was already having a deleterious effect on the population.[63]

At its sitting in May of 1932, the League Council adopted a report asking that, if the Liberians accepted the principle of the Liberia Committee's plan, negotiations on its adoption should take place in August. The result of these deliberations could then be confirmed at the September session of the council. Since success hinged on modification of the Firestone Company's agreement with Liberia, in August the British embassy in Washington urged the State Department to pressure the company to send representatives to the September meeting. J. P. Moffat confided in his diary: "I did not tell him [D. B. Osborne of the British Embassy] that we were urging the Firestones not to send representatives, but did indicate that his request would be pretty difficult in view of the generally unsatisfactory nature of the report and Liberian acceptance."[64] In October the State Department, following assurances from Geneva on Liberia's full acceptance and an adequate delegation of authority, endorsed the League plan and sent it on to Firestone.[65] But the company maintained its position of nonnegotiation and Moffat was forced to conclude, "For the sake of the record at least we shall have to send a fairly stiff letter to Firestone and then make clear to [Firestone] by telephone that what we are interested in is less the outcome of the negotiations than that such negotiations should be held."[66]

Soon afterwards Acting Secretary of State William Castle informed Harvey Firestone that his refusal to enter into direct negotiations brought on "a responsibility to public opinion both in [the United States] and abroad which the American Government [was] not prepared to assume on [his] behalf."[67] Firestone arrived the following day "in all his wrath" to demand that the department stand behind his refusal to negotiate. He was told that appearances had to be preserved. It was finally agreed that, if the State Department "could so arrange that the negotiations could not take place until after the elections [i.e., the American presidential elections of 1932], he [Firestone] would inform the League of his willingness to cooperate."[68] Firestone apparently hoped that, once the Hoover administration was assured of four more years in office, it would have greater freedom of action.

The State Department and the company then collaborated in Firestone's bid for time. The department informed the League that a representative of the company could not sail before around the first of November, and Harvey Firestone announced to the League that he was sending a representative to Liberia to collect direct information before beginning talks in Geneva.[69] The first of November came and passed and still Firestone had not sent his representative. Only on November 13 did he announce to the State Department that his emissary was departing and would arrive in Liberia on December 11. Just before the Firestone representative finally arrived in Monrovia, the Liberian legislature took an action which further complicated the already embroiled relations between the company and the Black Republic. On December 17, 1932 the Liberian legislature passed a joint resolution which suspended all payments on the Firestone loan until governmental intake reached $700,000 per year. It also reduced the number of personnel working for the receivership and lowered the salaries of the remaining officials.[70]

Harvey Firestone surmised that Barclay was relying on the League and Great Britain to defend Liberia from retaliation. The rubber tycoon had long been suspicious of Great Britain; his "idée fixe [was] that all the resources of Great Britain, both Governmental and business, are directed toward displacing [his] interests in Liberia and toward doing so under the guise of international action."[71] The American secretary of state thought the charge "ridiculous," but President Hoover took it seriously. Secretary Stimson observed that "the President himself had a fight against the British rubber interests some years ago when he was Secretary of Commerce and consequently he is rather inclined to believe one hundred percent Firestone's views."[72]

During a conference at the State Department in January of 1933, Firestone and his son, Harvey Firestone, Jr., maintained that there existed "a vast British conspiracy to do away with [their] rubber plantations in Liberia."[73] Reading from pilfered Liberian cabinet meeting minutes, the elder Firestone charged Lord Cecil with being a party to the machinations. Stimson listened but dismissed Firestone's request for more than "a blanket promise of general support."[74]

Unbeknown to Firestone, the British were not anxious to take the initiative in Liberia, and there was no clear congruence of ideas between Cecil, as an official of the League, and the British Foreign Office. In November of 1932, Cecil favored formal British recognition of the Barclay regime as a reward for Liberia's dropping its reservations to the League plan. A Foreign Office official noted, "Lord Cecil thought the present Government was the best Liberia could produce, and it was proposed that his Majesty's Government should recognize Liberia whatever the Americans decided to do." The Foreign Office disagreed and viewed this resolution of the problem as a bit too easy. It criticized Cecil's proposal as a confession of failure by the League. The Foreign Office suggested that Liberia be urged to submit to a European mandatory power. If Liberia refused to place itself under a mandate, which was likely, she would be formally warned that continued mistreatment of the indigenous population would call into question her right to remain in the League. It was felt that "once the League had endorsed any such declaration [on expulsion] . . . it would be easier to His Majesty's Government to grant recognition since we should have some assurance that the League would be prepared to expel Liberia next time she was guilty of serious misconduct."[75] Several days later an official wrote that Britain had two choices: "(1) to enforce the League Plan, and (2) in the event of (1) not proving possible, to urge the League to press Liberia to accept a European mandatory Power." It was reasoned that if the British would "go all out" for the first policy, its failure would still not rule out the implementation of the second.[76]

The Foreign Office sounded out other branches of the British government on its Liberian policy and received varying responses.[77] An interdepartmental meeting in March of 1933 resolved that if the League plan collapsed, the British should recommend—after first putting forward the idea of a League commission—that the Liberian government accept a mandate.[78] A Foreign Office official commented, "If the United States were to step in and put in an administration of their own, well and good, but one could not count on their taking this drastic action."[79]

In January of 1933 the United States informed Lord Cecil that Liberia's repudiationist actions amounted "in effect to the confiscation of moneys due to an American corporation and to destruction of the security on which funds were advanced. . . ."[80] Secretary of State Stimson suggested that the American "path would be much easier" if the League would inform the Liberians that the body did not support the Liberian moratorium. Cecil conferred with the Foreign Office, which noted "the Americans are making heavy weather over what they profess to regard as a British commercial intrigue to oust Firestone." The Foreign Office agreed that the Liberia Committee could not put pressure on the Liberians "on the strength of a one-sided account of what has happened. . . ."[81] Cecil, head of the Liberia Committee, informed the United States government of this position and strongly condemned the Firestone Company's previous dilatoriness in negotiation. He informed Stimson "that several members of the Committee have arrived at the conclusion that the object of the Firestone Company was, by insisting on the rigid execution of what was, after all, a very onerous agreement, to drive the Liberian Government into such straits that they would be at the mercy of the corporation."[82]

Stimson, caught in the middle again, reexamined the history of Firestone's relations with the League and heatedly informed a company representative that the firm had been deliberately uncooperative. Only if the rubber company collaborated with the League would the State Department aid it around the present impasse.[83] Harvey Firestone gave way a little. He consented to deal with the League if the State Department could bring about a lifting of Liberia's moratorium, and agreed to acknowledge a *de facto* moratorium on loan payments during direct negotiations. For its part, the Liberia Committee sent Barclay a cable asking for, but not strenuously demanding, a suspension of the moratorium resolution of December 17.[84]

In the waning days of the Hoover administration the Liberian government remained recalcitrant and the League remained cautious. Harvey Firestone attempted to brush aside these impediments by demanding an armed invasion. Between January 24 and February 14 the Firestones or their lawyers visited the State Department at least six times to demand that a cruiser be sent to Monrovia.[85] On January 21, 1933 the Liberians had added insult to injury (in the Firestone view) by demanding the resignations of all the officers employed by the receivership. The Liberians also dismissed the American superviser of internal revenue and stopped depositing customs revenues in the official depository. In response, a Firestone lawyer, Everett Sanders (also chairman of the Republican National Committee), demanded protection of American investment, putting considerable pressure on the outgoing administration. As a result, President Hoover reportedly informed his secretary of state "that if necessary he would go to extreme lengths to protect the rubber plantations, even to sending a naval force."[86] State Department officials

J. P. Moffat and William Castle drafted a note protesting the dismissal of the fiscal officers and the related actions. Later they saw Stimson, whose "final directions were to remember to be as strong as we could, but not to commit us to a situation where a naval ship would be necessary without letting him know."[87] Two days later Moffat reported that "the pressure from the Firestones is getting daily greater and they are more and more unmasking their designs to have this administration, during its forty days left, send a gunboat to Monrovia."[88] But a few days later the rubber manufacturer's pressure apparently backfired. The secretary of state balked when Everett Sanders came to plead for a ship. Firestone's lawyer was told that the State Department would not intervene militarily. Moffat noted, "Mr. Sanders left rather crestfallen and we are left wondering anew why the Firestones should employ the Chairman of the Republican National Committee five weeks before the Democrats come in."[89]

In early February the Harvey Firestones, Sr. and Jr., descended on the State Department and once again asked for direct intervention in Liberia. They were less insistent than usual. "The reason for their calm," Moffat said, "I think, may be summed up in one sentence, that they were convinced that events were forcing us around to their point of view and would, in a short while, force us to send a cruiser even though we might not agree with them as to the advisability of doing it at once."[90] But the State Department wished to avoid a drift in that direction. Stimson took some satisfaction in noting that the president "took the position that we had to make as good as possible paper record for [the Firestones], so that the coming administration would find it difficult to abandon good American interests out there; but that we should be very careful about sending a ship over." Hoover thought "the new [Roosevelt] administration would like nothing better than to reverse that kind of action on our part."[91]

In the prevailing deadlock of conflicting motives and interests, the League took a small step away from an impasse when on February 7, 1933 it insisted that Liberia withdraw its repudiationist legislation. Soon after Stimson learned of this development, the Firestones entered his office with their old demands. They dismissed the League's recent action and suggested as an excuse for sending a battleship ostensibly sending out a mediator. Firestone, Sr. reportedly maintained that "the only way in which Liberia could be convinced that America was prepared to stand up for its rights was to make a show of force and that this would give sufficient aid and comfort to Barclay's enemies, who were basically pro-American to take matters into their own hands."[92]

Stimson objected to Firestone's demands on several grounds: (1) the United States was collaborating with the League; (2) Liberia was not the only country to repudiate her contractual obligations; (3) American lives were certainly not at their greatest peril in Liberia; (4) "the sending of a warship to another continent would be almost certainly open to misinterpretation, and would create political repercussions not only in world public opinion, but more immediately among the blacks and other elements in [the United States]"; (5) the Roosevelt Administration would be coming in in twenty-five days.[93]

Harvey Firestone, however, remained adamant in his insistence on American intervention. Not content, Firestone went over the head of the State Department and visited President Hoover. Hoover, "remembering," according to J. P. Moffat, "that they [the Firestones] were among the largest Republican contributors and also that he personally played a large part in the initiation of their Liberian investment, tries in every way to please them and I rather gather the impression that he encourages them to put pressure on the Secretary while officially upholding the Secretary's hands."[94] The next time the two Firestones visited the State Department, the secretary "flatly refused" to see them.[95]

In its final days, the Hoover administration decided to send a commissioner to Liberia. The judge advocate of the United States Army, General Blanton Winship, a southern military gentleman, was dispatched in February of 1933, accompanied by Ellis Briggs of the State Department. Winship's mission was to remove the deadlock created by Liberia's repudiationist legislation.[96] It was a complicated task, since Firestone activities in Liberia were dimly viewed in many quarters. Winship had to persuade the Firestone Company to moderate its position; at the same time he had to encourage Monrovia to recognize the legitimacy of the Firestone agreements. While they were in London in March of 1933, the British foreign secretary bluntly informed the American negotiators that "it was, in actual fact, impossible to expect an administration which was budgeting for a revenue of under 500,000 dollars, to devote some 200,000 dollars to the service of the Firestone loan."[97]

Indeed, the British Foreign Office viewed the proposals put forward by the Firestone Company's representative in Liberia as "monstrous." An official complained that "not even the Liberian Govt. could be expected to accept them [i.e., Firestone's proposals], for their acceptance would mean that in all matters financial, neither Parliament nor the Govt. would have a say."[98] These proposals, put forward by Firestone's representative, L. T. Lyle, recommended that "the number, personnel and duties of the employees of the Financial Adviser and Fiscal Officers shall be such as the Financial Adviser may deem necessary and proper and shall be under the exclusive jurisdiction of the Financial Adviser as shall also the property and supplies acquired for the use of such offices and employees."[99] He further suggested that "for any year when no budget shall have become operative . . . a provisional budget shall be prepared by the Financial Adviser and be delivered to the President of the Republic of Liberia and should thereupon become operative [*sic*] and remain in effect for such year, or the balance thereof, [and] shall have been proposed and approved in accordance with the provisions of the Loan Agreement." Firestone's demands in effect aimed at setting up a financial dictatorship at a time when events were least favorable to the company's interests.

After five weeks of negotiations in Monrovia, Winship and Briggs did obtain certain modifications in the loan agreement. Winship reported this to the League and in June of 1933 conducted further negotiations in Geneva and London. The Firestone Company accepted a reduction in the interest rate from 7 to 5 percent, and agreed that the current expenses of government and the cost of the plan of assistance would have priority over the cost of servicing the Firestone loan. The Finance Corporation of America also agreed not to collect interest when Liberia's annual income was less than $500,000 a year. It promised to guarantee the salaries of the foreign advisers when these could not be met out of current revenues and agreed to make a $150,000 loan as initial capital.[100] These concessions would result in an estimated annual saving to the Liberian government of about $62,000.[101] The Firestone Company's acceptance of modifications in its financial arrangements, however, was contingent on the strengthening of the League's plan of assistance. The Liberia Committee accepted eight out of twelve Firestone-proposed changes in the plan, demanded as "sufficient guarantees." Under these changes, authority of the chief adviser over the provincial commissioners would be strengthened, and a two-thirds majority rather than a unanimous vote of the League Council would determine decisions on the application of the plan. Harvey Firestone now seemed to be moving swiftly toward the attainment of one of his major objectives, an American adviser; the State Department continued tacitly to support his stand, while avowedly neutral on the nationality question.[102]

In early June, Lord Cecil spoke with General Winship. The General disapproved of too much American control, but thought that the appointment of an American could be made under League auspices.[103] On June 23, 1933, J. P. Moffat optimistically reported, "The news from Liberia looks distinctly more hopeful with Winship actually succeeding in moderating somewhat Cecil's position."[104] "It looks now," he said, "as though a compromise would be made whereby an American should be selected as Chief Adviser, but responsible to and removable by the League." Cecil, the chairman of the Liberia Committee, spoke directly with Harvey Firestone, Jr. on the subject and stressed the need for truly international action in the Liberian situation. The League diplomat reported that "Firestone seemed to recognize the force of this, and undertook that if the nationality of the Chief Adviser was American, he would consider whether it might not be possible to arrange that the Financial Adviser and the Military Commander should belong to other nations."[105]

A sticking point remained: Liberian objection. Barclay's regime, it was reported to the British Foreign Office, remained adamantly opposed to an American adviser.[106] The Liberians did not want an American adviser, nor did they want strengthened League supervision over their internal affairs. Again the focus of negotiation shifted back to Monrovia. General Winship and Melville Mackenzie, the British representative on the Brunot commission, were dispatched to persuade Barclay that the plan devised was the best Liberia could hope for under the circumstances. Mackenzie had hopes of persuading Barclay to accept an American chief adviser on the condition that the president of the United States would nominate a non-American financial adviser.[107] The British Foreign Office also hoped to sweeten the pill for the Liberians by suggesting that Liberian acceptance of the League plan would result in official British recognition of the Barclay regime.[108] Lord Cecil, after some agonizing, reconciled himself to the idea of an American chief adviser, although he hoped to leave the question of the nationality of the adviser open in the Liberia Committee's report to the League Council.[109]

In August of 1933, Winship and Mackenzie set off to Liberia and on August 25 presented Barclay with a note containing the compromise plan intended to pull all of the parties into agreement. Barclay, however, continued to have reservations. In the face of this recalcitrance, Harvey Firestone agreed in September to countenance a non-American adviser if the League plan were accepted without modification. Winship, in Monrovia, was instructed "to see if in return for this concession . . . he could keep all the other Powers firmly aligned against reopening negotiations."[110] But Liberia did not seem to be moving toward acceptance of the plan. Moffat of the State Department wrote of the "total bankruptcy" of the American policy vis à vis Liberia and felt that the United States was "now faced with the alternative of dropping Liberia or letting it fall of its own weight or probably be absorbed by England and France or else of modifying the League Plan virtually leaving the Firestones to one side."[111]

The British consulate in Monrovia likewise viewed the prognosis as bleak and complained "that since the last return of Mr. Grimes from London and Geneva . . . the attitude of the Liberian Government has been decidedly unfriendly to all white residents and especially to this Legation."[112] This hostile attitude had "been accentuated by the failure of General Winship and Dr. Mackenzie to persuade the de facto President and his cabinet as to the advisability of accepting the last plan of assistance." The head of the British legation had recently been told "by Colonel Davis, the Aide de Camp to the President, that they feel that they have been 'let down by Lord Cecil.' " "I pointed out," he reminded them, "that in order to obtain concessions for Liberia, Lord Cecil was obliged to accept the condition demanded by the Finance Corporation."[113] But Barclay still had several major reservations to the League's plan, and they all revolved around the issue of Liberian sovereignty.

After several years of haggling, the Liberia Committee was down to its last concessions to the Black Republic. In October of 1933 it adopted a report agreeing that the chief adviser should be neither a United States citizen nor a national of a state having territory contiguous to Liberia. It also agreed that the portion of the national budget allotted in the League plan for running the Liberian administration should be increased from $300,000 to $325,000 with the extra amount being spent on education. Monrovia was given until the next session of the League Council to state whether or not it accepted the plan. Despite these concessions, Louis Grimes of Liberia protested that the arrangements arrived at in the autumn in Geneva were not the same as those that had been agreed upon in the summer in London.[114]

In the middle of October the American State Department was jolted by continuing Liberian maneuvering to thrust aside the League. The department received "a very disturbing telegram from Liberia indicating that the Liberians were preparing to reject the League Plan and then turn around and ask us to assume all adviserships."[115] When Winship and Briggs returned from Geneva in October, Moffat mused "whether or not to threaten Liberia into accepting the Plan."[116] "The advantages are obvious," he noted, "the disadvantages are that if we tell them that if they reject we will disinterest ourselves from them entirely, this may be taken as passive permission by the British and French to go in on their own." Winship and Briggs wanted to urge Barclay to accept the plan as a condition for continued American friendship; the State Department continued to hope that Monrovia would relent.[117] On November 19 the department issued a statement again reiterating its support for the League plan: "Should the present administration of Monrovia reject this opportunity, such action could only be construed as opposition to reforms the urgent desirability of which has been apparent for over three years, and as indifference to the welfare of the million and a half native people of Liberia."[118]

On January 12, 1934 the Liberian legislature accepted the plan of assistance subject to twelve major reservations diminishing the authority of the chief adviser and his foreign assistants. The Liberian reply came too late for the January meeting of the council, and the League then resolved to give Liberia until May to accept or reject the plan as presented in October. But the Liberian representative made it clear that his government would maintain its reservations. Harvey Firestone was very displeased. Moffat reported, "He is now hoping that the League will send an ultimatum threatening joint intervention on the ground that this is in accordance with President Roosevelt's policy."[119] Firestone, in fact, wanted the American government to propose such action to the League. A few days later Moffat telephoned Harvey Firestone, Jr. and pointed out that the League of Nations was empowered only to impose sanctions and that mandates were not joint affairs. A month later Firestone, Sr. was increasingly pessimistic about the future of his investment, fearing that the Liberians would next attack the plantation contract.[120] The only solution to the problem in his opinion was armed intervention. In April the Firestones had a conference with the new secretary of state, Cordell Hull, and came away thinking the secretary favored strong action in Liberia.[121] On May 25, therefore, Harvey Firestone again asked for force to reinstate the fiscal officials.[122]

But if external force was still not forthcoming, internal revolution might produce the same end. Factions opposed to Barclay grew more restive as the May deadline for Liberia's acceptance or rejection of the League plan approached. The American chargé wrote, "This growing pro-American faction is naturally looking to Firestone for support and this may prove a possible solution to the present impasse."[123] In February the American secretary of state met with a delegation of black missionaries concerning Liberia. Hull indicated his goodwill toward the Black Republic, but made evident his exasperation with the Barclay regime. This tack may have been designed to make the group think more positively of those elements inside Liberia inclined to be more cooperative with the United States.[124]

In early May of 1934 the State Department heard of a movement led by ex-Presidents Howard and King to have the Liberian government accept the League plan with the request that the chief adviser be an American.[125] The black newspaperman Lester Walton (later to be American minister to Monrovia) wrote to Claude Barnett of the Associated Negro Press that Barclay was under great pressure and might resign rather than accept the League plan.[126] Ex-President Howard issued a public "warning," hinting that Barclay and his colleagues might best be advised to hand over the government to others.[127] The American chargé in Monrovia was instructed to tell the Liberians that the United States would not come to their aid in the event of a foreign invasion if the League Plan were rejected. As a result, it was reported:

> They have for the first time become seriously worried and public opinion is running hard against the Administration. Arthur Barclay no longer wishes

his nephew to remain President and the latter is apparently considering resignation. The petition requesting immediate acceptance of the Plan is being rapidly signed and should be presented on the 10th [of May]. Ex-President King has threatened Barclay that if he did not immediately accept the League Plan, he would fight and would organize to do so if necessary. . . . Ex-President Howard, the elder statesman of Liberian politics and former protector of Barclay, has now come out against him. I don't want to be unduly optimistic but it almost looks as though the ice jam has broken after all these months.[128]

In late May—after the Liberian rejection of the League plan—Harvey Firestone, Sr. sought to use the rumors of an impending coup in Liberia to prompt the United States to forcible intervention. Harvey Firestone, Jr. announced that enemies of the Barclay regime were ready to strike, but needed encouragement from the United States. But the State Department was still not in favor of force, and Moffat reminded the younger Firestone that "to encourage a revolutionary body would be to incur a frightful responsibility in case it failed to work out."[129]

Before the May showdown at the League, Liberian Secretary of State Clarence Simpson took note of the U.S. State Department's hopes for an internal change in Liberia: "To my great disappointment I now discovered that the Americans, while increasing the official pressure on our Government in a last minute attempt to make us change our minds, were also seriously hoping that irresponsible elements claiming to be favorably inclined towards the 'Assistance' Plan would take over the Government as a result of what could only be a violent revolution." The secretary observed, "If anything, this revelation increased our determination to resist all pressure."[130] The optimism of the State Department was indeed premature. Eight days before the plan was to be accepted or rejected, Moffat reported "that the pressure on the [Liberian] Government was sagging off again as Barclay is spreading two rumors: one, that MacVeagh [the American chargé] was not accurately representing us and that he had not received confirmation [on the nature of the situation] from Lyon [the Liberian consul in Baltimore], and two, that the League was going to postpone consideration of the Liberian problem to a later session of the Council."[131]

The British House of Lords had met in April of 1934 and condemned Liberia in the harshest of terms. Earl Stanhope, undersecretary of state for foreign affairs, strongly attacked the government's treatment of its indigenous population.[132] Lord Lugard had circulated a denunciation of the Barclay regime in which he proposed expulsion of Liberia from the League. "Suppose, your Lordships," wrote Lugard, "that the U.S. or any other State declined any longer to be flouted by Liberia and resorted to force, is there any Member of the League which would be prepared to champion the cause of misrule . . . ?"[133] In the Lords debate Lugard presented a scheme for restricting Americo-Liberian authority to Monrovia and the coast. If this was not practicable, he suggested the African state be expelled from the League.

When the League Council finally met on May 18, 1934 the rapporteur from the Liberia Committee presented a report and resolution withdrawing the plan of assistance in view of the Liberian reservations. Anthony Eden asked for the expulsion of Liberia. In the British House of Lords, Earl Buxton concurred, arguing that the United States should now take responsibility for the country or that it should become a mandate.[134] Lord Cecil also said that expulsion might have to be considered.

But this was not by any means a clear option. In January of 1934 a British Foreign Office official had advised quite candidly, "It seems hardly open to us at this date to ask, or to expect, that the League should threaten anyone, even Liberia, with expulsion: and in that case our best policy seems to be to bring the dismal failure at Geneva to an end as soon as possible, or at least to disassociate ourselves as far as possible from it." Now that League assistance had been rejected, Britain could tell the Americans that Liberia was their concern (". . . the Americans are, after all, the last people who ought to sneer at the League for unwillingness to encroach upon sovereign rights").[135] There was some uneasiness at leaving the matter entirely up to the United States, but the consensus was that America would shoulder the responsibility.[136] In April, at a private Geneva meeting attended by representatives of France, Poland, the United States, and Britain, it had been agreed that while the expulsion of Liberia was desirable, it would be difficult to get unanimity on this subject in the League Council.[137] The League, as a body seeking to encourage the rule of law in international relations, was bound by its own legalisms. If Liberia, a sovereign state, would not accept the League's recommendations, the organization had no recourse but to abide by that decision. The League's impotence in other international disputes was mirrored in the Liberian situation. Legally there was no sanction which could be applied to Liberia. Even if sanctions could have been applied, it is doubtful the other members of the League would have united in carrying them out. And so, exasperated by Liberia's failure to meet its deadline, the League withdrew its proffered assistance on May 18, 1934.

After the withdrawal of the League plan, the future course of Liberian events was uncertain. The day after the League dropped the plan, the American representative to the Liberia Committee announced to the British that his government was willing to cooperate in joint international action on the Liberian situation.[138] Ten days later the British ambassador transmitted a letter to the American government which also promised cooperation "in any well-considered measures which the United States Government may consider appropriate to the occasion."[139] Liberian Secretary of State Simpson went to Geneva in September because "we still feared that the question of 'assistance' might again be raised. . . ."[140]

In certain Liberian quarters a more conciliatory attitude toward the Firestone Company was manifest. The Liberians had already shown unanticipated signs of willingness to mollify their creditor: in February of 1934, Monrovia unexpectedly paid Firestone $100,000 in monies due, and in July, the Monrovia *Weekly Mirror*, the voice of the True Whig Party, invited Harvey Firestone to Liberia.[141] The American chargé noted the article and thought it of interest

> because Mr. Firestone is as anxious as Mr. Barclay to keep the British out of Liberia and for the moment, the loan, the moratorium and the Plantation Agreement have, with both these, assumed places of secondary importance as compared to their anxiety to maintain the independence of Liberia; the one for the sake of his cheap rubber supply outside British limitation agreements, and the other to save his presidential chair which he hopes to occupy for another seven years.[142]

In July of 1934 the U.S. State Department sent Harry McBride, a former financial adviser to Liberia (in 1918), to undertake a special investigation of the republic.[143] In Monrovia, McBride reported that Barclay was drawing up his own plan of assistance.[144] In August of 1934 the Liberian president completed the three-year development plan. It was approved by the legislature in December, and in October, Barclay announced that two foreign specialists had already been engaged.[145] McBride analyzed Barclay's plan and found it somewhat deficient in the scope and quality of the advisers. Furthermore:

> the national financial structure upon which the successful development of the plan is dependent offers certain drawbacks. Liberian figures show that revenues during the first six months of 1934 amounted to $223,309, as compared with $217,077 for 1933, an increase of $16,232. As well over one-half of the annual revenue is collected in the second semester, these figures, if they are accurate, show that something over $500,000 is now being collected annually. Customs revenue shows a decline due to considerable extent to the increasing importation of Japanese merchandise. As the tariff is on an ad valorem basis the cheaper Japanese goods, especially footwear and cotton goods, cause a loss of customs revenue. On the other hand the collection of internal revenue (hut tax) has been intensified and shows an increase. There are charges of mal-practice on the part of Liberian

tax collectors in collecting these taxes, and some of them are undoubtedly well-founded, yet it must be taken into consideration that native tribes in most parts of Africa have constantly resisted the payment of any form of taxation, and that, if fairly collected, the Liberian hut tax of one dollar per year is not unjust or exorbitant as compared with similar taxes in the neighboring colonies.

The budgetary requirements for 1935 . . . call for an expenditure of $568,040, and there are reasons for believing that revenues may possibly equal this figure. Further, it is estimated that a surplus from the present year amounting to at least $70,000 will be carried over into next year's available funds.[146]

On his return to Washington, McBride concluded that the United States had two alternatives if it did not favor a trial of Barclay's plan. It could "countenance a continuation of the present state of affairs, which is most unsatisfactory, which offers little hope of definite improvement in the future and which certainly leaves Liberia's foreign creditor [the Firestone interests] in a most unsatisfactory situation with no guarantee of any sort that payments upon the loan will ever be resumed": or it "could confront Liberia with a show of armed force either . . . alone or by some international combination as a lever to procure the acceptance of the provisions of the League Plan in its entirety." The latter alternative seemed "out of the question because of the present policy of the American Government in its foreign relations."[147]

Several days after McBride's return from Liberia, J. P. Moffat of the State Department called the Firestones to Washington. They were informed that they would have to begin anew with the Liberians. Moffat told them that "for better or worse the Administration would not use force." He declared optimistically that the period when the United States "intervened in small countries bending governments to their will, particularly on behalf of commercial interests, was definitely over." The Firestones indignantly replied that the government had a "direct responsibility" to uphold them, but they consented to think the matter over.[148] The formerly close collaboration between the Firestone Company and the State Department was increasingly subject to strain. The American chargé in Monrovia took a dim view of the rubber company's activities and communicated his feelings to Washington.[149] Reviewing a conversation between the chargé and Walter Hines of the rubber company, Moffat was forced to observe that the company man was not only callous in his view of the Liberian situation, but had made "certain specific threats on behalf of the Firestones that if we do not do their bidding the Firestones will launch a press attack against the Administration and the Department which for advertising value would more than make up for the losses incurred in Liberia. . . ." Moffat mused, "The time may some day come when it will be useful to confront Mr. Firestone, Sr. with the expressed views of his agent."[150]

The Firestones did agree, in November of 1934, to come to a *modus vivendi* with the Barclay regime. The Dutch and the British had renewed their restrictions on rubber exports in April of that year, and with the increased cost of rubber the company became more anxious to reach an agreement with the Liberians. In December of 1934 the Liberian legislature approved Barclay's three-year plan of internal reform and authorized him to renegotiate the 1927 loan. On January 1, 1935 the Barclay regime signed Supplementary Agreement Number One (supplementary to the 1926 Loan Agreement) between the Liberian government and the involved American financial interests (the Finance Corporation of America and the National City Bank of New York). The new accord took note of Liberia's development plan and provided that Liberia would not pay current interest on the Firestone loan when annual revenue fell below $450,000—the "Basic Budget."[151] The Basic Budget included the salaries of the loan officials and advisers, in addition to regular administrative expenses. Interest on the 1927 bonds was lowered from 7 to 5 percent until the end of 1942. Should the national revenue rise above $450,000, the surplus would be applied to pay current interest. If this sum were not sufficient, the balance of the yearly interest would be cancelled. Income beyond what was necessary to pay the interest would apply to amortization and also to the liquidation of the floating debt.[152]

The Liberian government promised to issue bonds worth $355,000 to clear up interest payments due as of January 1, 1935. At the end of three years (December 31, 1937) the provisions of the 1926 agreement would be automatically revised. Supplementary Agreement Number One's implementation was contingent on the repeal of the 1932 moratorium and other violations of the 1926 agreement. This the Liberian legislature proceeded to do. In March of 1935, Liberia and Firestone concluded a supplementary plantations agreement (Supplementary Plantations Agreement Number One). The new agreement enlarged the value of tax exemptions granted Firestone. Some Liberians complained that the value of these new tax exemptions was much greater than that of reducing the interest rate from 7 to 5 percent, but in return for the exemptions the Firestone interests returned to Liberia cancelled bonds to the value of $650,000.[153] Of this sum, $400,000 represented an advance on land rent and $250,000 was in connection with tax exemptions. The Firestone Plantation Company received the exclusive right to explore and mine minerals in the area of its lease, subject to a royalty of not more than 10 percent on valuable minerals. It also got the right to operate a radio communications system and its own airfields.

In May of 1935, President Franklin D. Roosevelt approved the granting of formal diplomatic recognition to the Barclay regime.[154] The next month the Liberian legislature ratified the new agreements and repealed all repudiationist legislation. By the opening of 1936 it appeared that the Barclay regime, so imperiled just a short time before, had weathered severe external criticism. But an internal storm was still raging. The *West African Review* had already noted: "Liberia not having agreed to commit suicide, the basic issue has been thrown in the background. American financial interests have superseded the interests of the 2,000,000 natives who were and are being, exploited, tortured and killed." The paper added: "The American Government has forgotten, at least it seems so, that natives were ever maltreated by the corrupt oligarchy at Monrovia."[155] The American government may have forgotten, but the Liberian government could not forget. Monrovia had outlasted its battle with the Firestone Company and the League. It remained to be seen—as Chapter Six will demonstrate—whether it could outlive its battle with its own subjects.

4· The Liberia Lobbies

The Negro community in the United States appears to be misinformed regarding the true state of affairs in Liberia. We can understand and even sympathize with their desire to prove to the world that the Negro race is capable not only of self-government but of governing a subject people; but the fact that Professor Johnson, an American Negro, was one of the Christy Commission, which exposed the slave-dealing and misrule, should show them that so far from establishing the prestige of the Negro race in the eyes of the world by championing the cause of the Liberian oligarchy, they are seriously injuring it. [Lord Lugard, British House of Lords, April 25, 1934]

An analysis of the Liberian crisis has convinced one observer "that black Americans are likely to be most successful in influencing the foreign policy of their country when: (1) the area of the world is one in which they have manifested a traditional interest and with which they have had historical or long-standing sentimental ties, (2) the area is perceived by policy makers as lying outside of the sphere of significant American national interests, (3) the interests of other American groups in the area are minimal, (4) the question at issue can easily be dramatized in terms of traditional American values and foreign policy principles, (5) organizations exist within the black community which, as a result of continuous study of international developments, can readily articulate an Afro-American position and rally the black community in support of that position, and (6) Afro-Americans establish a tradition of injecting foreign policy issues in which they are concerned into political campaigns, especially on the congressional and presidential levels."[1]

The first and second of these points are the most significant. Afro-Americans had great influence in the Liberian crisis because it was perceived by many policy makers as a "black issue." From the start, much black opinion was poised against the interventionist designs of the Firestone Company. As Firestone's influence waned in the face of a prevailing anti-interventionism, leaders of black opinion and white anti-imperialists had little stiff opposition. Once it was obvious that there would be no American military intervention in Liberia, there even came to be a certain congruence between the position of Firestone and those Afro-American groups interested in the Liberian question. Neither Firestone nor the black groups were willing to see a European mandate over Liberia. In the period following the withdrawal of the League plan, the rubber company and those blacks interested in keeping Liberia open to Afro-Americans shared a common opposition to any real or supposed threat to impose such a mandate. Thus both black opinion and that of somewhat chastened American capital were powerful influences against United States withdrawal from the Liberian imbroglio. In early 1933, Secretary of State Stimson had reasoned that Liberia was not important enough to merit even the thought of invasion. A year later the State Department was lamenting its inability to disassociate itself completely because of the insistent claims of black groups. Combined with the continuing demand for an "All-American" source of rubber, these claims were potent forces to contend with by the mid-thirties.

What then was the Afro-American response to the Liberian crisis? It differed considerably from both that community's response to Marcus Garvey's Liberian emigration program of the 1920s and its reaction to the Italian invasion of Ethiopia in 1935. In both these cases, some form of mass response was elicited from American blacks by an issue involving Africa. Garvey's Universal Negro Improvement Association (UNIA) gained widespread support because it offered a solution to the very real problems faced by blacks in post-World War I America. Garveyism sought and got widespread black involvement in a black movement. The Ethiopian crisis elicited a widespread black response to a broader international issue. Black Americans (as well as West Indians and Africans) for once saw an African problem thrust to the center of the world stage and made the subject of extensive coverage in the mass media. It was an issue which could capture national headlines and easily be dramatized in terms of white versus black.

The Liberian crisis, however, involved neither mass black involvement in a black movement nor mass black involvement in an international issue. The mass of Depression-weary Afro-Americans were not perfervid in their defense of Liberian sovereignty. There were few public demonstrations and the organization of *ad hoc* support groups was rare. However, the organizational scope of the Afro-American response to and defense of Liberian sovereignty was much broader than that of

Garvey's UNIA. Established organizations, working separately or in tandem, vigorously lobbied and petitioned on behalf of Liberia. Their leaders could claim to speak for millions of members. The black churches, which strenuously argued that Liberia remain open as a field for black missionary enterprise, represented a broad segment of the black population. The National Baptist Convention (which could claim 3,196,623 members in 1931), the African Methodist Episcopal Church (545,814 members in 1931), and the African Methodist Episcopal Zion Church (456,813 members in 1931) all, at various times, spoke to American officialdom on behalf of Liberian sovereignty.[2] Highly visible organizations like the National Association for the Advancement of Colored People (NAACP) made repeated and frequently successful attempts to influence foreign policy decisions. In this they were aided by the tendency of some officials to view the Liberian crisis as a black scandal of peculiar concern to American blacks.

Afro-Americans could not help but be aware that race was a determinant in the attitude of white America toward black Liberia. Likewise, the Liberian and American governments were both aware that racial considerations impinged on their relations. Although the American State Department sought to maintain the fiction that such considerations did not intrude, in actuality the racism permeating American life had a very definite effect on these relations. To most American officials Liberia was a "demigovernment" run by a race considered lacking in the requisite skills and capacities for national self-government. In the mid-1920s an American official in Liberia could express the opinion that all Liberians sensed their inferiority vis-à-vis white men; later an American customs receiver could say, "You never really know where you are with a negro."[3] In 1934, President Roosevelt's emissary, Harry McBride, noted that Liberia's confrontation with the League had increased Liberia's own race consciousness:

> President Barclay's lone stand against the League Plan has naturally brought him a certain amount of admiration among his faction. Up until his regime there was never in Liberia any pronounced "social problem." Liberia was a black man's country and no more was thought about it. Mr. Barclay, however, in rather violent attacks against white supervision has succeeded in kindling a certain amount of race hatred. His friends quite openly insist that they will never *give* white men any special rights of extra-constitutional authority in their government and say, "if they want it let them come and take it."[4]

Former Liberian President Howard told McBride that Barclay was interested in working toward a settlement with the United States, but Howard protested the attitude of the Americans working for the receivership who, according to the former president, made statements about "starving out the dam [*sic*] niggers."[5] A month after the United States officially recognized the Barclay regime, the American chargé in Monrovia wrote to McBride:

> There can be no doubt that all the Liberians from Barclay down are genuinely pleased to have recognition. Barclay's reaction is, of course, easy to understand. It is a great personal triumph for him here and I suppose we can't blame him for a somewhat arrogant pride that he has brought the white colossus to his own terms. Both pride and vanity are well developed qualities in his make up, as in fact they are with all Africans, but once that fact is recognized and accepted it should cause no difficulty. It simply means that no proposition, however simple, can be presented frontally. . . . Eugene O'Neal [*sic*], without ever having been to Liberia as far as I know, interpreted it perfectly in Emperor Jones.[6]

Although the State Department sought to stress the dichotomy between national prejudice and national policy, its need for a stronger defense against the charge of racism was obvious. Early on, therefore, the department sought to involve Afro-Americans in its indictment of the Black Republic. In 1931 the black writer George Padmore warned: "It is important for every Negro worker to take note that, whenever the American or other white capitalists have some dirty task to perform in connection with Negro countries like Haiti and Liberia, they always secure the service of some black lickspittle who is supposed to be a 'big' leader of his race, pay him a few dollars or give him some petty office and thereby get him to do the job for them." Padmore added, "The usual policy in America is to have the President take his photo with the Negro in question or have a glass of tea, and the whole betrayal is settled."[7] To a certain extent this was true. In selecting a member of the 1930 commission of inquiry such considerations played a part. For example, the secretary of state wrote to President Hoover in the autumn of 1929 saying, "In considering the nature of the recommendation to be made to you in the premises the Department has been inclined to believe that it would on the whole be preferable to recommend a colored man for the position [American member of the commission], assuming that a suitably qualified colored man of sufficient standing and prominence was available."[8] Soon thereafter, Undersecretary of State William Castle reiterated the advantages of a black candidate, saying the department "felt that, from many points of view, it would be better if we could get the right kind of colored man. . . . If the investigation proves that slavery, or something like it, exists with the connivance of the Government, it would make a much better impression among the negroes of this country if the report were signed by a man of their own race."[9] Secretary of State Stimson considered for the commission Dr. Emmett Scott of Howard University, formerly secretary to Booker T. Washington and "for a number of years . . . prominent in negro affairs and in national Republican activities."[10] It was also suggested that W. E. B. DuBois be considered, a department memorandum by Henry Carter noting: "In spite of the radicalism and bitterness which marked him in previous years, I think he has calmed down very considerably and there can be little question as to his ability and distinction. He might prove somewhat difficult to handle but I think that in the present circumstances it would be well to consider him pretty seriously."[11] The man finally selected was the less problematical Charles Johnson of whom J. P. Moffat observed, "He is an intellectual negro, quiet and unassuming on the surface, but I suspect him to be haughty and autocratic."[12]

The 1930 commission of inquiry was itself influenced by racial considerations. Johnson said his colleague Christy felt Africans were "standing still and [were] 100 years behind England . . . and France . . . , that U.S. Negroes were 100 years behind whites."[13] The black sociologist "suggested . . . that with all of Africa gone [i.e., under European domination] this little 40,000 square miles might well be an experiment in Negro self rule, citing the case of Ireland on the British Isle [sic] which was just as far behind England, and only in the last 10 or 15 years had started ahead."[14] The two men disagreed on how best to alleviate the problems found in Liberia; Johnson noted that "after mutual agreement on corruption and lack of standards, he [Christy] ventured it was a situation that could not correct itself now by American Negroes, because they could not have the standards."[15] Christy favored administration by white men; Johnson thought that black self-rule should not be imperiled and that American blacks might play a significant role in rehabilitation.

Among many Afro-Americans there was early a feeling that some plan was needed to ameliorate conditions in Liberia. *Opportunity*, the journal of the National Urban League, wrote that "since the United States government has acted in concert with the League of Nations in investigating slavery and conditions of forced labor in that country, there is no valid reason why it should not continue to act with the League until the distressing conditions revealed by the report have been completely eradicated."[16] In March of 1931, Alain Locke, professor of philosophy at Howard University, called for United States cooperation "in some international plan of supervision and assistance" which might demand "the modification of terms of the Firestone concession and the surrender of our present receivership" in Liberia.[17] In November of 1932, Rayford W. Logan, assistant to Carter C. Woodson of the Association for the Study of Negro Life and History, supported the original League proposals, even if they implied a temporary curtailment of Liberian sovereignty.[18] In the same month Walter White and W. E. B. DuBois of the National Association for the Advancement of Colored People gave their support to what was, in DuBois's words, "the excellent plan of reform drawn up by the League."[19]

Black churches voiced similar opinions. In March of 1931 a delegation of black clergymen representing the National Baptist Convention petitioned the secretary of state, asking the United States government "to do everything in its power, through the Committee of the League of Nations recently appointed to help Liberia, and also through the representatives of our Government in Liberia, to the end that all the unwholesome conditions of forced labor, slavery and other oppressions may be removed, that health conditions may be improved, and that the Republic of Liberia may retain its place as an independent self-governing nation."[20]

It was evident that black groups were troubled by the charges of the 1930 commission. But it was also increasingly evident that they opposed the idea that the price of amelioration of Liberian problems should be white control. If forced to decide between "cleaning up" Liberian conditions through white agency or maintaining the sovereignty of the Black Republic as a symbol of black achievement, most black groups favored the latter course. In March of 1932, Dr. J. E. East, executive secretary of the Foreign Mission Board of the National Baptist Convention and a former missionary, visited the State Department along with a colleague and stated that black Americans would oppose any plan of assistance unless its administrators were black. Placing whites in such positions would be viewed by the black population in America as evidence Liberia had been surrendered to white rule. Any such possibility would lead black citizens to call for American intervention to control the situation (with the presumed participation of black Americans).[21]

In September, Rev. W. H. Jernagin, paster of the Mount Carmel Baptist Church in Washington, D.C., and three other black pastors delivered a letter to the State Department expressing grave concern for Liberia's sovereignty and indicating that the destruction of Liberian independence would be a great blow to black missionary enterprise in Africa, since most European powers restricted Afro-American missionary activity. The State Department was urged to aid Liberia in carrying out its own program of reforms. Jernagin stressed black opposition to a white chief adviser and a strong desire that Liberia remain black-ruled.[22] On September 9, Secretary of State Stimson wrote to E. H. Coit, Chairman of the Foreign Missionary Board of the African Methodist Episcopal Church, disagreeing with the clergyman's assertion that Liberia had cooperated in reforming itself.[23]

Many white missionary and educational organizations, on the other hand, favored a firm American presence in Liberia and supported the Firestone family's version of the crisis. Harvey Firestone, Jr. was a member of the Advisory Committee on Education in Liberia and the Firestone Company was a contributor to various philanthropic and religious groups.[24] In the summer of 1933, President Roosevelt was informed by the State Department, "Our policy has the present strong backing of the Advisory Committee on Education in Liberia, a group which spends $250,000 annually in Liberia and contains the Colonization Society, the Phelps-Stokes Fund [an educational foundation], and the Boards of Foreign Missions of the Episcopal, Methodist, Lutheran and Baptist Churches."[25] Opinion in many philanthropic quarters was that the Firestone investment was a godsend for Liberia. Thomas Jesse Jones, for example, educational adviser to the Phelps-Stokes Fund, believed strongly in the desirability of that investment and had in 1928 delivered a rebuttal to Raymond Buell's Williamstown address attacking Firestone. During the crisis of Liberian independence, Jones tended to urge strong American initiatives, being aware at the same time that such a stance might jeopardize his position with the existing Liberian regime. In August of 1931, for instance, Jones wrote that, in light of the division of opinion among groups active in Liberia, "the policy of the Advisory Committee on Education in Liberia and other organizations concerned in the welfare of the Republic seem[s] to require cooperative relationships with President Barclay, including as much friendly pressure as possible upon him so that he may request and encourage international participation in Liberian affairs."[26]

In August of 1932, J. P. Moffat at the State Department reported the visit of Dr. Robert Patton of the Episcopal Foreign Mission Association and Henry West of the American Colonization Association. West, described as a "hard-boiled newspaper man of some sixty years of age . . . [with] the hobby of African missions," was about to go off on an inspection tour of Liberia to determine what financial and other policies the missionary boards should maintain.[27] In January he called again and stated that he entirely supported the State Department's policy in Liberia.[28] Indeed, West was probably more "pro-American" than the department. He wrote a pamphlet in which he characterized the Firestone Company as a boon to the Black Republic and maintained that "an American pilot [chief adviser], insisted upon by the Department of State, could steer Liberia into a harbor of prosperity and security. . . ."[29] The British Foreign Office took notice of the pamphlet and its author and concluded, "The pamphlet is based on a mass of lies and might have been written by Mr. Firestone himself, so strong is its pro-Firestone bias."[30] Ellis Briggs of the State Department met with the Advisory

Committee on Education in Liberia and received a similar impression: "It was an amusing experience . . . , since the three representatives used almost word for word, gesture for gesture, the statements and motions executed interminably by the Firestones during recent interviews with the Secretary and with us at the Department."[31] The Liberians also were suspicious of ties between the Firestone Company and philanthropic interests. A white employee of the Booker T. Washington Institute in Liberia wrote Thomas Jesse Jones of the Phelps-Stokes Fund that the Liberians were aware of the institute's links with Firestone and that this seriously impaired its effectiveness.[32]

Indeed, throughout the Liberian crisis the Advisory Committee on Education listened to Harvey Firestone's version of his troubles. The Phelps-Stokes Fund archives contain a memorandum on the situation which clearly mirrors Firestone's obsessions.[33] As a solution to the Liberian crisis, the memorandum, drafted during the Hoover administration's final days, "recommended that an agent of the United States Government proceed promptly to Monrovia to deal with the increasingly serious conditions in Liberia and that he be sent on an American naval vessel to ensure his timely arrival."[34] The next month J. P. Moffat had to write "a letter to the missionaries who are asking for more aggressive action toward Liberia including a warship at Monrovia. . . ."[35]

The warship was not sent, but the close contact between company and missionaries continued. On May 5, 1933, Thomas Jesse Jones met with the Firestones and reported them "very much perplexed."[36] The following day, Jones wrote to Dr. Robert Moton, the venerable patriarch of Tuskegee and Booker T. Washington's successor, inviting him to Washington to lobby for a stronger defense of American interests in Liberia. On May 12 a missionary delegation that included Moton met with Undersecretary of State Phillips to ask that the United States retain its dominant position in Liberia. Moffat described Moton as quite effective: "It was[,] I suppose, a case of atovism [sic], where the descendent of Wendell Phillips [nineteenth-century abolitionist] once again was touched by the appeal of the oppressed negro."[37]

By the summer of 1933, when the League was debating the Liberian issue in London and Geneva, the battle-lines on the Liberian issue had been drawn in the United States. The American undersecretary of state noted that the State Department had the support of George Schuyler, a black writer at the Pittsburgh *Courier*, and "the approval of the more conservative negro elements, such as Dr. Moulton [Moton], President of Tuskegee, and several other prominent negroes such as Dr. Johnson of Fisk University, and Mr. [Lester] Walton."[38] On the other side, the government was being criticized by a group of "aggressive negroes" and white anti-imperialists. Among the blacks were W. E. B. DuBois of the

National Association for the Advancement of Colored People and Carl Murphy, the editor of the Baltimore *Afro-American*. Among the white anti-imperialists were the Foreign Policy Association and the Women's International League for Peace and Freedom (WILPF).

The NAACP was chief among those organizations which came to support the cause of Liberian independence as a symbol of black rule. As early as March of 1931 the organization showed interest in the findings of the Christy-Johnson commission.[39] But its concern for Liberia really began in earnest in early 1932.[40] In an effort to prod the State Department into a more conciliatory attitude toward the Barclay regime, the association, early on, attempted to enlist the aid of Charles Johnson, American representative on the League of Nations' commission of inquiry, as the black most intimately involved with the details of Liberian labor conditions. Unfortunately for the NAACP, Johnson refused to make a public statement: "My assumption," he wrote, "whether or not completely founded in fact, has been that my services were originally sought primarily as an investigator and social student, and there is nothing more than consistency in my insistence that it not be made by me a matter of racial protest."[41] Another Fisk University sociologist, E. Franklin Frazier, thought Johnson could be involved in a public discussion of the Liberian matter by asking the State Department why he was not being consulted. Frazier reasoned, "It may be that this course of strategy will reveal any recommendations that Johnson might have made to the State Department which have not been made public."[42] The NAACP followed this course and was icily informed by the State Department that the sociologist was not being consulted at the present time but that, if he wanted to give the department his views, they would be pleased to receive them.[43]

The NAACP was highly suspicious of the Firestone Company's activities and issued an anti-company statement by Howard Oxley, former educational adviser to the American Advisory Committee on Education in Liberia. The association noted that Oxley "challenged Secretary of State Stimson's statement that 'the Firestone interests have no immediate connection with the present problem,' " and "expressed great surprise that such a statement should come from the State Department because the Firestone Company has put more pressure behind the movement for reforms in Liberia than any other organization."[44] The State Department did not answer the group's letter but privately expressed the opinion that Oxley was attempting to embarrass the government.[45]

The NAACP warned the secretary of state that "should the League adopt the American suggestion of imposing upon the League Adviser dictatorial powers the result would be, in our opinion, a destructive occupation similar to that which the United States has carried out in another

Negro Republic, namely Haiti;"[46] and they insisted that "the League of Nations in our judgement cannot possibly adopt any such plan." The association believed that if the American government persisted in its attitude of demanding an all-powerful chief adviser, the League would probably discontinue its efforts to aid Liberia and the United States would unilaterally intervene to protect the Firestone interests.

For its part, the association made clear the kind of adviser it wanted: an American, but not one subservient to the Firestone interests; and the man selected should not be a racist, but should have full faith in black capacities.[47] The State Department attempted to assuage the ire of the organization, assuring it that the United States had never insisted on an adviser of any particular nationality.[48]

In keeping with the proposal for a "just" American adviser, Walter White of the NAACP wrote to Liberian Secretary of State Grimes opposing the selection of a European (White suspected it would be a Belgian) and suggesting that a competent American be chosen.[49] Grimes rejected the idea of an American adviser, however well disposed, because he believed any American would ultimately reflect the position of the American State Department.[50] Nevertheless, the idea persisted, and in June of 1933, White cabled Grimes that Prof. Raymond Buell, the political scientist, would be an ideal and impartial appointee.[51]

A major ally of the NAACP in its combat with the State Department and the Firestone Company was the Women's International League for Peace and Freedom (WILPF), an anti-imperialist and internationalist organization. The WILPF's initial involvement with the Liberian situation came about when Liberians in Geneva made contact with one of its officers, Anna Graves.[52] By the fall of 1932 the WILPF was in touch with the NAACP and the WILPF's executive secretary, Dorothy Detzer, was radiograming from Switzerland, "Negro protests against American plan needed."[53] In June of 1933 Anna Graves wrote Walter White of the NAACP urging immediate action on behalf of Liberia. The next month she cabled to urge the NAACP to send a representative to Geneva while General Winship and the Firestone representatives were there.[54] In August, Graves again wrote to White complaining that the NAACP had not answered her letters between December of 1932 and July of 1933. "If," she wrote, "Liberia disheartened gives in and becomes a peon state—gives in because she had so little moral support—practically none, until this last minute from American Negroes—I think her fate will be partly the fault of the American Negroes' lukewarmness from December 1930 until July 1933."[55]

The WILPF, of course, did not confine its efforts to chiding the NAACP; it also vociferously lobbied the State Department. In January of 1933, Detzer and Graves visited the department and confronted

Moffat, who complained that Graves was "a combative old maid, extremely well versed in certain phases of the problem and well documented. . . ."[56] He felt that "although her facts were pretty correct, she drew one wrong inference after another, steadily impugned the motives of the American Government and the Firestones and accepted as gospel truth everything that had been told her by Cecil, Madariaga, Grimes [and] Ligthart." On June 6, Detzer visited again and spoke with Undersecretary (then Acting Secretary) Phillips, who supposedly told her he would take no action on the chief advisership until, in her words, "he had given an opportunity to some of us who are opposing an American in that place, to discuss the matter after Winship returns."[57] On July 17 she met with the general and voiced opposition to the League's plan as representing "a form of paternalism." She attacked Harvey Firestone's insistence on an American chief adviser, who would "either represent an agent of American imperialism or Firestone imperialism."[58]

On July 31, 1933, a group of prominent blacks and some members of the WILPF met Undersecretary Phillips at the State Department. The group included, among others, President Mordecai Johnson of Howard University, W. E. B. DuBois, Dorothy Detzer, Rayford Logan of the Association for the Study of Negro Life and History, Charles Wesley of Howard's history department, and Emmett Scott, secretary of that University.[59] Several days before the meeting Wesley and Logan had drafted a statement on Liberia. They defended the Black Republic's repudiation of its debt and urged the creation of a supervisory commission which would be liberal in its approach and include a Liberian and an American black. They attacked a proposal that education in Liberia be completely turned over to missionary societies. They contended that black Americans would not be content until they had heard Liberia's side of the controversy, and maintained that the American black population was solidly behind the maintenance of Liberian sovereignty.[60]

Undersecretary Phillips began the meeting with a brief outline of America's historical interest in Liberia, adding that as a great-nephew of Wendell Phillips, the nineteenth-century abolitionist, he had a special interest in Liberia. Phillips indirectly blamed Liberia's present financial plight on the previous American administration. While the United States supported legitimate interests in Liberia, he said, the Roosevelt administration would not sacrifice Liberia simply to appease American business.[61] DuBois, acting as spokesman for the group, read his own prepared statement. The black elder statesman declared that "the darker world had become convinced that it is being used and exploited by Europe and America for the benefit and power and luxury of white folk and at the expense of poverty, and slavery for yellow, brown and black."[62] DuBois warned that as greater numbers of blacks received university degrees they were becoming more impatient than ever before of racism. DuBois said blacks did not believe Washington wanted a "New Deal" for black states and compared Haiti and Liberia. He asked that the League's plan of assistance not be rammed down the throats of the Liberians and urged that the proposed Liberian budget under the plan be amended to include funds for education: "We have too often seen missionary enterprises as the hand-maiden of capitalistic and imperialistic designs and we are sure that the Christian people of America will not wish to supplant Government education by Church education in Liberia any more than in the United States."[63] DuBois also requested that the United States support the appointment of a chief adviser acceptable to Liberia, that no ultimatum be sent on Liberia's acceptance of the plan, and that the United States officially recognize the Barclay regime.[64]

The selection of General Winship as American commissioner produced some sharp exchanges between DuBois and Phillips and between Phillips, Mordecai Johnson, and Dorothy Detzer. DuBois suggested, just before the delegation left, that it might have been better to send a black instead of a white southerner. Phillips reportedly answered, "Yes, it might have been wiser."[65] But Rayford Logan reported that "when a member of the delegation told him [Phillips] that Negroes are alarmed by Winship's present role in the negotiations because of his Southern antecedents, and attempted to point out how disastrous has been the policy of appointing Southern white men to similar posts—the lessons gained from Haiti and from the appointment of such men to command in colored regiments during the World War furnished glaring examples—the acting secretary remarked that 'we will not go into that.' "[66] Logan believed that, although the delegation had not moved Phillips away from the appointment of an American chief adviser, there was at least hope that a Southerner would not be selected. He felt that "to appoint to this post a man with the 'ideals' of the Southern gentleman of 1860, as Miss Dexter [sic] . . . so aptly described him, would bespeak either a crass ignorance or a determination to flout the earnest appeal of nearly fifteen million American and Liberian Negroes."

After the visit of the delegation, the State Department released to the press this account: "Mr. Phillips stated . . . that he would be glad to give careful consideration to the views of so large a group of friends of Liberia and that he would transmit them to Major General Blanton Winship, the present American representative on the League Committee, for his consideration and such suggestions to the Committee for alterations as might seem feasible."[67] In reality neither Phillips nor the members of the delegation were entirely pleased with the outcome of the interview. Logan wrote that "the delegation derived little satisfaction from its audience. . . . In the last analysis, protection of American interests abroad is entrusted to American marines."[68] Detzer thought the conference might speed up processes already in motion: three days afterwards she wrote to White, "I am told confidentially that they are worried inside the State Department about further publicity and agitation on this question of Liberia and are going to sign and seal the League plan as quickly as possible."[69]

Inside the department, Secretary of State Cordell Hull decided to seek the opinion of President Roosevelt on the Liberian matter. Moffat drew up the memorandum to Roosevelt, noting to himself, "There is no policy in the world that has not got its critics and personally I do not take the criticisms of either the radical negro groups, the pacifist groups or the professional anti-imperialists, such as Raymond Leslie Buell, too seriously."[70]

In early September of 1933, Walter White wrote to Buell, after the latter reported that the secretary of state was sticking to his previous position. "It was probably naive of me," White mused, "but I had hoped that the long interview we had with Phillips on July 31 might result in some change, however slight, on the part of the State Department."[71] Phillips himself reviewed the interview thusly: "The suggestions which I obtained from this conference are two in number: (1) The desirability of an allowance so that the state will not be deprived of a certain amount of education under the auspices of the state; (2) That if the Firestones could be induced to spread their loan over another group of bankers, the Department would be in a far stronger position in its efforts to see justice done in Liberia."[72]

For his part, Phillips believed the United States had three alternatives: take control of Liberia, withdraw completely, or collaborate with the League of Nations. The undersecretary favored adoption of a League plan with a strong chief adviser, a slight readjustment downward of the Firestone contract, and the advance of new money by Firestone. "Perhaps I should also add," he wrote to Roosevelt, "that the Liberian plantation, which is from all accounts one of the best rubber producing units in existence, is our only major source of rubber independent of the Far East and hence a very important consideration in our national defense."[73]

However, the delegation's requests were not entirely in vain. The United States did push for more funds for education in the revised plan of assistance presented in the fall. Phillips also seriously considered ways of spreading the financing of the Firestone loan among various financial groups, thus lessening the rubber company's dominance. He discussed the matter with Winship, who suggested that the members of the delegation to Phillips might be sounded on their willingness to take on the loan through the purchase of Finance Corporation of America bonds.[74]

The critics of the State Department's Liberian policy had, as Detzer suspected, caused uneasiness in official circles. Moffat complained in his diary that he and his colleagues were "in a bit of a jam as the radical negro groups are accusing us of imperialism and have worried Hull by writing in the *New Republic* and *The Nation* that the permanent officials of the Department, without his knowledge and understanding, are continuing to destroy Liberia for the benefit of American vested interests."[75] Soon thereafter he reported that the critics were "continuing their attacks on our Liberian policy . . . indicating that Mr. Hull is an honest man surrounded by the machiavellian and sinister influences of 'the careers' who after all are nothing but tools of Wall Street and the vested interests and out of sympathy with the philosophy of the New Deal."[76] The articles Moffat was referring to actually were not written by "radical negro groups," but by the white liberals Raymond Buell and Mauritz Hallgren. In August of 1933, Buell had attacked American policy in the *New Republic:* "Under the previous administration, one could not have expected the State Department to be firm with Mr. Firestone, because it was Mr. Hoover who joined with Mr. Firestone in a campaign against the British rubber 'monopoly,' and it was Mr. Firestone who contributed $20,396.74 to Mr. Hoover's 1932 campaign."[77] But looking at current policy, the political scientist had to conclude: "The only possible explanation is that pressed with more immediate duties, the political heads of the new administration have had no time for Liberia and have entrusted this question entirely to subordinate permanent officials who apparently have no understanding or sympathy with the New Deal."[78] Mauritz Hallgren had protested in *The Nation* that "Liberia, having already been reduced to helplessness through the financial dictatorship of the Firestone rubber interests, is now, with the aid of the League of Nations and consent of the American State Department about to be placed in complete servitude."[79] He argued that Liberia's government had lost its financial independence through the 1926 loan agreement, "which the State Department compelled it to accept against its will." Soon the Black Republic was "to be stripped of its administrative independence and cultural autonomy as well."

The WILPF and the NAACP continued their lobbying effort after their less-than-satisfactory call at the State Department. In late August of 1933, Dorothy Detzer received a cable from Geneva which said the British and the Americans had offered to recognize the Liberian administration if it would accept the compromise plan worked out by General Winship. She immediately confronted Ellis Briggs at the State Department, and after much sparring Briggs showed her a joint note which had been sent to the Liberians on the previous day by the British and American legations.[80] Detzer despaired of the State Department and sought to reach the president directly. On August 30 she appealed to Felix Frankfurter, asking him to intercede with Roosevelt on her behalf. In her memoirs, the denouement of the Liberian situation hinged on this appeal, which received the reply, "Your letter has been read by the highest authority."[81] As Detzer recalled: "Early in October, the press announced that the President had requested Secretary of State Hull 'to review the United States' Liberian policy.' And a few weeks later when the Council of the League met, the Council endorsed a greatly revised plan of assistance submitted to it by the Roosevelt Administration, and this plan Liberia promptly signed."[82] In actuality, Detzer was doubly mistaken. Liberia did not accept the League plan and Roosevelt's response was, as transmitted through an aide: "Send for this lady, see her and explain how and where she is wrong."[83] The Roosevelt administration had taken a slightly new tack on the matter, however. In keeping with Roosevelt's views, the State Department told Harvey Firestone in late September that the United States would not tacitly support his continued request for an American chief adviser.[84]

In that summer of 1933, Firestone's missionary supporters and his detractors were directly confronting one another. Liberian Secretary of State Grimes wrote Walter White urging action on behalf of Liberia and warning that Henry West of the Colonization Society, Thomas Jesse Jones of the Phelps-Stokes Fund, and Bishop Campbell of the Protestant Episcopal Mission were "dancing attendance on Mr. Firestone."[85] The Federal Council of Churches in Christ in America had already sent the State Department a copy of a resolution which urged an American chief adviser.[86] The council held that "the Government and people of the United States, have, we believe, a definite and unique contribution to make to the advancement of Liberia and Liberians, a contribution which has vital significance also for the whole continent of Africa."[87] Dorothy Detzer wrote Walter Van Kirk of the council that she was shocked by the resolution.[88] In September, Walter White wrote to Raymond Buell saying that he, DuBois, and Detzer "had a long and somewhat acrimonious discussion with representatives of the Federal Council of the Churches of Christ. . . ." White and his colleagues found the churchmen "abysmally ignorant of recent developments."[89]

A meeting of black and white missionary groups convened in Washington on February 7, 1934. Thomas Jesse Jones, the great exponent of a firm American presence in Liberia, was reportedly confident that the gathering "was a really serious group which was thoroughly in accord with the policy of the United States regarding the present Liberian situation, and felt that they [the black missionaries] might be trusted to keep in line."[90] In a conference with Frederick Hibbard of the State Department, Jones expressed the view that the black missionaries should be allowed to follow their own lead, as the appearance of government interference might subject the department to criticism.[91] Most of the whites present (including Jones and Harvey Firestone, Jr.) urged the group to recommend that Liberia accept the League of Nations plan. Two black clergymen, Reverend Walter Brooks, a Baptist pastor from Washington, and Bishop William W. Matthews, resident bishop of the A.M.E. Zion Church in Liberia, strongly disagreed.[92] To reconcile opposing views a committee of concerned blacks, consisting of Matthews, Emmet Scott, Lester Walton, and the Reverend W. H. Jernagin, drew up a number of resolutions which the conference subsequently adopted. The missionary groups stated their support for Liberian independence and called for reconsideration of the League plan of assistance "in the light and spirit" of Monrovia's reservations. As might have been expected, it was asked that missionary activity in Liberia "remain under the guidance of American influence."[93] One resolution also requested an American chief adviser.

Bishop Matthews was particularly persistent in his efforts to have the State Department normalize relations with Liberia. The day before the conference he met with William Phillips and strongly urged this course of action.[94] At the conference itself he reiterated these views and attacked the United States for assailing Liberia on the slave trade issue but failed to castigate Spain. When labor conditions in Liberia were brought up, he was quick to draw a comparison with the treatment of black labor in Mississippi. Inside the State Department, J. P. Moffat took note of the conference and commented, "We are preparing ammunition to explain why it is impossible to recognize, in the present circumstances, and how lacking are any efforts of Barclay to take our wishes or recommendations into consideration."[95] It was Moffat's own feeling that "it was a mistake not to have recognized Barclay but [I] do not see how it could be done while he is engaged in slapping us in the face." On February 14, 1934 Cordell Hull received a delegation of black missionaries and Moffat prepared a short reply for the secretary to deliver, which Hull "embroidered on in a very humorous and understanding way, sending them away convinced of his good will toward Liberia in general, but his thorough annoyance toward the cavalier attitude of Barclay in particular."[96]

J. E. East of the National Baptist Convention was another black participant in the Washington meeting who expressed reservations about the course of action being urged on black missionaries. On May 1, East wrote to the Advisory Committee on Education in Liberia and the Board of Trustees of the Booker T. Washington Institute in Liberia. Regretting that he could not attend the joint meeting of these two bodies, he nevertheless wanted to give them a black point of view. In East's opinion blacks were almost unanimously opposed to any move that would force

Liberia to accept a plan of assistance. He stated that, in spite of the array of evidence presented by the white delegates at the Washington meeting, many blacks were still unhappy about the conference's recommendations. He urged the holding of a broader conference in which various black groups (churches, fraternal organizations, educational institutions, and the press) would be better represented, and he said Afro-American groups would attempt to take their appeals directly to President Roosevelt.[97] "It is also proposed that we will have all of our associations and conventions, both large and small throughout the country . . . flood our State Department and White House with a suitable petition, urging that Liberia will not be forsaken now by our own Government for the sake of her 12,000,000 colored citizens." East proposed drawing in Harvey Firestone and urging him to use his influence. "He certainly would gain millions of friends and customers among our group for his products," observed the clergyman. East's letter had some impact; writing of the meeting to which East had addressed his comments, Thomas Jesse Jones observed that the letter had convinced him of an important point: if white philanthropists tried to cajole blacks into pressuring Liberia to accept the League's plan of assistance, the attempt would probably backfire.[98]

Later in May of 1934, Reverend East and other representatives of black missionary boards visited the State Department and lobbied for continued American interest in Liberia regardless of the outcome at Geneva (in Moffat's view "a series of rather nice sentimental appeals on behalf of the continued interest in Liberian welfare").[99] A little thereafter the State Department had another meeting with East and his confreres, who asked that the United States undertake the entire supervision of the Liberian affair and, interestingly, appoint an American chief adviser.[100]

The bishops of the African Methodist Episcopal Church met at the annual conference of the Foreign and Home Mission Board in June of 1934 and considered the Liberian matter. Again the formula of sovereignty with reform was endorsed. The meeting maintained that Liberia should never be surrendered as a mandate to any European power; instead the United States, while respecting the sovereignty of the Liberian Republic, should provide a plan of assistance under American auspices.[101] Although Undersecretary Phillips refused to give assurances as to the future course of American policy, prominent blacks, such as Robert Moton, continued to ask the State Department to come to Liberia's assistance.[102]

The lobbying efforts of these various American groups raises this question: what effect, if any, did they have on the actual course of American foreign policy? The view has been expressed that such activities, especially among blacks, were exiguous and had almost no effect on the outcome of policy. According to one recent analyst: "If Africa is of relatively small concern to the United States, it is surely also true that the Negro attitude in the United States toward Africa has only a marginal bearing on American policy there. . . . To put it in crude terms, there is no reason to assume that anybody can deliver a sufficiently substantial Negro vote on African issues to affect the outcome of significant elections."[103] Looking specifically at Liberia, another observer maintains, "Liberia's political independence was not saved because of any fear of the black vote or the protests of white liberals, although those factors sometimes influenced the timing of State Department actions (as did other domestic political considerations)." Instead, "the Department of State chose to subordinate the narrow interests of the Firestone Company and its demands for armed intervention to the expansion of American trade in Latin America."[104]

It can be effectively argued that the United States was withdrawing from direct intervention in Latin America, its traditional sphere of influence, during the early 1930s and that this almost certainly precluded embarkation on a policy of armed intervention in another continent. Looking at overall United States policy in this period one does detect a noticeable shift. Armed intervention for profit appeared an increasingly dubious proposition by the late 1920s. Americans had intervened in Latin America twenty-one times betweeen 1898 and 1924 and yet failed to firmly establish a hegemonic *status quo*. The Hoover administration defined a less belligerent policy.[105] Intervention in Liberia would have been both a turning away from this demarche and an economic error. The State Department knew "the establishment of a virtual American colony in Africa might render the continued espousal of the Monroe Doctrine difficult to justify, and would unquestionably arouse the suspicion of Europe and South America."[106] At the same time it noted that such a policy, "while doubtlessly justified by many on philanthropic or racial grounds, could not fail to arouse the hostility of others as imperialism."

But while American blacks and their friends did not set policy on Liberia, they delimited it. In 1930 the State Department had rejected the idea of letting Liberia fend for itself. William Castle thought, "Negroes would be furious and would turn bitterly against the administration."[107] Around the same time, however, the State Department decided against calling in black leaders and outlining its Liberian policy to them. Ellis Briggs of the State Department said that since he was "inclined to believe, American negroes will oppose any monkeying with Liberia on the grounds that we are helping foreign imperialists to smother that scorbutic nation for whose birth we were, alas, responsible, . . . little could be gained by taking them [i.e., Afro-Americans] into our confidence in advance."[108] In his opinion, the government should take its own course of action "and let them yell."

In setting its own course, however, the State Department constantly looked back over its shoulder at black opinion. An emerging policy of nonintervention does not preclude the possibility that such opinion was a major influence in the handling of the Liberian situation.[109] The State Department was well aware that it was under scrutiny by segments of the black public. In the autumn of 1932, Secretary of State Henry Stimson was told by the NAACP, "We are sure that the negroes of the United States will vigorously resist . . . intervention not only because it will impose a great injustice upon the Republic of Liberia but because it will be utterly inconsistent with the recent opposition expressed by the United States to the intervention of Japan in Manchuria. . . ."[110] The secretary of state was warned, "If the Department does not change its attitude on a question of vital importance to colored voters in the United States we should not be able to avoid attributing its position to the hostility of the Hoover administration to the negro race." The warning appears to have had effect. When, in early 1933, Hoover said that if necessary he would go to extreme lengths, even naval force, to protect the Firestone Company's investment, Secretary Stimson opposed him. According to Moffat, this was because "he can see, probably more clearly than the President, the howl this would produce in Europe and among our blacks in this country, and the ease with which it could be made to appear inconsistent with our Manchurian policy."[111] In February of 1933, Stimson pointed out to Harvey Firestone that armed intervention in Liberia would probably have severe repercussions among American blacks. And after it was decided to send General Winship to Monrovia, Moffat noted, "The trip will receive little space in the white press, but as the Negro papers will play it up big, it [has] to be drafted with meticulous care."[112]

The American government was well aware, therefore, that much black opinion not only did not favor American occupation of Liberia, but also opposed the abandonment of Liberia to European powers. In the spring of 1934, Moffat said that, in his view, Britain and France would not stand by indefinitely and see the Barclay regime defy them. Fighting between indigenous groups and the Monrovia government certainly gave them an opening for direct intervention, and it was very difficult for the United States to urge others to pursue a hands-off policy. However, because of "political and sentimental elements involved," the United States could not wash its hands of the Liberian affair.[113] A month later Moffat was more explicit: "The Secretary is anxious to issue a press statement less with a view to influencing public opinion in Liberia than to influencing negro opinion in this country."[114] Undersecretary Phillips lamented that "unfortunately the word was circulated not only in Liberia but in this country that Liberia's sovereignty was involved, and the fears of the colored population have been played upon."[115]

If in fact the State Department took great cognizance of black opinion, the question of why they did so remains. Many blacks felt that black opinion and voting power were crucial vis-à-vis Liberia. In 1925 W. E. B. DuBois had warned that "the Firestone Plantations Company wishes it can repeat in Liberia all the hell that white imperialism has perpetrated heretofore in Africa and Asia. There is only one power that can in the slightest degree curb this and that is the black American with his vote."[116] Eight years later the black journalist George Schuyler wrote the NAACP scoffing at its possible advocacy of a Scandinavian chief adviser. Schuyler pointed out "that there are no Negro voters in Scandinavia to bring pressure on either the governments of Norway or Sweden in case the man selected turns out to be a s.o.b."[117]

In January of 1931, J. P. Moffat of the State Department expressed great concern about the publication of the report of the League's commission of inquiry: "The whole question is so dangerous from the point of view of party politics in the United States, including the negro vote, that it has to be handled with special care."[118] Because of Undersecretary of State William Castle's great desire to keep black support for the Republican Party, the American chargé in Liberia, Henry Carter, wrote directly to President Hoover in 1930 with his request that the United States temporarily intervene. He went over Castle's head because he feared Castle would veto his ideas out of deference to black opinion.[119]

Concern with the black vote during the Liberian crisis may have stemmed from changes taking place in the relationship between the two American political parties. If the crisis burst on the scene at a time when overt Dollar Diplomacy was falling into desuetude, it also came at a time of electoral shift. In 1920 and 1924 the twelve largest cities in the United States, taken together, elected a Republican majority. In 1928 they selected Democrats.[120] The Northern urban black vote may have been relatively small and unmobilized, but in a shifting political situation it loomed large in the minds of certain State Department officials (especially William Castle).

Thus, it was against this background of shifting party politics that the Liberian crisis took place. In 1932, when the NAACP stated its strong rejection of a "dictatorial" chief adviser, the State Department was alarmed by the organization's stance, fearing that publication of this position would "raise the devil with the colored people," and lose the Hoover administration support among blacks.[121] Walter White of the NAACP wrote black sociologist E. Franklin Frazier on the same issue, noting that the United States had accepted a compromise text on the authority of the chief adviser. "Fortunately," said White, "this matter arose just prior to what seems will be a very close election and at a time when the Administration is very much worried about the Negro vote being 'off the reservation.' "[122] Harvey Firestone also attempted to use the issue of black votes as a lever to obtain policies favorable to his interests; unless the Liberian matter was taken away from consideration by the League, he claimed, the United States would not only lose its independent source of rubber, but the Republican administration would also be "embarrassed with the negro race during the Presidential campaign of 1932."[123] Moffat, considering these arguments and counterarguments, complained of "the mental gymnastics of trying to carry two pails, one filled with negro votes and the other filled with Firestone campaign contributions. . . ."[124] In the autumn of 1932, Moffat predicted that Firestone would not push the administration on the Liberian issue until after the November 8 presidential election, when Hoover, if he won, would be under no compulsion to cultivate the black vote.[125]

When the Roosevelt administration came in, however, concern for black votes continued. In 1933, Dorothy Detzer felt that black electoral strength was very important to the resolution of the whole matter. She told Anna Graves that this was true "particularly as Farley [James Farley, Democratic National Chairman] is touring the South in order to try to gain southern votes because of the loss of the prohibition issue." She thought that if the Democrats alienated blacks at the same time it would "be bad political strategy."[126] The following year, in the British House of Lords, Lord Snell took issue with Lord Lugard's belief that the United States would take strong governmental action in Liberia, reminding his audience "that as practical politicians we should remember that there are 2,000,000 negro votes in the United States of America, and that therefore it is not easy to assume that that does not present a problem to the United States Government."[127]

Having seen how various black groups sought to influence the foreign policy apparatus from without, we still face the question of the role of blacks *within* that apparatus. In 1976, Senator Frank Church remarked that "no agency in government . . . has less black influence than the State Department, and that's why we're in trouble in Africa."[128] A very different viewpoint was expressed by black sociologist E. Franklin Frazier in 1959. Frazier voiced the opinion that Afro-American participation in the American foreign service apparatus would have little positive impact on Africa policy. In an extremely negative appraisal of the Afro-American role, he said, "Negroes lack any political philosophy except a narrow opportunism." Furthermore, he continued, "An increasing number of American Negroes may go to Africa as advisers and specialists, but they will go as Americans representing American interests, not African interests." He saw "evidence that middle class Negroes in such positions are deriving great satisfaction from what they regard as a new status and acceptance in American society."[129] Frazier's highly critical appraisal of blacks in the foreign policy apparatus highlights the point that the absolute number of blacks in the State Department is subsidiary to their perception of their role as black representatives of white America on a black continent. The careers of the black United States ministers to Liberia in the early 1930s amply demonstrate the ambiguities of their position.

The ministership to Monrovia was traditionally assigned to an Afro-American. The office was a political plum which fell to one of the black Republican or Democratic party faithful. During the Liberian crisis the State Department frequently questioned the wisdom of this policy, arguing that any black in this office would be plagued by pressures which would hamper his efficiency. This was well demonstrated in the case of Charles Mitchell, who was appointed in 1930.

Mitchell, who had been business manager of West Virginia State College, was sent to Monrovia in February of 1931. Being black certainly did not guarantee him smooth relations with the Barclay regime. During the early months of his tenure, Mitchell urged the State Department to recognize the regime, but Barclay, without that recognition, refused to accord the minister the status or cooperation he thought he deserved.[130] Relations between the two men became embittered and when Liberia undertook its repudiationist measures, Mitchell strongly advocated American intervention, urging the United States to take control of the country and compel the lifting of the offending legislation.[131]

In Washington, opinion of Mitchell was somewhat less than supportive. J. P. Moffat wrote in the summer of 1932 that Mitchell was "an extremely intelligent negro and a kindly one,—perhaps too kindly."[132] Unfortunately, Mitchell had "been double-crossed by Barclay and reluctantly admits that he sees no chance of development in Liberia unless some outside Power dominates the show." By January of 1933, Mitchell was "our poor negro Minister, who is bearing the brunt of Barclay's wrath and who is out-maneuvered about once a day by the latter's superior intelligence. . . ."[133] Moffat noted "the Secretary could not forbear giving a good chuckle in appreciating the situation which our politics of requiring a darky Minister inevitably produce." In February of 1933 the president of Liberia demanded that Mitchell be recalled on the grounds that the minister "had overstepped the bounds of courtesy in writing personal letters to the President of Liberia which were so offensive that they could not be overlooked."[134] Mitchell was removed (he left on March 22, 1933) and replaced by the mission of Winship and Briggs.[135]

The question of a replacement naturally arose. The chargé in Monrovia wrote Moffat in September urging that a black minister not be appointed:

> In my opinion, while I do not doubt that many high class Negroes would like to be appointed Minister and Consul General here, their desire for the appointment is based primarily on the utter ignorance of conditions as they are, and I am convinced that they are not able to give, when here, the best that is in them; they cannot help being discouraged, and disgusted for that matter, at the flat failure of the Liberian Negroes to meet the standards of living, politics or learning that the American Negro now stands for. Also, I question that the Liberian feels or shows the respect due to the educated American Negro.[136]

In his view the post "should be administered by a career white officer who has not had too much experience in the Far East, where questions of caste and color are predominant. . . . [He] should be able to meet the principal Liberians in a friendly way, yet without familiarity or loss of caste." Almost two years later, with no minister yet appointed, a new chargé wrote the State Department, "Barclay has intimated that he would prefer this [i.e., a white envoy] and I feel that a sympathetic well qualified white would be of greater use to both governments for the next year in formulating and launching Barclay's plan."[137]

But the Roosevelt administration stuck to the appointment policy of previous administrations. While chargés in Monrovia were debating the merits of a white man in the post, the next minister, Lester Walton, wrote to Claude Barnett of the Associated Negro Press: "You asked me in a previous letter about the State Department's attitude in sending to Liberia a white chargé d'affaires. . . . When the time comes a Negro will be sent as U.S. Minister."[138] In July of 1933, Walton told his colleague, "Confidentially, I heard from [James] Farley [Chairman of the Democratic Party] this a.m.," who "did not speak of [the] collectorship but spoke of me being given consideration for [the] Liberian post when time comes."[139] Walton assured Barnett, "No Minister will be named for several months, what the brothers say notwithstanding."[140] By the beginning of the next year, Walton, back from a trip to Liberia, was even more confident. "So far as [the] Department of State is concerned," he wrote Barnett, "I can confidentially say to you that I need not worry." The department was "not going to stand for any Tom, Dick or Harry going."[141] When, in the summer of 1935, the American chargé in Monrovia learned that Walton had achieved his ambition, he wrote Harry McBride, the special investigator of Liberian conditions called in by the State Department the year before:

I am sorry you could not get a white man with all the qualifications but I appreciate the difficulties. In the face of them I don't think we could have gotten a better man than Walton. His friendship with Barclay, however, will be both an advantage and a detriment. As long as things go well he will be alright [*sic*] but in the matter of suggestion or advice he will be handicapped as no Negro, or at least no Negro here, willingly takes advice from another. They are born individualist in their own race. They will sometimes take advice from whites as no matter how much they dislike us they realize that we have had more experience and advantages. When the pressure comes Barclay will expect Walton to side with him as a member of his race and not oppose him as a representative of the United States. Failure to agree with him will bring enmity as Barclay is emotional like all of them.[142]

Walton arrived in October of 1935. The British consulate in Monrovia described the new American minister as "a very agreeable and intelligent negro subject of America." It drew, however, an erroneous conclusion—that Walton's appointment was unfortunate since "he has to protect American white interests here and there is always the possibility of a clash between the Firestone organization and the Government. . . . Mr. Walton's position would be very complicated by his race and colour. . . ."[143] In fact, Walton's economic opinions were not dictated by considerations of race and color; he saw the role of blacks in foreign policy as auxiliary and not contradictory to that of American economic interests. In 1933 he made his pro-business stance quite clear; invited by newspaper columnist Drew Pearson to meet with Dorothy Detzer of the Women's International League for Peace and Freedom, he expressed fear that Detzer might be of the same stamp as another WILPF member, Anna Graves, whom he had met in Geneva: "I grew tired of her wild talk and told her so far as the colored American was concerned, capital had done more for him than labor, which bars members of my race from trade unions. . . ."[144]

Walton had close ties to the pro-Firestone Phelps-Stokes Fund and had actively sought to become a pro-company propagandist. At the time of the investigation of 1930, Walton, then a journalist for the New York *Age*, was already receiving money from the Phelps-Stokes Fund through the Commission on Interracial Cooperation in Atlanta. Shortly after the stock market crash of 1929, the head of the commission wrote to Anson Phelps-Stokes of the Phelps-Stokes Fund praising Walton's usefulness.[145] But as the Depression deepened, the services of the black journalist seemed less essential. In early 1931 a representative of the fund wrote to Anson Phelps-Stokes complaining that although "during the past five or six years (or possibly seven years) the Interracial Commission has paid Mr. Walton a regular monthly salary of $83.33. . . . I am not sure that Dr. [Will] Alexander [of the Interracial Commission] and his associates place the same value on Mr. Walton's services that we do."[146] Although

he did not always present the views of the commission, Walton's articles
on Liberia were seen as having a salutory effect on black public opinion.
A month later the philanthropist Phelps-Stokes wrote the commission,
noting that the body had cut Walton's salary. The black journalist was
described as "greatly distressed" at this and at "the uncertainty as to the
future." Phelps-Stokes asked that the old salary be continued. He commented: "We do not, of course, however, make the continuance of our
help to the Interracial Commission in any way dependent upon the
employment of Mr. Walton. That would be manifestly improper."[147]
Ten days later the commission informed Phelps-Stokes that Walton
would be paid for February and March. The commission also promised
to speak with Dr. Robert Moton of Tuskegee about Walton's future.[148]

During the uncertainty over his emoluments, Walton wrote to
Phelps-Stokes outlining his plight. "On one or two occasions," he wrote,
"I have suggested to Dr. [Thomas Jesse] Jones that the Fund pay me
outright." Walton said Jones had advised him "that you [Phelps-Stokes]
were unalterably opposed to such arrangements, as you did not want the
fund to go on record as paying for publicity."[149] But, the embittered
Walton wrote, "It should be kept in mind that all the time I devote to
writing and releasing stories on Liberia or Hampton, etc., is distinct and
separate from any financial arrangements with the New York *World* [one
of the papers to which he supplied articles]."[150] Moreover, at great cost to
himself, the journalist had defended the best interests of his race:

> A few weeks ago the President of the Dunbar National Bank expressed
> himself perturbed over Soviet Russia's program of seeking to stir up strife
> and discontent among colored Americans. It cannot be denied that an organ-
> ized effort is being made to rally Negroes under the communistic banner and
> that the scheme is meeting with questionable success. Lynching, unemploy-
> ment, discrimination against the Negro in labor unions and even in the
> North, are being effectively emphasized. Dr. Jones well knows that I believe
> in progress and want to see my race advance as fast as possible, but I believe
> this will come about by evolution rather than by revolution. To me it seems
> the height of folly for men in high places to sit in smug complacency without
> turning a hand to combat a sinister campaign of a nation to create discord and
> disloyalty among one-tenth of our country's population.[151]

In May of 1933, Walton wrote of his continuing efforts to present
the cause of Firestone to the black American public: "While there [Wash-
ington] I had a talk with friends [presumably Firestone] relative to their
getting a correspondent. They pointed out that if such a step were taken
the identity of the correspondent would be discovered sooner or later
with calamitous results to them."[152] In July of 1933, L. A. Roy of the
Phelps-Stokes Fund noted that it would be excellent if funds could be

found for some American black with the correct views to accompany a representative of the fund on a trip to Monrovia.[153] In the same month Walton went to Liberia as a correspondent. On his return to America, Walton embarked on a lecture tour and gave an essentially pro-Firestone view of the troubles with the Barclay regime. After his appointment as American representative to the Liberian government, Walton continued his intimate relations with the Phelps-Stokes Fund and kept its members abreast of Liberian developments. When in 1935 the Liberian cabinet received a salary increase, he told an officer of the fund that he hoped Harvey Firestone would not be "unduly pessimistic" about this action and felt the American capitalist would "be justly compensated for all that he has gone through."[154]

As minister, Walton, with some opportunism, seemed quite able to balance the conflicting forces around him. While remaining an intimate and hidden friend of the Firestone interests, he was also able to gain the confidence of Barclay. In November of 1935 Walton wrote to Claude Barnett: "Confidentially the most cordial and confidential relations exist between President Barclay and me. By working together informally, you can do so much more than going through formal procedures."[155] However, five years later Walton was to express a much more jaundiced view of the Barclay regime, complaining that the Liberians would never accept advice unless it was delivered with a hand "of iron in the silken glove."[156]

Walton, who came to view himself as the black expert on Liberian affairs, clearly seems to have maneuvered successfully through the Liberian crisis on the basis of self-interest. As the protégé of the Phelps-Stokes Fund, he assiduously sought to ingratiate himself with white philanthropic interests, who at certain times granted him emoluments, and with the Firestone Company. His position as a loyal Democrat stood him in good stead after the advent of the Roosevelt administration. His guiding principle during the crisis was self-advancement rather than adherence to any of the aims of the various black groups debating the Liberian issue. His success in attaining the ministership was vivid proof of the rewards to be gained by tenacity. At the same time, his success highlights the ambiguities surrounding the role and allegiance of the black diplomat in Africa.

Walton and some of his predecessors in Monrovia represented no black consensus, or even constituency, on African affairs; they emerged from the infighting of American partisan politics, and they offered no substantive black input in American African policy. What input there was came from black individuals and groups who were motivated to defend Liberia by missionary ardor or racial solidarity. Another factor, however, was blacks' concern for their economic opportunities in Liberia, and this remains to be explored.

5· The Hope of the Diaspora

I want you to realize what the Republic of Liberia means. We are to a
great extent solving your destiny [cheers]; we have assumed a very great
responsibility; a few of the people on the West Coast of Africa have
assumed the responsibility of at least 400 millions of people; it is a very
great responsibility. We are always conscious of the fact that our efforts
one way or the other must affect the great and weighty interest of the
race at large and therefore how careful we should be in executing the
great task of our work. . . . The criticisms that may be levelled upon
the Liberian Administration will not be confined to Liberians only but
on every black man whether he be of Sierra Leone, the Gold Coast,
Nigeria, the West Indies or the United States of America. . . . [C. D.
B. King, Address at the Grammar School, Freetown, Sierra Leone,
1925]

During the crisis of the early 1930s, Liberia stretched forth its hands to
blacks in North America and the Caribbean. The appeal affected both
those who viewed the Black Republic as the symbol of black independence and those who viewed it as a field for black enterprise. To the first
group, the threat represented by European and American diplomatic
intervention seemed obvious. As we have mentioned, Liberia was widely
seen as a test case of racial capacity. A writer in *Current History* declared:
"The American nation has cooperated through one of its most distinguished Negro citizens in the work of inquiry and is officially eager to
see that these inquiries become the basis of a real work of reconstruction. . . . In a real sense the Negro race in Liberia is on trial before the
world."[1]

To Afro-Americans the importance of the Liberian scandal seemed
clear, but the initial response to it was mixed. The charge that "slavery"

was a going concern in Liberia, with blacks enslaving fellow blacks, was disturbing; if this situation did exist, it constituted racial betrayal. Afro-Americans had long been ambivalent toward Africa: was it a proud ancestral home or a land of savagery? This ambivalence could only be heightened by revelations which seemed to bolster assertions of black racial infantilism and incapacity for self-rule. The molder of black opinion in the United States faced the problem of what tack to take on the Liberian issue. If the Liberian elite was corrupt, it should be condemned. Yet condemnation fell in very nicely with the charges of white racists and might threaten the independence of the lone republic on the continent. The deep desire of many blacks in the Diaspora to keep Liberia open as a black man's country encouraged them to defend Liberia even in the face of lingering doubts about the aims and methods of the Liberian elite.

The difficulty was increased by entreaties from Liberia itself. Americo-Liberia found itself poised between blacks in the Hinterland and blacks in the Diaspora. After 1930, in hopes of gaining support from overseas blacks, Liberia made a strong appeal to racial solidarity. President King said in defense of Liberia: "In view of the attitude of other administrations in Africa toward slavery and forced labor, it is difficult to understand the reason for this outburst of general criticism against Liberia, except it be because of her weakness or to serve as an excuse on the part of the enemies of our race to blot out the existence of a State in Africa which holds out to millions of Negroes in Africa, the United States, and the West Indies, the brightest hopes for the realization of their highest political and racial aspirations."[2] King's successor, Edwin Barclay, echoing the Gettysburg Address, defiantly maintained, "No coerced admission of failure and incompetency, nor inspired misrepresentation of administrative conditions, no treasonable political propaganda either at home or abroad shall force us voluntarily to submit [to] the fiat, that this nation, founded by black men, should perish from the face of the earth."[3]

The need to protect Liberia against racist censure was apparent. As the crisis proceeded, this need frequently led many of Liberia's most ardent defenders to paint a roseate picture of the Liberian state, increasingly envisioned as the repository and fulfillment of the hopes of millions of blacks in the Diaspora. In the forefront of these defenders were many Pan-Africanists—writers and thinkers dedicated to emancipating Africa from colonial rule and to improving the condition of black people in both Africa and the Americas. The most notable defenses of the Liberian regime came from W. E. B. DuBois in the NAACP journal *The Crisis* and B. N. Azikiwe in his book *Liberia in World Politics*, as well as from George Padmore in the Afro-American press. Azikiwe, who later became president of independent Nigeria, was hyperbolic in his praise of the Black Republic. He believed the Liberia of the 1930s was to be the fountainhead of African cultural renaissance: "German *Kultur* and *Kulturkampf* are possible in Germany; Japanism is realizable in Japan. If African *Kulturkampf* must be consummated—it is inevitable, despite all attempts to stifle national consciousness and self-determination—then the incubator for hatching the egg of a great national awakening, toward the establishment of a black hegemony, is the Republic of Liberia."[4] W. E. B. DuBois maintained that "indeed, the record of peace, efficiency and ability made by this little poverty-stricken settlement of the rejected and despised, sitting on the edge of Africa and fighting the world in order to be let alone, is, despite querulous criticism, one of the most heartening efforts in human history."[5] In an article entitled "Pan-Africa and New Racial Philosophy," DuBois warned his readers against racial divisiveness, pointing out that the white world painted a distorted picture of the nonwhite world "which with engaging naivete we accept and then proceed to laugh at each other and criticize each other before we make any attempt to learn the truth."[6]

George Padmore was equally tenacious in his defense of Liberia. The West Indian-born writer was one of the leading enunciators of Pan-Africanism as an anticommunist alternative for the liberation of Africa. In his work *Pan-Africanism or Communism* he bluntly stated that Pan-Africanism was "an independent political expression of Negro aspirations for complete national independence from white domination—Capitalist or Communist."[7] Padmore had joined the Communist Party in the 1920s, but became increasingly disenchanted with the party's positions, particularly on colonial questions. By 1934 he had left the Communist International and its subsidiary organization, the International Trade Union Committee of Negro Workers, denouncing the International's failure to rally to the defense of the Monrovia regime. He believed that the maintenance of Liberian independence was essential to the anticolonialist struggle. In 1938 the London-based International African Service Bureau, of which Padmore was chairman, wrote to Barclay through its treasurer T. Ras Makonnen:

> This organization . . . takes a special interest in the condition and progress of the State of Liberia. . . . Those of us in the Western world follow its career jealously, because, although some of us may never have seen Africa, we know that equality for the Negroes in the Western world is inextricably bound with the emancipation for the African people. This organization has in the past and may, in the future, pass severe criticism on the condition of the Liberian people or on certain aspects of its Government, but we take this opportunity of assuring you, and the people whom you govern, that such criticisms are made in the interests of the Liberian people and of the

Negro race as a whole. Whereas we stand for the complete emancipation of every part of Africa from European domination, we stand firmly for the national independence of the State of Liberia. Liberia is not an Imperialist State. We unhesitatingly condemn all whose criticisms have as their aim, direct or indirect, the bringing of Liberia into the orbit of the European dominion of Africa. We urge and advocate the necessity of Africans and peoples of African descent, and all their allies and representatives, fighting, if necessary, with arms in hand, for the independence of Liberia. Not only that, but we shall seek always to bring before all members of the Negro race and all other persons likely to be interested, the importance of Liberia to the cause of African emancipation, the necessity of being vigilant in its defence, and readiness at all times to take whatever steps are necessary for that aim.[8]

In 1941 Padmore wrote, "I have always considered it my special duty to expose and denounce the misrule of the black governing classes in Haiti, Liberia, and Abyssinia, while at the same time defending these semi-colonial countries against imperialist aggression."[9] This carefully balanced position would have been eminently reasonable, but in the 1930s it was increasingly difficult to maintain. For many blacks in the Diaspora, the choice was of the either-or variety: support sovereignty under the existing black governing class or see the independence of Africa's only republic ended or diminished. The decision was not an easy one. If Liberia disappeared from the map, would this not influence the future course of decolonization? The perception of many Pan-Africanists—such as Padmore, DuBois, and Azikiwe (who returned to West Africa from America in the mid-thirties)—that the destruction of Liberian sovereignty would affect the future of West African nationalism is probably correct. The failure of an African state with a Western model constitution would have been used by colonial apologists as an argument to delay African independence: the need for continued foreign tutelage would have been emphasized and played upon. If, in the mid-thirties, the League of Nations plan had been accepted, or if Liberia had fallen under a European mandate, the country would have been under non-African supervision at least until the eve of World War II. The issue of independence might well have been held in abeyance during the war, and one cannot say whether an independent Liberia would have reemerged.

Moreover, the defense of Liberia was, by 1935, influenced by reaction to the Fascist attack on Ethiopia. In 1936, President Edwin Barclay proclaimed that Liberia would "maintain her status as a Negro State in the age of imperialistic conquest."[10] The Accra (Gold Coast) *African Morning Post* warned its readers that Liberia would follow Ethiopia as the next victim of European colonial aggrandizement.[11] In the summer of 1935 the British consulate in Monrovia informed its Foreign Office that Liberians were showing great interest in the fate of Haile Selassie's government.

The consulate thought the Italian invasion would make the Liberians more jealous of their independence and, at the same time, more amenable to outside advice.[12] In the same summer William Jones of the Baltimore *Afro-American* told his readers that it was "of deep significance . . . that just at this time when Abyssinia is the focus of world diplomatic relations, the United States Government steps in and announces recognition of the only other parcel of land not under colonial rule in that great country [*sic*]."[13] From Baltimore, Liberian Consul-General Ernest Lyon had already reminded Barclay that Liberia was the only black ruled state in Africa. In his view Ethiopia was independent, "but Abyssinia is not Negro."[14] The conquest of Ethiopia at least removed the significance of this debatable point. The International African Service Bureau told Barclay, "Today [now] that Abyssinia has been made a subject State and the last of the ancient African Kingdoms is destroyed, Liberia becomes of special importance as a symbol of African independence."[15]

Despite the Pan-Africanists' support of Liberia, there was continued ambiguity in the relationship between the Liberian ruling elite and blacks in the Diaspora. One evidence of this ambiguity can be found in the issue of migration to Liberia. Although the Christy-Johnson commission had officially recommended Afro-American emigration and the Brunot commission had expressed the "hope that some of these foreign [League of Nations] specialists may be recruited from among the representatives of the negro race,"[16] there was no torrent of Afro-American emigration to Liberia in the wake of the 1930 League investigation. Monrovia was suspicious of immigrants and required them to post a bond of $100. By this means the possibility of emigration was closed to impecunious Afro-Americans, who formed the majority of American blacks in the period 1929–1936.

Doubts about the relationship between Liberia and the wider black world were present throughout the period of the scandal. Late in 1934 Claude Barnett, of the Associated Negro Press, expressed his misgivings: "We have helped to make Negro public opinion have confidence in the present [Barclay] administration in order that [the American] government might feel the pressure of aiding the Republic and yet there is considerable question of how much confidence we have in them."[17] Ten years before, W. E. B. DuBois had attempted to silence such doubts by telling Afro-Americans, "There is not a thing that American Negroes can tell Liberians about the needs of Liberians that Liberians do not know and have not discussed and desired for fifty years, and they are bitter when the descendants of slaves who meekly submitted to their slavery presume to ladle out loads of obvious advice to people who for a hundred tremendous years have dared to be free."[18] Yet complaints about the Black

Republic continued to be heard from various Afro-Americans. In December of 1933 the Pittsburgh *Courier* published an account of the experiences of Mrs. Elizabeth McWillie, an Afro-American emigrant who had returned in disgust to the United States. Mrs. McWillie said immigrants were the victims of extortion and that several groups from the West Indies had been left destitute. The woman reported that many immigrants from the United States were "so fed up on Liberia that they would kiss a Mississippi cracker if he could only get them away from there."[19] She criticized the delegation, led by DuBois, which went to the State Department to plead Liberia's case and declared, "Lots of people in Liberia wonder why DuBois keeps on talking about Liberia. He knows nothing about the country nor the conditions existing there." Claude Barnett received a letter, originally sent to Dr. L. K. Williams of the National Baptist Convention, in which the writer, an Afro-American, said, "I have never in my life seen black people hate other black people as this Administration and the so called leading people in Liberia hate the American Negroes; they do not want any American Negroes out here in large numbers."[20]

Was there any substance to Afro-American doubts as to the sincerity of the Americo-Liberian elite or were such fears simply the result of the misadventures of a few disgruntled individuals? There are indications that, from the mid-1920s at least, as a result of Marcus Garvey's abortive scheme for large-scale Afro-American emigration, the Liberian elite was wary of too great an Afro-American presence. Garvey, a Jamaican by birth, had established the Universal Negro Improvement Association (UNIA) in 1914 and by the end of World War I had attracted a considerable mass following in the United States.[21] One of Garvey's aims was the eventual liberation of Africa from European rule. A part of his program called for the strengthening of economic ties between Afro-Americans and Africa and the emigration of large numbers of American blacks to the continent. Liberia was to be his base and in 1920 he sent a delegation to confer with the Liberian government.[22] Monrovia was informed that the UNIA wished to transfer its headquarters to Liberia and the government was asked to aid the organization in securing land. The UNIA agreed to raise funds to pay Liberia's debts, which amounted to $2,210,807.53 by September of 1920.[23] The mayor of Monrovia, Gabriel Johnson, President King's son-in-law, along with a member of the Liberian Frontier Force, visited New York in the same year and was given an important post in the association. Garvey sent a delegation to Monrovia in December of 1923 to complete plans for the first phase of the emigration scheme. The UNIA group offered to transport from 20,000 to 30,000 black families to Liberia per year. President King appointed a committee, which included the vice-president and the chief justice, to act as liaison with Garvey's American organization. A phased settlement scheme was proposed: in the initial stage 3,000 immigrant families were to be settled in six settlements of 500 families each (two on the border of British-controlled Sierra Leone and four along Liberia's boundaries with French-controlled territory). The UNIA was granted a beginning concession of 500 acres (but not along the borders).

Beginning in February of 1924 relations between the Garveyites and the Liberian government quickly went awry. Before the end of February three members of the UNIA had left Liberia, expressing their great disappointment with the Liberian situation.[24] Garvey intimated in March that immigrants would arrive in Liberia in the autumn, but the attitude of the Liberian government toward Garveyism continued to deteriorate. King definitely turned against the association and refused to meet its delegates. In June, Secretary of State Edwin Barclay informed the Elder Dempster steamship line that no members of the UNIA were to be permitted to land in Liberia and promised that if they were landed they would be deported at the company's expense.[25] When three Garveyites arrived in Monrovia in late July they were promptly arrested and deported on a German ship bound for Hamburg.[26] Farm machinery and other goods belonging to the group were seized by customs in Cape Palmas. In December of 1924 the Liberian legislature hailed C. D. B. King as "a far-seeing, patriotic statesman" and lauded him for deporting the UNIA members and thereby "demonstrating the correctness and soundness of his policy and political principles, with which the national legislature is in full accord."[27]

Why did the Liberian government make its *volte face?* Several reasons can be adduced for the subversion of Garvey's "Back to Africa" scheme. The Liberian government maintained that Garvey's militant anticolonialism imperiled its relations with the British and the French. Liberian Secretary of State Edwin Barclay acknowledged that both of these powers had inquired as to Monrovia's attitude toward the UNIA and the Liberians went to great pains to assure them that Liberia would not become a hotbed of anticolonialist agitation. An article found in the Liberian National Archives amply expresses this view: "Some misguided negroes consider Liberia a suitable *point d'appui* for launching and indulging in animus against the white man, unmindful of the fact inter alia Liberia as a nation knows no race antagonism, and like her European neighbors is engaged in the same undertaking towards the uplift of the indigenous Africans within her territory; and as such requires the amicable and sympathetic co-operation of her white brethren if she ever hopes to succeed in the accomplishment of her ideals."[28]

The United States government and groups within the United States also took a dim view of Garvey's activities. In May of 1921 the American minister in Monrovia was told to keep an eye on the UNIA and to provide information on the character and activities of Gabriel Johnson, the association's chief Liberian member.[29] The American attitude was probably also influenced by that of Garvey's great antagonist, W. E. B. DuBois, editor of the NAACP's *The Crisis*. In January of 1924, DuBois, who viewed Garvey's plans as utopian, visited Liberia as the American representative at President King's second inaugural. On return DuBois gave a favorable report of the Liberian administration and urged the United States to give Liberia developmental aid, aid which would, no doubt, be an alternative to that being proffered by the UNIA.[30] Shortly after his return from Liberia in May of 1924, DuBois attacked the head of the UNIA as "without doubt the most dangerous enemy of the Negro race in America and the World."[31]

Perhaps the most salient reason for the abortion of the Garvey scheme was the threat that it presented to the Liberian *status quo*. The Americo-Liberian elite became increasingly aware that an influx of Garveyites would present serious problems of control and political authority. Initially the elite may have viewed Garvey's seemingly grandiose schemes as unfeasible. However, by the mid-1920s the UNIA had begun a shipping line (the Black Star Line) and bought three ships. The prospect of further funds being raised in America brought the achievement of part of Garvey's aims within reach and raised the very serious question of how the UNIA would relate to the existing administration. The head of the organization had already assumed the title "Provisional President of Africa" and had bestowed the title "Supreme Potentate" on its chief Liberian representative, Gabriel Johnson. The question of how the supranational and Pan-African Garvey organization would interdigitate with the constitutional structure of the Black Republic aroused grave misgivings in Monrovia. The Monrovia regime was aware of the revolutionary potential of groups of Garveyites settled separately on the country's borders, and proposed that instead the Garveyites should be distributed among existing Americo-Liberian settlements.[32] A large influx of Afro-Americans also raised the spectre of an unemployed and discontented population of politically aware citizens. In 1920, President King alluded to this danger in his inaugural address when he noted that immigration must "be carefully safeguarded" and that immigrants should not come unless they could obtain profitable employment.[33]

Between the local "Potentate" of the UNIA and the delegates sent out from America there was also mistrust and jostling for position. In June of 1921 one of the emissaries from the United States, Cyril Critchlow, complained that Gabriel Johnson was "a government official who is Liberian first and then anything else after that."[34] Critchlow maintained that the "Potentate" took little interest in the association's work, his time being "largely devoted to his private business—his boat and other personal affairs." The emissary thought Johnson was endeavoring to link his own business interests to those of the UNIA and felt that, in general, Americo-Liberians looked forward to bilking the proposed immigrants. On the other hand, an article now in the possession of the Liberian government attacked the highhandedness of Garvey's delegates and said "His Highness the Supreme Potentate' found himself controlled and hedged in by secret instructions. . . . 'His Highness', *because he was a Liberian* could not be trusted to carry out the secret purposes of the 'President General' [Garvey]."[35]

Most damaging to the Garveyite cause was its attitude on the "Native Question." Elie Garcia, one of Garvey's lieutenants in the 1920 delegation, drafted a report on "The True Conditions in Liberia." Garcia's report was a damning indictment of the Liberian regime and eventually fell into the hands of the government. The Americo-Liberians were chastised as parasitical and lazy. Garcia charged, "They buy men or women to help them and the least little insignificant Americo-Liberian has half a dozen boys at his service—for he, himself, will not even carry his own umbrella in the street, said article has to be carried by a boy, and so, for the smallest parcel."[36] The settler-indigene problem was left for the future; for the present, Garcia advised that the exercise of "modesty" and "discretion" on the part of UNIA would "remove any possible idea of opposition and will not prevent us, after having a strong foothold in the country, to act as we see best for their [the Liberian population's] own betterment and that of the race at large."

In the aftermath of the failure of Garvey's scheme, the Liberian regime kept a wary lookout for further Garveyite attempts at settlement. In 1929, President King made it quite clear that he did not want the American selected for the League commission to be connected in any way with the Garvey movement.[37] King and others maintained a somewhat jaundiced view of Afro-American participation in Liberian affairs, Garveyite or not. In 1934 the American chargé asked the then ex-president if King felt there would be less friction if the financial or administrative officers appointed under a plan of assistance were black. King replied that he felt white men would be preferable because they would be more detached and because it would be easier to find suitable white candidates.[38] In the same year Ernest Lyon, the Afro-American who was Liberian consul-general in Baltimore, wrote to the Liberian secretary of state saying "it is commonly rumored that Ex-President King opposed the employment of American colored men by the Firestone Corporation."[39] Later in 1934 Henry West of the American Colonization Society wrote that he "had looked forward to an all-Negro staff at Kakata [site of an educational institution], knowing that Dr. East, Dr. Jernigan and other of our colored friends, including Mr. Walton [of the New York *Age*], were desirous that this experiment should be tried," but he noted that the opposition of Kakata's Liberian advisers was "very emphatic."[40] In 1936, when Walton was American minister in Monrovia, reports were received that a large group of Afro-Americans wanted to emigrate. The minister and President Barclay agreed to issue a statement that skilled artisans were welcome but "as Liberia is autonomous, it has been compelled to take a definite position regarding the coming of organized groups, having as their object the making of the country the base of international antagonisms."[41] The fears of the Liberian government were, in all probability, aroused by the neo-Garveyite Peace Movement of Ethiopia, which had been organized in Chicago in 1932 and which was actively encouraging black emigration to Liberia.[42]

But there were some kinds of Afro-American involvement that the Liberians would tolerate. Liberia had long been touted as a place for the unfolding of the black economic destiny, and during the crisis of the 1930s the Americo-Liberian elite, while discouraging schemes for massive immigration, continued to play on the theme of Liberia as a frontier of economic opportunity. For many blacks in the Diaspora, Liberia was something more than a symbol of black self-rule—it was the one area where black enterprise might flourish.

Recently, Ian Duffield, looking at West Africa and Afro-America in the interwar period, has been led to conclude that "by the late 1920s, Pan-Africanism based on produce-trading began to decline, initially signalled by the loss of faith in black American partners and their replacement by white Americans. . . ."[43] Duffield is speaking particularly of British West Africa. But a close examination of the Liberian situation reveals that any such generalization for West Africa as a whole is dangerous. In the twenties and thirties economic Pan-Africanism (linking Liberia and the Diaspora) remained an important element in the thought of both Afro-Americans and Liberians.

For example, in late 1933 the Liberians proposed to send a commission to the United States to solicit financial and moral support from American blacks, as well as from white American corporations.[44] The major response to such appeals was bound to come not from the broad mass of Afro-Americans, but from the "black bourgeoisie." The individuals and organizations that espoused the cause of Liberia were, for the most part, from the articulate and relatively more comfortable segments of the community, segments that had always been opposed to Garvey. The Americo-Liberian elite which had rejected the proffered aid of Garvey and Garveyism in the 1920s was, in the next decade, quite ready to solicit the aid of Garvey's enemies. Unlike Garvey, who commented that the Americo-Liberians were "afraid" of him because "they have no colleague in me to exploit the labor of the unfortunate blacks and build up class distinctions, based on education of the wrong sort,"[45] the American black bourgeoisie posed no threat of immediate inundation through emigration or of destruction of the entrenched position of the Americo-Liberians. With the promise of an independent Liberia as a field for black economic exploitation, the support of some segments of this black bourgeoisie could be maintained. Although there was no actual upsurge of Afro-American investment in Liberia in the early 1930s (a time of general economic distress), there was a proliferation of schemes for, and interest in, Afro-American participation in the economic development of the Black Republic.

Well before the scandal of 1929 there had even been some hope that the spread of American *white* capitalism to Africa would benefit black America. In 1924 DuBois sought to reconcile profit with enlightened philanthropy when he wrote the American secretary of state suggesting that "the United States should send a small commission of experts to Liberia to examine and report on her agricultural and industrial possibilities and the best methods of realizing them." The commission "should include not simply business men, but men also trained in anthropology and economics, who have in mind not simply the possible profits to exploiters of the country, but the ultimate welfare of the Liberian State, its people and its native races." The men sent out should "be colored American citizens."[46] In 1933 DuBois remembered:

> On my return to the United States [after visiting Liberia in 1924] I wrote to him [Firestone]. I know what modern capital does to poor and colored peoples. I know what European imperialism has done to Asia and Africa; but, nevertheless, I had not then lost faith in the capitalistic system, and I believed that it was possible for a great corporation, headed by a man of vision, to go into a country with something more than the mere ideal of profit. . . . I tried to point out that by using trained American Negroes he might avoid this situation [i.e., exploitation] in Liberia and have a more normal development by putting in the hands of people of the same race, local and immigrant, such power over the invested capital as would divert it, at least to some extent, towards ends of social welfare as well as towards profit.[47]

Still DuBois appears to have been dimly aware at this time of the danger of exploitation of blacks by blacks; already, in 1921, he had pointed out the "danger to black France . . . that its educated and voting leaders will join in the industrial robbery of Africa rather than lead its masses to education and culture."[48] But not even DuBois was immune to the tendency to see Africa as a zone for economic penetration by Afro-

Americans, and this tendency could, as in the Firestone case, be manipulated by white America. When, in early 1924, DuBois attended the inauguration of President King, he was accompanied by William Henry Lewis, an Afro-American attorney, leading Massachusetts Republican, and assistant attorney general in the Taft administration. Lewis had proposed that DuBois be designated the representative of the United States at the inauguration, believing that it would assure the Republican administration "the support of the *Crisis*, the most widely read publication among the colored people, or stultify it, if it should come out against us."[49] In Monrovia, DuBois met the American receiver of customs, Sidney de la Rue, a man who soon felt that it would be most useful to rally "the negro element" in support of the Firestone concession. He advised the State Department that such support would be increased if the American company would grant posts to black graduates of technical schools. If this were done, he asserted, "we should have all the radical press controlled by DuBois also on our side."[50] No doubt DuBois wanted to use Firestone for the purposes of Afro-America; however, it is equally obvious that those urging the Firestone concession were also prepared to use Afro-Americans for their own ends. DuBois's great antagonist, Marcus Garvey, envisioned Liberia's development as dependent on an influx of black capital and talent, largely unencumbered by ties with white investment. Garvey attacked DuBois's espousal of the Firestone concession and, in August of 1924, Garvey's Universal Negro Improvement Association petitioned the Liberian legislature to reject the advice of "the man W. E. B. DuBois" and not grant a land concession to Firestone.[51]

In 1925 a writer in the Chicago *Defender* praised Harvey Firestone as a "great man with great wisdom" whose plantations would benefit not only Liberians but also Afro-Americans. Black Americans, he believed, might find an outlet for their talents under the auspices of the company: "It is our chance. Let us be prepared for it when it comes."[52] In the same year another newspaper elaborated on such prospects:

> At the Census of 1920 only one colored man in the entire country gave his occupation as that of a forester; fifty reported themselves as architects; eighty as civil engineers and thirty-one as mechanical engineers . . . due to the fact so few of our young men have taken up these professions, because of the difficulty of obtaining employment. It appears that the Firestone Company may be obliged to select a mixed, if not all-white administrative force to put over this great piece of constructive work in the black Republic, in whose progress all of us are greatly interested.[53]

The Newport News *Star* ran a story headlined "Firestone $100,000,000 Puts Republic of Liberia Definitely on Map of World . . . New Field

Affords Outlet for Negroes, Skilled Artisans, Mechanics, Physicians, and Others to Be Taken to Liberia."[54] The following year the New York *News* inaccurately said that Firestone was employing blacks in Liberia. In its enthusiasm the paper falsely announced, "Firestone Carries 500 Students from Tuskegee—Hampton Group to Exploit Africa's Wealth."[55]

While some Afro-Americans believed that their interests were best served by working in tandem with large-scale American capital, there were others who felt that Liberia might provide an opportunity for blacks to build up an independent economic base. A leading example of the successful black immigrant entrepreneur (and politician) in Liberia was Thomas J. R. Faulkner, who had emigrated from Baltimore some time before 1910.[56] Faulkner eventually operated the only hotel in Monrovia, an ice cream parlor, and a restaurant. The Afro-American introduced the ice machine and the telephone, and also constructed an electric power plant. In 1927 he ran unsuccessfully for president as head of the People's Party. In July of 1930 he left Liberia for the United States in hopes of getting black backing for a bank to replace the Bank of British West Africa.[57] In Washington it was noted that Faulkner aimed not only to found a bank, but also "to interest American negro capital in furnishing money for the construction of a railroad northwest from Monrovia into the interior."[58] The businessman's plans also included "certain harbor improvements at Monrovia and other development enterprises in the vicinity of the capital."

Although Faulkner had emigrated to Liberia and achieved a fair degree of economic success, his post-1930 large-scale projects did not reach fruition. Many similar plans hatched by blacks in the United States or the West Indies were even more Utopian. A year after Faulkner announced his banking scheme, William Edgenton wrote in the *Atlantean*, "The Liberian Development Association which constitutes most of the Negro millionaires of America and the neighboring islands, with the greatest talents of modern development, has stretched out her hand to rescue her and offer the little republic aid in a cure for her economic and financial ailments—not to criticise or scandalize her present existence, but to convert the so-called slave ground of Liberia into a land of peace and plenty, where the eastern and western Negroes will co-operate in all business lines, and her factory whistles will call the laboring natives instead of the Spanish steamers."[59]

In January of 1934 Dr. S. P. Radway of the Afro-West India Round Trip Association wrote to Edwin Barclay from Martinique and proposed "a mammouth [*sic*] Industrial Scheme" which would be "Auxiliary to the African Industries Company Ltd." of Monrovia. Radway argued that blacks in the West Indies had skills and capital which their colonial status did not allow them to develop. In answer to his own query—

"Where then must we go?"—he replied that Liberia provided the only hope. Perhaps remembering the Garvey debacle, he promised that proposed immigrants would not be a burden to the state and would not upset the established order.[60] In the same month a black man in Liberia's Montserrado County urged the president to prohibit the entry of white concessionaires and, instead, to embark on an extensive propaganda campaign in the Diaspora. Cash cropping should be begun on a massive scale, he advised, backed up by a fund of $40,000.[61] In the summer of 1934 a black prospector, J. T. Betts, informed Barclay that he was going to do surveys in the Hinterland, his efforts being motivated by "racial interest in this Negro Republic."[62]

By far the most ambitious program to furnish black economic aid for Liberia was a partial result of the efforts of the Liberian consul-general in Baltimore, Ernest Lyon. Lyon, an Afro-American and former minister to Liberia, assiduously cultivated Afro-American moral and financial support, while opposing schemes for mass emigration.[63] In June of 1933 he informed the Liberian secretary of state that he was about to launch a campaign to counteract adverse comment in American newspapers. Lyon adopted the tack that Liberia's economic troubles were traceable to her participation in World War I and said that prominent Afro-Americans were beginning to rally to her defense.

The consul-general encouraged William Jones, whose paper the Baltimore *Afro-American* had initially taken a very dim view of the "slavery" scandal, to take an active interest in the welfare of West Africa's only republic. In November of 1933 Jones arrived in Monrovia as a "goodwill" delegate from the "Save Liberia Movement," a group representing fifteen prominent Afro-Americans.[64] The editor had come to the view that ties between Afro-America and Liberia must depend on more than sympathetic race feeling. In his view, economic self-interest would, in the future, bind both peoples together and provide a vent for American black capital. Money would be raised in America for Liberian development and unemployed Afro-American professionals would find employment in Liberia. Jones made contact with Thomas Faulkner and held discussions with the Liberian secretary of the treasury. Before the legislature and public groups, the newspaperman put forth a plan of financial and technical assistance. His program had several parts: an educational campaign would be launched to generate interest in Liberian development; an annual development fund of approximately $1,000,000 would be raised; a Liberia-America trading and banking company would be established; fifty scholarships would be granted in the United States to young men and women pledged to do developmental work in Liberia; "foundational aid" would be organized for farm development and educational work in Liberia.[65] Jones proposed to raise some of the money through direct appeal. Teachers and students might contribute small sums of money (a "Save Liberia" button could be given to every child who collected more than a dime).[66]

Jones also planned to appeal to fraternal organizations and churches. The money raised "would be regarded as kind of a subsidy, such for instance, as the colonial Governments have given to develop their large coast towns, harbors and roads, and would be used by the Liberian Government to do similar development." Money would also be raised by issuing of bonds of a projected American Liberian Trading Company.[67] "Thousands of fathers and mothers of young boys could," Jones reasoned, "be induced to buy a $5, $10, or $25 bond for and in the name, perhaps of their children, which would mature 20 years from now just when their children would be in the prime of life." Such bonds would strengthen the links between Afro-America and Liberia because they "would give such boys and girls a permanent interest in the development of the country."[68] Afro-American capital, in Jones's view, would counterpoise the forces ranged against the Black Republic: "Instead of the white dictators urged by the League of Nations, the [Liberian] legislature voted for a plan calling for colored advisors, an open door to immigration from the U.S.A, co-operative trade relations, and assistance for internal development. . . ."

By early 1934 Jones had returned from Liberia and wanted a meeting with prominent blacks to draw up a program which would eventually be presented to President Roosevelt.[69] In January, Carl Murphy, the president of the *Afro-American*, announced that he was going to convene a Washington meeting of prominent blacks to devise ways of alleviating Liberia's economic troubles. Later in the month, Jones, Willard W. Allen, Grand Master of the black Masons, and Consul-General Lyon met at the State Department and outlined a plan for saving Liberia. Subsequently, the *Afro-American* came up with a long list of names of prominent blacks prepared to submit a program to the American president.[70]

Like many schemes for Afro-American and Liberian cooperation, the Jones plan did not progress far beyond the planning stage. The State Department did not support the plan and many Afro-Americans opposed it.[71] The Pittsburgh *Courier* attacked Jones's plan as "incredible philanthropy" in view of the social and economic hardship already endured by the Afro-American population.[72] By August of 1934 it was obvious that Jones's ardor had cooled considerably. When it was proposed that the editor aid in the formation of an "Americo-Liberian Society," Jones "seemed to be very timid about the idea because he did not know how it would be received by the leaders in the United States of America."[73] A year later it was obvious that the journalist had despaired of black capital being able to develop Liberia on its own. He hoped that the American Departments of Labor and Commerce might promote trade with Monrovia and use Liberia as an opening through which to promote cotton trade in Africa.[74]

The Jones plan of 1933 was vociferously attacked from the left. Harry Haywood, a black Communist, denounced the scheme as an attempt by the black bourgeoisie to serve as lackeys of American imperialism in Africa.[75] The class motives of the program were attacked and it was denounced as a scheme to allow the black petite bourgeoisie to play a comprador role in Africa. Haywood argued, "This can be seen in the statements of one of its leaders, 'we are beating our hearts and souls trying to break through the thick wall of prejudice which bars us from the higher brackets of big industry here in America, when there is a virgin field which [we] can develop in Africa."[76] He maintained that the plan to protect an independent Liberia avoided mention of the role of United States capital in the Liberian economy. He questioned the underlying rationale of any program to bail out Liberia and concluded that the Jones plan's "propaganda was aimed largely at the ghetto petite bourgeoisie—themselves driven into poverty by the Depression."[77]

In addition, Haywood specifically attacked George Padmore for his supposed support of the Jones plan. According to his detractors within the Communist Party, it was Liberia which caused Padmore's break with international Communism and his espousal and elaboration of Pan-Africanism. Padmore was attacked for allegedly failing to "recognize the fact that the condition of the two million natives in Liberia is not the same as the condition of the ruling stratum of the Americo-Liberians and that the natives must also fight against these black oppressors and imperialist lackeys."[78] He was expelled from the International Trade Union Committee of Negro Workers, of which he had formerly been secretary. The new secretary denounced Padmore's supposed interest in the Jones plan and wrote that "the actions of Padmore could have but one result; to undermine the unity of Liberian workers in their struggles against exploitation and oppression by the Imperialists and the Americo-Liberian ruling class; to weaken the working class movement under the slogan of race unity instead of class unity, thereby strengthening the hands of the Imperialist oppressors and their Negro allies."[79]

The whole idea of Afro-America coming to the aid of the Americo-Liberian elite was excoriated in the Communist organ, the *Negro Worker*, and Padmore's supposed backsliding on the Liberian issue was deplored.[80] According to the *Negro Worker*, Padmore had "become one of the most zealous organizers of the Roosevelt-Jones 'Committee of Aid'. . . ." The entire idea of defending the Black Republic was ridiculous. "Can the freedom of the native workers," asked the *Negro Worker*, "be purchased by raising five million dollars or any other large sum?" The journal asked, "Does freedom come through such a utopian plan?"

and answered, "As long as the higher strata of the native population can be bribed by the big corporations and landlords, it is child's play to think that the imperialist bandits will give one concession without it being forced from them by the mass struggles of the toiling population."[81]

In the acrimonious debate which followed Padmore's split with the Party, it became clear that the Jones plan per se was not the cause of the Pan-Africanist's explusion from the Communist ranks. Rather it was Padmore's espousal of racial solidarity across class lines (mixed with intraparty conflict) which resulted in the break. In late 1935 he attacked the Communist International for fabricating charges against him on the Liberian issue. "Why," he asked, "did the C.I. not accuse me of this years ago, for the last article I wrote on the Liberian question was in January, 1932, when I was still *persona grata*."[82] The secretary and chief executive of the American Communist Party, Earl Browder, retorted that the real reason for Padmore's expulsion was his espousal of the notion of race war and his acceptance of Japan's role as the protector of East Asia against white imperialism.[83]

The Liberian crisis does demonstrate that by the mid-1930s Padmore's thinking followed a Pan-Africanist, rather than a Communist, logic. Early in his career he had held that the actions of the Americo-Liberian elite proved the fallacy of Garvey's belief in black entrepreneurs.[84] And in 1931 he attacked "the diplomacy of the white imperialists in using the Negro national reformist leaders—like Marcus Garvey, . . . Dr. DuBois . . . and others—as their agents in paving the way for increasing attacks upon the standard of life of the Negro masses."[85] However, by 1934 he could write to DuBois that "Liberia has her faults, but since white politicians are no better than black ones, it is our duty to save the 'black baby from the white wolves.' "[86] There is little proof that Padmore was the motive force behind the Jones plan (as the party seemed to allege), but the party was correct in thinking that he was more concerned with preserving the integrity of the Black Republic than with overthrowing its oligarchy. Padmore attacked the party for being blind to the fact that "Liberia is an economic colony of American imperialism, and as such it is the duty of American Communists to defend Liberia" despite that country's failings.[87] The Jones plan met with Padmore's approval because it promised to provide the aid which the party steadfastly denied the Monrovia government.

At a fundamental level there was, from the beginning, an inherent contradiction between the "self-improvement" aim of Afro-American settlement in Liberia and the propaganda of African "redemption." If Africa was the land in which the blacks of the Americas would advance their economic position, it should have been obvious that such advancement was not necessarily consonant with the economic interests of the indigenes. Early in the Liberian scandal a State Department official queried the American emigrant Thomas Faulkner: "I asked how he reconciled his attitude towards the conditions which he alleged existed in the Republic with his desire to raise capital for [Liberian development]." Faulkner's reply on this point was vague and immediately involved him in generalities regarding his belief that the "American negro should be the salvation of the Black Republic."[88]

It has been said that given the contradictions in the stated aims of Liberian settlement, the nineteenth-century settlers cannot be faulted if "though there was much talk of 'brotherhood' and 'uplifting the race' . . . the 'race men' from the U.S. actually had little scruple when it came to using whatever force and deception was necessary to deprive the natives of their land and resources."[89] The harassed settlers from the New World were only obeying the logic of settlement. Thereafter, the perpetuation of the view of Liberia as a land of opportunity ignored the conflicts inherent in the creation of a settler society. Black capitalism would demand black workers. The potential antagonism between the two could only be partially papered over by the creation of the notion of a homogeneous black racial community.

Liberia seemed to hold out to Afro-Americans the promise of transforming a dispersed and marginal black bourgeoisie into a national one. However, the promise was largely chimerical. For one thing, American blacks possessed little capital. But the great failing of the proposed economic linkages, little realized at the time, was that black entrepreneurship in Liberia did not jibe with the ongoing policy aims of the Liberian elite. J. Gus Liebenow has noted that this elite has tended to discourage Liberian business and encouraged the entrance of foreign groups other than blacks at various levels of economic enterprise.[90] In the 1930s Bishop William Matthews of the African Methodist Episcopal Zion Church also noted this, but dismissed its significance, asking Afro-Americans, "How is it that the Jew and the Greek and the Italian have more business firms right in our own segregated communities than we have?"[91]

The Bishop failed to realize that in Liberia the small scale of black entrepreneurship—apparent even today—may reflect the conscious decisions of the ruling elite. Since non-blacks cannot become citizens of the Black Republic, this has created a situation, especially in terms of small retail trade, in which a mercantile minority (i.e., the Lebanese) has been allowed in at the sufferance of the ruling group and is dependent upon the goodwill of that group. Although it was suggested in the 1930s that capital from America might prove to be the answer to the "Syrian Problem" (the Lebanese), the attitudes and long-range interests of the entrenched elite opposed the creation of a group of black entrepreneurs with citizenship rights and interests which might run counter to theirs.[92] The career and political aspirations of a man like Thomas Faulkner amply demonstrated the difficulties the Liberian elite had in controlling the activities of emigrant black entrepreneurs. Although some Afro-Americans viewed (and still view) Liberia as a land of economic opportunity, it is obvious that their aspirations were not consonant with the attitudes and established economic arrangements of the Americo-Liberian ruling group. While elements in the Diaspora may have looked to Liberia for their economic salvation, it is now obvious that the Liberian elite would have been loath to permit their aspirations to upset the Liberian *status quo*.

6· The Unresolved Problem: The "Native Question"

... the Liberians as hungry wolves search their prey but our hope is fixed to the League of Nations. [Juah Nimley to British Consulate (Monrovia), 1934]

In spite of the hopes of various segments of "tribal" Liberian society, post-1930 events did not end the dominance of the Americo-Liberian elite. Although there was some amelioration in the administration of "Native Policy," there was still a "Native Policy." Some Western educated indigenes had looked upon the year 1930 as the dawning of a new era in which the reins of power would be transferred to their hands. However the Barclay regime (and with it, the Americo-Liberian elite) managed to weather the storm presented by both internal and external opposition. No basic changes were brought about by the events of 1929–1936. There was no radical redistribution of power inside the country and no imposition of externally fostered reforms. Barclay skillfully manipulated both the internal and the external situation. Cloaked with the legitimacy bequeathed him by the doctrine of national sovereignty, he steadfastly and successfully maintained that there could be no interference in the internal running of Liberia. By 1936, as chief executive of the one remaining independent state in Africa, he also drew on prevailing sentiments of racial solidarity and anti-imperialism abroad. The crushing of "native" resistance in 1936 was by a paradox converted by many foreign observers into a symbol of the triumph of African statehood.

After 1930 Liberia did attempt to appease world public opinion. As

[127]

we have seen, the legislature enacted laws prohibiting labor export and the pawning of human beings. A public health service was created and the Hinterland administration was reorganized. However, the public relations value of such actions was largely negated by the news that the Monrovia government was forcibly attacking the Kru and Grebo for testifying before the League's commission of inquiry. The people of Sasstown, especially, resisted, under the leadership of Kru Chief Juah Nimley (Senyo Juah Nimene). This struggle gave rise to stories of a calculated policy of genocide on the part of the Barclay regime. Resistance continued until 1936, when the "rebel chief" was captured and exiled.

In early 1930, Thomas Faulkner, the defeated Liberian presidential candidate, wrote to Sir Eric Drummond of the League of Nations and warned of "a bloody fight or a revolution," if the organization did not intervene.[1] The following year League investigator Charles Brunot was informed that the indigenous population would revolt if outside assistance was not forthcoming and it was feared that, deprived of funds for ammunition, the Monrovia regime might topple.[2] The Liberian government and various foreign observers maintained that a "provocateur," one "John Stuart, alias Major Frank or Major Ford," went to Sasstown and announced that the authority of the Monrovia regime was all but defunct.[3] After Stuart departed from Sasstown, the district commissioner himself hurriedly abandoned his post and from July 1930 until October of 1931 there was no local representative of the central government. In order to resolve inter-Kru disputes and to assert the power of the Barclay regime Colonel Elwood Davis was sent to the Kru Coast. He arrived in May but was unable to establish his authority immediately.

Davis was a black American from Indianapolis, who had emigrated to Liberia around 1919 as part of what the British legation cryptically referred to as the "Zionist Mission." The same source animadverted, "He very soon turned into a fake medical officer, in which career he was supported by President King . . . [and] continued his careers as an imitation Public Health Officer and an imitation soldier under successive Administrations."[4] These strictures were probably misinformed. Charles Johnson of the 1930 League commission reported that Davis had served against Mexico in Pershing's Tenth Cavalry and later as a troop trainer in World War I.[5] In spite of, or perhaps because of, his military experience, Davis proceeded cautiously on the Kru Coast. He waited ten weeks, writing letters to defiant tribes in hopes of avoiding a confrontation.

In July, at Pallipo in Liberian District Number Five, Davis found the people insubordinate, supposedly due to the propaganda spread by "Stuart."[6] There was also an outbreak of internal strife at Nana Kru. The feuding there was only a prelude to the violence which was to erupt in and around Sasstown in 1931. The reasons given for the violence are many and various. Initially the trouble may have involved border disputes between Sasstown and Picaninny Cess.[7] Liberian garrisons in the two areas may have taken sides in the dispute and become involved in armed conflict. The Monrovia government, for its part, attributed the disturbances to the tyrannical practices of Paramount Chief Juah Nimley, who was invited to Monrovia and lectured on the conduct expected of him.

According to Monrovia, this was to no avail. On August 27, 1931, President Barclay wrote to Davis telling him that the collector of the port and the customs guards at Sasstown had been driven away and asking him to go in and reimpose order. In November of 1931 actual fighting began between the Sasstown Kru and the Monrovia government. Davis had been unable to treat with Nimley, who would accept neither messengers nor letters. A delegation of educated Kru sent by Barclay arrived in Sasstown to help mediate the dispute between their kinsmen and the government, an action which Nimley may have interpreted as a divisive ploy. While the delegation was holding a palaver with Davis and Nimley, the chief's men surrounded the conference hall. The knowledge that Nimley's men were without caused consternation within. According to the Liberian government, when Davis began to address the assemblage, "Major Grant [one of Davis's officers] stepped outside[,] returned and said to [the] Paramount Chief and the Council: 'Chief Nimley, you have informed us that you have no war with the Government, and we have come here with that assurance.' " The major then asked, "How is it that when I stepped outside, I observed several hundred of your men armed and in war dress, secreting themselves in ambush and behind trees and houses?"[8] At this point the meeting broke up in disorder. Men fled outdoors and fighting began. The Liberian officials moved to New Sasstown (separated from Old Sasstown by a stream). Fighting continued for the whole of the first day and was resumed on the morning of the second when the supporters of Nimley withdrew. The town was burned, along with two nearby fishing villages. For the rest of the month punitive operations were carried out by government troops against Sasstown's surrounding farms. Meanwhile, villages allied to Sasstown attacked villages loyal to the Monrovia government.[9] Near the end of December, Colonel Davis and Major Grant went to the capital to report on the situation. During their absence, the followers of Nimley made an unsuccessful attack on New Sasstown, their only offensive of the war.

Juah Nimley's resistance to the Monrovia regime was based on his objection to the policies of the central government and sustained by his fear that the government would treat him as it had the "rebels" of 1915–1916. Early in 1934 he wrote Lord Cecil, chairman of the League of

Nations' Liberia Committee, stating his fears: "It is most certain that we will be arrested like the Nana Kru Chiefs who are now in Custody at Sinoe, and in the end we may be killed like the 75 chiefs who were invited to a 'Peace Conference' at Sinoe but who were seized and executed in 1916."[10] Nimley feared that if he did not comply with the president's order to disarm this would be used as an excuse for further attacks on his people. While resisting, Juah Nimley continued to maintain that he was a loyal adherent of the central government. In 1931 he expressed this to a Special Peace Delegation from Monrovia:

> The rumor that has reached the Government that we do not want to pay taxes is false. We know that it is our duty to pay our hut taxes annually as same is for the upkeep and benefit of our land. . . . We do not really refuse to pay the taxes for the year 1931 but due to the financial depression throughout the world, produce, our chief supporter [sic], has no value and hence we could hardly get means to pay the taxes.[11]

In 1932 Juah Nimley complained to a British investigator that the government was deliberately spreading stories of his intransigence. He protested that "after the International Commission of Enquiry left Liberia there was no native man who said there is no Liberian Government. . . . What else can the native man do to show that he recognizes the Liberian Government? He pays taxes, he pays customs duties."[12]

The Sasstown troubles received much international publicity. In some quarters it was reported that 600 unarmed civilians had been butchered by the Frontier Force.[13] The Kru managed to communicate their grievances to the world fairly effectively. In 1931 the American minister noted that he had received numerous complaints from various parts of Liberia including the Kru Coast. "The legation is conscious of the fact," said the minister, "that some of the complaints coming to us may be exaggerated, yet it is believed that the attempted institution of reforms by the Government so far does not meet the requirements necessary to insure safety of life in districts where soldiers are stationed."[14]

The *West African Review* of January, 1932 said Barclay had demanded of a conference of Kru chiefs that they divulge the authors of an appeal for outside aid which read: "We appeal to the League of Nations through the United States and Great Britain for our protection, the protection of our lives, our wives and children, also for our continued survival, as we are being slaughtered and inhumanly treated in every instance now, and unless something is done, and that immediately, we are certain that we will not be able to survive very much longer under the inhuman treatment of this administration.[15] After the chiefs all denied knowledge of the document's authorship, Barclay supposedly had them sign a statement denying its allegations. In the following month, with widespread atrocities still being reported internationally, a group of Kru residents in New York appealed to the State Department for aid.[16]

In January of 1932 the British consul wrote the Foreign Office: "I receive disquieting reports concerning Kru war, indicating unabated serious warfare, destruction of towns, depredations and killing of natives."[17] The Barclay regime was reportedly encouraging civil strife and "establishing terror by hunting and exterminating Sasstown tribes." He urged "definite action if Kru tribes are to be saved from extermination or permanent disorganization." On January 30 the representatives of the American, British, and French governments told the Liberia Committee that Barclay's government was taking draconian measures against indigenes. On March 7 these governments protested what was reported as a calculated policy of genocide.[18] The British, American, German, and French governments sent notes to the Liberian Government and asked that an investigator be sent to examine the situation in detail. The Liberians accepted the investigation, but expressed their doubts about foreigners' rights to interfere. Barclay told the British legation that his government had taken no reprisals. "Explicit assurance is, however," Barclay announced, "that no action will be taken against the Kru tribes concerned so long as they refrain from attacking neighbouring peaceful tribes and threatening foreign interests established under the protection of the Liberian Government."[19]

On March 14, 1932, the British vice-consul was sent to the Kru Coast to report on conditions. A week later Barclay sent his own commission, consisting of one American—Winthrop Travell, a loan official—and two Liberians—Reverend F. A. K. Russell, a Grebo, and J. F. Coleman, editor of the Monrovia *Weekly Mirror*. These inquires produced three individual reports (Travell submitted a minority report), which were published in Geneva in May of 1932. Even before their publication the American State Department was afraid they would "endeavor to whitewash the administration by laying the blame for the outrages upon the truculent behaviour of one of the tribes which 'had been misled' by the spreading of propaganda that the coming of [the] International Commission meant [the] end of Liberian Government authority."[20] The official Liberian reports did indeed attribute the troubles on the Kru Coast to the seditious activities of outside agitators and to the desire of the indigenous people not to pay tax. The latter charge was, no doubt, often true. But what looked like obduracy to Monrovia must have seemed a justified rejection of outside exploitation to many of the peoples of the Kru Coast.[21]

British Vice-Consul D. D. Rydings' report was more authoritative.

He dismissed the rumor of genocide and calculated that forty-one villages had been burned and a total of 141 men, women, and children killed.[22] He concluded that before the outbreak of hostilities Colonel Davis had acted with restraint, but that "after the outbreak of hostilities . . . operations against the disaffected tribes appear to have been conducted in a ruthless, callous and brutal manner without regard for the lives of innocent women and children as will be apparent from casualty figures which were supplied to me by the dissident tribes."[23]

In April of 1932 the American representative to the League of Nations' Liberia Committee informed the State Department that, according to British sources, grave abuses were still being committed on the Kru Coast.[24] The following month the League Council, in agreement with the Liberian government, sent Melville Mackenzie, former member of the Brunot commission, to Liberia to further investigate conditions and, if possible, bring peace. The Liberians, although approving of the visit, complained that the tone of Mackenzie's commission was dictatorial (he arrived on a British naval vessel and the Liberians were warned not to make reprisal against the indigenes).[25] On July 12, 1932, the League representative arranged a truce between the Monrovia government and the Kru and Grebo and between warring factions of the indigenous population. In September of 1932 he reported to the League on his mission. Peacemaking had, for the time being, succeeded: the truce was to last one year and the people were to be allowed to return to their farms. Monrovia promised to inflict no reprisals. Mackenzie emphasized the temporary nature of the peace. It was urgent, in his opinion, that foreign administrators be appointed before the end of one year, since the disarmed population would be at the mercy of the Frontier Force at the end of that period.[26]

On July 1, 1933, the Mackenzie truce expired and in the last days of August intratribal warfare broke out betwen the Fishtown and Nimeah sections of the Grebo, with twenty-eight Nimeah men reportedly killed.[27] Nevertheless, in his annual address in October, Barclay set forth a roseate official view of the internal situation: "The Secretary of the Interior reports a state of absolute political tranquility throughout the Republic, even in the district which was in a disturbed condition two years ago."[28]

In the spring of 1934 Barclay undertook a tour of the Kru Coast. Former Secretary of State Louis B. Grimes wrote to Lester Walton, telling him "that while the noble lords [i.e., the British House of Lords] were discussing the massacre of the tribesmen in Sasstown President Barclay was in Sasstown with his wife and other female relatives, and was being not only loyally and enthusiastically, but even affectionately received."[29] Barclay himself viewed his trip as proof of the high esteem in which he was held by the Kru populace.[30] According to the Liberian government, Kru friendly to the government supposedly offered to arrange a palaver between Barclay and Nimley, but Nimley refused. The president thought that "many of the followers of Juah Nimley were anxious to return to their homes on the beach, but were deterred from doing so by the wicked manner in which he enforces his orders that they should not submit."[31] The Sasstown leader was accused of executing members of his community who urged submission to the central authority. According to the government, "loyal" Kru could not understand "why, in accordance with the McKenzie [sic] . . . Settlement, they should be deprived of access to their plantations which are being profitably exploited by the rebellious portion of the tribe who, through Dr. McKenzie's [sic] arrangement, have access to the Coast while the loyal people lose the proceeds of their plantations."

Barclay attacked British stories of atrocities as mere inventions and announced that none of the 300 chiefs he had spoken to in a council at Grand Cess had confirmed reports of atrocities. As to the reports of harsh proceedings against the people of Sasstown, the president said that Liberian forces had taken offensive action against no one and that, instead, dissident Kru had attacked government forces who were out on patrol.[32] Barclay said the canoes of dissident tribesmen had been seized "as a measure of precaution and given over to the loyal chief at Sasstown for safe-keeping." Barclay maintained that he had freed the suspect tribesmen upon their giving assurance of their loyalty to the Monrovia regime. "That is," said the President, "all there was to this charge of atrocity alleged to have been committed by the Frontier Force against unarmed tribesmen."

Mackenzie strongly disagreed with Barclay's analysis of the Kru situation. He received information from an anonymous Swiss trader who said that conditions on the south Liberian coast were in a state of turmoil. According to the trader, the president, who had been accompanied by troops and 500 carriers, was met by such hostility that he had had to ask for a British cargo steamer to stop at Sasstown and take him off to Monrovia. According to the anonymous source, "King Niminyio" of the Grebo had taken to the "Bush" to organize resistance. The Swiss informant predicted that when the Kru and Grebo realized that the League was not going to send administrators, there would be a general uprising, beginning at Cape Palmas. "He [the Swiss] adds," Mackenzie assured a League official, "that the white residents will be in no danger at all, as the tribes have no quarrel with the whites, and indeed are only anxious to be administered by them, in view of their knowledge of conditions, particularly in Sierra Leone, where large numbers of them have worked on the ships."[33] The British consulate in Monrovia did not give much credence to Mackenzie's information. It did inform the Foreign Office, in October of 1934, that the people of Picanniny Cess had recently fought among themselves and that the Frontier Force had been sent in.[34]

In spite of Barclay's claims that conditions in Liberia were essentially normal, the American legation was suspicious. "Although members and partisans of the administration," commented the Chargé John MacVeagh, "maintain their denials that there have been any unusual disturbances on the Kru Coast, it has been admitted by the commanding officer of the Frontier Force to friends in Monrovia that the soldiers have been engaged against the tribesmen."[35] In March of 1934 the legation got word that soldiers led by Captain Henry Dennis, the brother of the secretary of the treasury, had in the previous month, without warning, attacked several villages and taken prisoners to Sasstown.[36] The American legation could give no comfort to Kru petitioners for protection and the chargé noted that "one of the messengers, who was a very dignified old subchief or headman, thereupon burst into tears saying they would all be murdered if no outside assistance was forthcoming." The legation complained that the Monrovia government was arming tribe to fight tribe and predicted that fighting would soon erupt again.[37]

The failure of the League of Nations' plan of assistance in the spring of 1934 threw the plight of Liberia's indigenous population into high relief. Would anything be done? British Foreign Minister Sir John Simon was already deeply concerned about the whole matter. "We have, I understand," Simon wrote, "definite news . . . that the tribes whom Dr. Mackenzie disarmed (Heaven knows why) are in danger. . . ." Fearing adverse publicity he urged that a strong note be sent to Liberia on the subject.[38] Simon wrote the British consul in Monrovia asking that he get assurances that mistreatment of the indigenous population would end. "His Majesty's Government will not content themselves," he wrote, "with an empty denial."[39] The outcome of this pressure was not reassuring. On April 18, Earl Stanhope, undersecretary of state for foreign affairs, told the House of Lords that the British consulate had delivered a note to the Liberian secretary of state. "In his reply," Stanhope informed the Lords, "the Liberian Secretary of State stated that he had no knowledge that any such events were happening and that he denied that the assurances given in the Liberian Note [of 1932] had been disregarded; and he made rather impudent suggestions that the protest was made in regard to Liberian subjects and not in regard to British subjects, and therefore he did not quite see what cause we had for interference."[40]

At Geneva the Liberian representative, M. de Bogerde, implied that the sources of Britain's information were probably biased and influenced by Liberian electoral politics.[41] The Liberian secretary of state, Clarence Simpson, maintained that "since the British communication advanced no fresh evidence to substantiate the charges which had been categorically denied by the Liberian Government a year earlier, and since the situation in the Kru districts at the time was perfectly quiet and normal, the British communication seemed to have more relevance to the events taking place at Geneva than to those supposed to have taken place around Fishtown [in Grebo country]."[42]

Sir John Simon continued to urge some kind of action on the Kru question in spite of official Liberian denials of maladministration of "native" areas. The British Foreign Office informed the American government that it would take "any well-considered measures which the United States Government may consider appropriate to the occasion," for it "would be a dereliction of duty to civilisation if the misgovernment of the native tribes by Liberia were to be allowed to continue. . . ."[43] American policy on the "Native Question" was nebulous. In April of 1934 the American chargé in Monrovia advised that no action be taken until after the May session of the League (although he did recommend that an international police force be set up or that France and/or Britain should take the country on as a mandate).[44] In May the British Foreign Office spoke to an American embassy official in London and suggested a division of responsibility: "The native tribes were our chief concern, while the negroes in Monrovia and the financial chaos were perhaps America's business."[45] The British were not anxious to intervene, but neither did they wish to abandon Nimley to his fate. A Foreign Office official said, "It is abundantly clear that Chief Nimley counts still on the League and on us to mediate between him and the Government and I think it is up to us (and/or the League) to see that he gets no raw deal. . . ."[46] In November of 1934 the Foreign Office interviewed one of the American fiscal officers, P. J. Fitzsimmons, while he was in London, noting that he felt the United States did not want any responsibilities on the other side of the Atlantic and "realised that the Krus were our [Britain's] main interest and his advice was for us to get out of Liberia and take the Krus with us to Freetown [Sierra Leone], where they were wanted and would be useful."[47]

After the collapse of the League plan and with the Firestone Company nearing a *modus vivendi* with the Barclay regime, the Kru had become an increasing embarrassment in some quarters. Sir John Simon, the British foreign minister, still concerned about the "Kru Problem," informed his ambassador in Washington that the British and American legations should put pressure on Barclay and Nimley to come to some kind of settlement and that recognition of the Barclay regime would depend on such a settlement.[48] Four months later the British were complaining that the American chargé had not received explicit instructions on the type of message to be sent to Nimley.[49] The British suspected that the United States was moving unilaterally toward recognition of the Liberian regime. They admitted that the Barclay regime might be trying to reform itself but felt that the settlement of the Kru difficulties was the key to recognition.[50]

The American legation's conception of how to effect such a settlement differed increasingly from that of the British. The American chargé complained that "due to some inexplicable confusion between Yapp [of the British consulate] and the Foreign Office, the latter felt that a joint suggestion to Barclay by us here would bring the protagonists together and Yapp was even instructed to proceed on that basis." The American felt that such a course would produce no results and prided himself on bringing his British counterpart around to his way of thinking. They agreed to send a Catholic priest with a message for Nimley (after getting the chief a safe-conduct from the Liberian government).[51]

The British representative drafted a letter to Nimley similar to British advice to the Kru during the 1915–16 uprising: "I deplore the continued absence of friendship between you and the Liberian Government and it would be well if you and your followers were to make your peace with that Government."[52] But the Liberian government, ever sensitive to interference in its internal affairs, raised objections to certain aspects of these peace preparations. Secretary of State Simpson rejected British use of the terminology "peace palaver." The solution of the "Kru Problem" was an internal matter between the rulers and the ruled and not a negotiation between equals. "The Liberian Government," Simpson noted, "would regard any doubt as to its *bona fides* in this matter as unwarranted."[53] Soon thereafter the American chargé announced, "The [Liberian] Government intends to have no conference with Nimley which will properly settle the difficulties." The chargé concluded that it was perhaps best for the United States not to communicate with Nimley.[54]

Thus, the United States, having sounded its alarm in 1929 about the condition of Liberia's indigenes, had by mid-1934 begun to wash its hands of them.[55] By 1936 the Sasstown insurgents had come to the conclusion that "the friendly Diplomatic [*sic*] relationship between the Government of Liberia, and that of the United States of America [is] tantamount to Firestone's personal interest and not that of the poor suffering Natives as theretofore."[56] The United States sent a letter to the British in April of 1935 inviting them to recognize the Barclay regime (which was repealing its anti-Firestone legislation).

In Monrovia the American legation took a somewhat jaundiced view of the indigenes they supposedly had originally intervened to help:

The Kru tribe is one of the more intelligent of the native tribes, certainly more warlike and less tractable to government authority than many of the others. They are proud and their traditions as an organized tribe go back for centuries. They are satisfied with their tribal government and while intensely clannish and faithful to tribal law and tradition they have no feeling of brotherhood to other African tribes and certainly little, if any, patriotic feeling toward Liberia as a State and nation. They object to interference with tribal chiefs of their own choosing and see no reason why they should subject themselves to any other negro, particularly one whose forebears came to Africa less than a century ago and who in consequence is an alien to them. White domination they can understand but their sense of government has not been sufficiently developed to accept domination by any other black. Hence there will be friction for many years to come between this tribe and the Liberian Government.[57]

The American chargé maintained that the Kru were no more oppressed than any other indigenous people in Liberia. It was their greater sophistication which was responsible for their greater notoriety: "The fact is that as coastal people they have worked on ships for generations and being more intelligent than many of the tribes in the interior they are more vocal and use this opportunity to acquaint the world with their grievances."[58] Frederick Hibbard, the chargé, blamed the British for implanting the idea of external assistance in Nimley's head and thus encouraging his continued resistance. Hibbard complained: "That idea [i.e., outside assistance] is firmly fixed and how it got there doesn't matter much. I do not think the British entirely blameless for its presence but they make it evident now that they intend to do nothing to make it a reality so we must start from there." In Hibbard's view the truce negotiated by Mackenzie had left more problems than it had solved. The chargé told Washington that the negotiator had "undoubtedly wanted to be the Chief Adviser under the League Plan." Although Mackenzie had denied promising Nimley the return of any representative of the League, Hibbard opined, "I am sure he felt that within a short time the Liberian problem would be effectively under the control of the League and that accordingly within the year's time limit he set there would be a white man on the scene to make final arrangements of the points at issue." Besides, even if Mackenzie had not had ulterior motives, he had failed to take into account the "native" mentality. Hibbard reminded the American investigator Harry McBride, "You know from your own experience how easy it is for these people, with their vivid imaginations unaffected by fact, to construe or interpret any statement according to their wishes or ideas." The truce of 1932 had in reality weakened the chances for a real *modus vivendi* between all the parties concerned, because "it is not possible for a bush Negro to distinguish between the League of Nations and the British Government when the representative of the former is a subject of the latter, arriving on a

British gun boat and accompanied by a British army officer on political service in Freetown who insisted on being kept thoroughly informed of all proceedings and even attended some of the palavers."[59]

The Americans lived in hope that the entire "Kru business" would blow over. Hibbard wrote, "The British . . . just as we, have many more vital preoccupations in their foreign policy and are glad to have someone show them a graceful exit from a situation which viewed from any other angle can only be settled by actual intervention." Very prematurely, the official concluded, "They will therefore, be glad to follow us in assisting Barclay in his plan and in extending recognition."[60] To a certain extent American hopes were justified. A British Foreign Office official wrote the embassy in Washington, "Now, to be perfectly frank, we are just as anxious as are the United States to be rid of the Liberian question, if only for a year or two."[61] However, before the whole issue could be ignored the Kru question had to be resolved. Early in 1935 the British made the same point to the Americans: "As the United States Government are aware His Majesty's Government's main preoccupation in Liberia relates to the position of the Kru tribes. . . . Any agreement which might be reached must thus necessarily entail a return to the tribes of at least a reasonable proportion of their arms."[62] One member of the Foreign Office took the view "that we would look peculiarly foolish if, after all the interest we have displayed . . . in the trials and tribulations of the Krus, we were to renew official relations with the Liberian Government without having obtained any kind of guarantee that these unfortunate natives will no longer be persecuted by the Monrovian blacks."[63]

Where appeals to reason failed the Americans hoped appeals to economic interest might succeed. The chargé in Monrovia confided to McBride in Washington, "One powerful factor which may influence the British toward recognition . . . is the recent visit here of one of the managers of the [British] Consolidated African Selections Trust. . . ."[64] Here was the economic lever which the chargé hoped would consign the Kru Question to oblivion. A British diamond mining concession in Liberia presumably would stifle British complaints about the conditions on the Kru Coast. "If Consolidated African Selections Trust," the chargé wrote, "thinks the concession is of sufficient value, and they appear to at present, they will put pressure on the British Government to regularize its relations with Liberia by recognition and the trade opportunity will outweigh any humanitarian feelings the British may have for the Krus, Lord Cecil and the Archbishop of Canterbury not withstanding."[65]

The British Foreign Office was interested; an official minuted that an officer of the Trust (a body supported by the Colonial Office) had pointed out the benefits to be gained from recognition.[66] Later the same official noted "there is no reason why British interests like the Consolidated African Trust should not play a leading role [in Liberia]," but "to do so . . . would mean the loss of our good name on the west coast of Africa, besides laying His Majesty's Government open to the most violent criticism in the country."[67] The British representative in Monrovia, a supporter of recognition, lamented, "Our trading interests are not developing here and unless the Consolidated African Selections Trust come in I think the time is rapidly approaching when Liberia will be of little interest to us though I suppose it may be necessary to keep someone here for strategic interests or as it were 'a look-out' man."[68] He added that Britain's policy in Liberia had been a failure: "Nothing would please any of the three [the Americans, the Germans, the Dutch] more than to see us embroiled further—who else troubles about the Kru people besides ourselves . . . in my own mind, I am satisfied that the Krus are being left in peace and are suffering little or no hardship but that they are definite mischief-makers."

The question of British recognition hung in the balance. As long as the Sasstown Kru continued to resist, recognition seemed to promise embarrassment. After official American recognition of the Barclay regime in 1935 a Foreign Office official, weighing the pros and cons of recognition, complained, "It is in many ways a pity that our freedom of action should be hampered by our previous commitments in support of these troublesome tribes, but I submit that the arguments in favour of recognition do not at present outweigh those against such a course." The British were, indeed, wrestling with the problem of how to end the Barclay-Nimley impasse. One Foreign Office official mused, "Mr. Nimley is a sick man and it is possible that he may die before long. He is 62. His demise would of course from our point of view be a fortunate event."[69]

In the spring of 1935 the American chargé complained that the British had "a number of vociferous old ladies who ask embarrassing questions at odd times about the situation on that Coast; questions often based on erroneous information, some of which unfortunately has come from Foreign Office sources."[70] The British Anti-Slavery and Aborigines Protection Society did view Liberia as a prime case of all those evils which it sought to eradicate. In 1931, Sir John Harris, parliamentary secretary of the society, pointed out with pride that Britain had opposed Liberia's entry into the League of Nations. According to Harris the subsequent course of events had been one great fiasco, and the Black Republic had demonstrated its complete unfitness to govern Liberia's indigenous peoples.[71] In 1934 the society decided to ask the Foreign Office whether papers could be published about the Liberian question and whether it was possible to send a delegation to speak with the American ambassador.[72] The Foreign Office did not favor this approach, but said that it would not stand in the way. The Foreign Office proposed that the Society get in touch with the corresponding organization in America. Harris, however, visited the Foreign Office and indicated that he did not wish to work through the American philanthropic groups, but instead would approach the American Society of Friends. Early in 1935, Harris considered pushing the idea of a new commission of inquiry to explore allegations that those who had testified before the Christy commission in 1930 had since been mistreated.[73]

But as the final phases of Nimley's resistance approached, even the humanitarians began to adopt a less strident tone on the issue of atrocities in Liberia. The International Bureau for the Protection of Native Races held its seventh biennial assembly in Geneva in September of 1935 and said Liberia had failed to abide by Article 23 of the Covenant of the League of Nations relative to "primitive populations" administered by members of the League. But later a report of the bureau noted that "the Liberian Government was able to master the situation, the disturbances having been most likely the last stages of a revolt undertaken by some tribes in their fight for their independence, or even for the establishment of a native Home Rule."[74] The bureau was willing to give the Barclay regime the benefit of the doubt. Its report spoke "of a work of reform begun by President Barclay, after peace was established, for a complete reorganization of the administration of his country, and the appointment of natives to high Government posts." The Anti-Slavery and Aborigines Protection Society was still dubious, recording that it did not give the report full credence. Yet, with the gradual isolation of Nimley, even the most ardent humanitarian had to fall into line. In the summer of 1936 Lord Cecil, who had previously been in accord with the Anti-Slavery Society, urged recognition based on the premise that if Liberia should lapse into future abuses recognition might be withdrawn.[75]

With the failure of the League Plan, the Sasstown rebels' hope for outside intervention dwindled and their evaluation of their plight became more pessimistic. In the summer of 1934, after the plan's abandonment, they managed to cable directly to the secretary general of the League. They complained of Frontier Force provocations, saying that if they retaliated the Liberian government "would tell the League that they are justified to attack us because we are wild uncontrollable people, when, in fact, most of us are seafaring and law abiding men who have travelled a good deal and we are not wild at all, as the Liberians have tried to represent us."[76] Their petitioner said that Lord Lugard, a member of the League Mandates Commission, could vouch for them as respectable seafaring folk.

In June the Kru community of Accra, in the Gold Coast, appealed to the secretary general and in July a Kru petitioner wrote to British Foreign

Minister Sir John Simon for aid.[77] "Your kind intervention has recalled memories," wrote the Kru, "of the old relationship which has long existed between the Kroos and the English-speaking world under which impression I have always believed that, although the League of Nations has the matter in hand, you English-speaking nations whose Christian feeling from a moral point of view in the interest of humanity for the protection of the weak has made you the police of the civilised world, will not fail in an action against the intruder of your old friends as they entirely depend on you for help."[78] Other appeals from the Krus and their friends bombarded the League and the British and American governments.[79]

Juah Nimley told Lord Cecil of the Liberia Committee in early 1934, "Our hearts are broken since we heard that the Liberians have rejected the League's Plan. . . ."[80] Cecil gave the letter to the British government and replied, "I am afraid that I have no power to interfere in any way." Six months later Nimley again appealed to Cecil and said, "Disappointment and sorrow ran throughout the whole of Liberia when it was found out that President Barclay alone with his first cousin, Mr. Grimes, had turned down the League's Plan which all of us wanted. . . ."[81] "We understand," said Nimley, "that the Liberian question has been handed over to the American Government, if this is true, we must humbly beg of your Lordship to use your influence with the American people and the League to prevent this [i.e., further 'reprisals']."

In February of 1935 the still-unconquered chief appealed to the British in Monrovia and was ignored. Nimley complained that "as the small guns and weapons I have in my possession have been taken from my hand by the League Councillors . . . that causes my little shaking in body and in natural spirit and even there is no way to escape . . . I shall be in torture together with my people and states."[82] Frantic appeals went out to British humanitarian and philanthropic interests in a last-ditch effort to spur British intervention. In May of 1936, Lady Kathleen Simon, of the Anti-Slavery and Aborigines Protection Society, received a letter from a Liberian stranded in Paris, who pleaded in awkward yet moving terms: "The present-day conditions in Liberia is as such that the situation is just as before in toto and the only solution to abolish the atrocities would be a collective security with[in] the frameworks of British Justice under Great Britain Mandatory Power, this I can assure you is the wishes of the people of Liberia and the only solution to save the Natives from the existing masscrition [massacre] throughout."[83]

By August of 1936, Nimley's position had become serious. A refugee from his camp, C. J. Julius, escaped to Accra and attempted to enlist humanitarian support for the chief who for over five years had defied the Monrovia regime.[84] In August, Julius appealed to the British Foreign

Office; his message received a cold response. An official thought it, "to say the least . . . , inconvenient that we should receive this petition from the Krus at a moment when . . . it has been decided that the time has come to recognize the Liberian government."[85]

On July 12, British Consul Yapp had reported that Barclay had been informed that all of the tribes supporting Nimley had surrendered and that the chief himself was in flight. Liberian Secretary of State Simpson proudly announced that the victory had been bloodless.[86] The Foreign Office quickly reconciled itself to this denouement of the Kru affair. Suspicion lingered that the crushing of the "revolt" had not been completely bloodless. "If blood *is* unfortunately shed in the process," said a British official, "I submit that this would give us no more right to protest than the civil war in Spain would entitle us to protest to Madrid against the measures taken against General Franco."[87] On September 9 it was announced that Nimley himself was in government hands and on October 6, Nimley and two of his leaders arrived in Monrovia as prisoners. The three men were interviewed at the War Department and then sent to confinement at Monrovia's military camp. The following day Nimley and his headmen were interviewed for three hours by their great antagonist, Edwin Barclay himself. The British representative, who had long viewed Nimley as a diplomatic nuisance, had to confess: "Dressed in native costume he bore himself with much dignity as he marched through the town under escort. I am told that the crowd assembled to watch his progress was the largest ever seen in Monrovia and that he was the recipient of hearty cheers. Everyone was anxious to see the 'wonderful Nimley,' as he was called."[88] The British representative admired Barclay's tactics as much as he admired Nimley's bearing. Barclay's great strategy had been, in his eyes, the "encirclement plan" which made the women dissatisfied enough to desert the fighters. The consul warned the Foreign Office that the area might still prove troublesome in the future when the Liberian government got around to collecting taxes.[89]

Barclay magnanimously declared that Nimley, previously accused of being a butcher of his own people, had only been led astray by educated members of his tribe.[90] The chief and his two headmen, Santi and Parle Weah, were sent to exile in Gbanga, Saniquelli, and Belle Yella respectively. In 1937 the chief, leader of a five-year war, was allowed to return to Sasstown as a common citizen and died shortly thereafter. Nimley, "wonderful Nimley," had been defeated.

In his annual message of 1936, Barclay, in a clement mood, proclaimed, "It is clear Juah Nimley himself attempted to persuade his people from the course upon which they had determined and had been overborne by his advisers and particularly by the so-called 'civilized' element of the tribe."[91] According to Monrovia, the war on the south coast had been fueled by the seditious propaganda of outside agitators. In the spring of 1934, Barclay had already stated this rationale for the recurring violence on the south coast:

> Dr. McKenzie [sic], in his report to the Government on his mission to Sasstown, attributed much of this unrest, more or less, to the civilized Krus who reside in Monrovia. He is quite correct in this because facts which are reported to the Government by certain foreign agents in Monrovia are absolutely unknown in the places to which they claim to refer. It is known that each tribe on the Kru Coast has a colony in Monrovia, and so it is possible for a man claiming to be a Dio or a Wissapo man, who, however, may never have been at Dio or Wissapo nor had any communication therefrom, to have communicated to the British Consul alleged facts [of atrocities] set out in his despatch.[92]

The Barclay regime saw Didwo Twe, an ex-member of the legislature, as the evil genius behind Kru resistance. Twe viewed himself as the chief spokesman for his people. As early as December of 1930 he had written to Charles Johnson, American member of the League's commission of inquiry, protesting raids on the Kru Coast.[93] In April of 1932 he wrote to the American minister saying he feared deportation because of his role in exposing abuse on the coast and because of his absolute refusal to be coopted by the Barclay government.[94] According to Twe, Barclay had made dire threats against "educated Africans": "On the first of May 1931, in the presence of the Hon. M. Massaquoi, Rev. D. W. Harman [Herman], Mr. G. F. Sharpe, Chief Kpade Boi, Dappe Togba and myself, President Barclay said to Paramount Chief Blogba Togba: . . . 'I will burn down the whole Kru Coast, if you don't stop talking about "white man," "white man".' " Barclay, according to Twe, warned, "You take it from me as an order and send word and tell your people that I say there will be only two months of peace on the Coast and no more." When Twe attempted to interject, he was supposedly told, "You damned civilized natives who ought to be leading your people properly are misleading them."[95]

The British consulate had a low opinion of Twe, as it did of most "educated Natives." In 1935 it described him as "an astute but unscrupulous individual" who had been expelled from the House of Representatives during King's presidency."[96] Eight years before, the American legation had made a careful compilation of the extant facts of Twe's life. He was

> a member of the Settra Kroo Tribe, [and] was born in Monrovia. There is no record of the exact date of his birth but he appears to be about forty years of age. He started his education in Monrovia under Miss Mary

Sharpe, an American missionary, and Doctor Paulus Moort. In 1900 he went to the United States for further education and remained there up to 1910. Congressman William W. Grout of Vermont helped Mr. Twe to obtain an education, and Mr. Twe attended St. Johnsbury Academy at St. Johnsbury, Vermont, and the Rhode Island State College of Kingston, Rhode Island. After the Congressman's death, Senator John T. Morgan of Alabama and Samuel Clemens became interested in Mr. Twe. It is very unfortunate that both Senator Morgan and Mr. Clemens died before Mr. Twe could finish his education.

I have been told that Mr. Twe, while in America, contributed articles to the "American Journal of Psychology," edited by Doctor G. Stanley Hall and to "The Boston Transcript." Since 1910 he has been a district commissioner for a number of years on the Sierra Leone frontier and has assisted the Anglo-Liberian and Franco-Liberian boundary commissions. At present, he is assistant to Mr. Robert A. Farmer, American Engineer, in constructing a coast telephone system.[97]

After the first reverberations of the slavery crisis were felt, and with the increasing harassment of dissidents within Liberia, Twe fled to Sierra Leone in November of 1932 and the Liberian government issued a writ for his arrest on charges of sedition.[98] Late in 1934, Twe wrote to a friend in England advocating armed revolution. He argued that it was certainly within the Kru's power, "But in order to . . . succeed fully . . . hold their independence intact till recognition, acceptance of the League's Plan and the arrival of white specialists, the Kru people ought to have at least 6 machine guns and 500 rifles with sufficient ammunition." According to the Kru nationalist, "This is now the only obstacle in the way to free a million people from oppression. . . . We hope the Lord could touch the hearts of some good men to come to the assistance of our people to bring about the establishment of the 'Kru Republic,' which the people want."[99] The British consulate in Monrovia, which favored recognition of the Barclay regime, harshly condemned Twe's opinions, viewing him as "a thorough-paced scoundrel." Yapp of the consulate suggested that "if he disappeared . . . no one would be the worse off."[100]

By the autumn of 1934, Twe realized that the Liberian matter had been almost completely dropped by the international community. Nevertheless, he suggested that if the Great Powers did decide to send out a caretaker, he, Twe, should accompany him. He wrote Lord Cecil that "England certainly has been very sincere throughout . . . and she really wants to relieve the oppressed people, but the League is no good at all."[101] Unfortunately for the Kru exile, Cecil replied, "I am afraid I see nothing that the British Government or I myself can do more to help at the present time."[102] Twe continued to agitate from Sierra Leone and was in correspondence with Sir John Harris of the British Anti-Slavery and Aborigines Protection Society. Harris sent Twe a letter via Graham Greene who was on a tour in Liberia. Twe advised Greene to visit the Kru Coast (the novelist was already carrying a letter from Harris to Juah Nimley).[103] The message to Nimley never got through. Greene altered his course before reaching Nimley's area.[104] By early 1936, Twe's resistance was broken. He returned unexpectedly to Monrovia from Freetown and asked for the protection of the British consulate. The Liberian secretary of the interior ordered Twe to leave the country and the consulate informed him that it could not intervene. Barclay did receive Twe in audience and eventually gave permission for him to stay in Monrovia on condition that he refrain from political activity.[105]

The conflict on the Kru Coast was not only a struggle between Monrovia and the Kru and Grebo. It was also a struggle between the Western-educated portions of those peoples and the Americo-Liberian elite entrenched in the central and county administrations. From the point of view of the Kru and Grebo, the Monrovia regime had endeavored to hobble them educationally and socially. Americo-Liberians were accused of discouraging literary education among the indigenes. In 1916 a meeting of Kru chiefs in Freetown complained that educated Africans, especially those educated abroad, were ostracized by the Americo-Liberian elite.[106] Western-educated Africans who sought individual title to land often had arguments with Americo-Liberian surveyors. Among the Kru, Sasstown and Grand Cess were the earliest towns to have missions and schools, and, for this reason, their residents were prominent among educated indigenes.[107] All along the Kru Coast the government taxed for education, but neglected to provide schools. In 1912 the people of Settra Kru petitioned the United States government directly and expressed their urgent need for instruction.

In Maryland County in 1875 mission-educated Grebo (largely trained by the Protestant Episcopal mission) outnumbered Americo-Liberians by a ratio of three to one.[108] However, they found entrée into the county administration barred to them. In 1873 educated Grebo had joined with their illiterate countrymen to proclaim the Gebebo Re-United Kingdom. In the 1880s the Grebo and Kru became entitled to representation in the Liberian legislature, as they were the only groups who paid more than a specified amount of taxes. Educated Grebo remained loyal to the Monrovia regime for a number of years because of this measure, but grew restive as few, if any, could reach the rank of senator. In 1910 the educated Grebo were again reported leaders in the war against the Monrovia government.[109]

In 1931, Al-Haj Massaquoi, the eldest son of Momolu Massaquoi (a Vai and former Liberian postmaster general), wrote to Lady Kathleen Simon of the Anti-Slavery and Aborigines Protection Society to complain:

> We the Natives except a few isolated cases are denied Offices in the Government and even in these isolated cases only unimportant positions are granted. Americo-Liberians with no Education whatever fill the highest posts—as a matter of fact without any prejudice and exaggeration 99% of Liberian Government Officials are uneducated, that is, cannot even boast of ordinary elementary school education and this not excluding those in the highest Offices including Cabinet Ministers—it will not be going too far to say that there are not more than half a dozen Lawyers in the entire Republic within the proper meaning of the term although so-called lawyers abound in plenty.[110]

Barclay was deeply suspicious of educated "natives," as he demonstrated during mediation efforts in October of 1931. As mentioned earlier, the president sent a special delegation of Kru to the south coast. Under the leadership of Reverend D. W. Herman, the group asked for the recall of Colonel Elwood Davis and his replacement with a certain Major Grant or another officer. The delegation felt that the Kru did not actually want war and told Barclay that they would meet with the recalcitrant Sasstown people in early November. Barclay's reply to this offer was: "Your radiogram lays down conditions which government cannot accept as it is beyond the scope of your instructions. . . . the people of Sasstown must in their own interest submit immediately to [the] Government and keep the peace. . . . you were sent to impress this upon them and not to make conditions."[111] Monrovia gave its reasons for rejecting the suggestions of the Kru delegation: "As neighbouring and loyal tribes were being threatened by this hostile combination [Dio, Wissipo, Borroh, Bettu, and Sasstown under the leadership of Chief Blogba Togba of Nana Kru and one Wesseh Cooney—opposed to Niffu which was 'loyal'], a retreat as suggested by Mr. Herman, the Chairman of the Delegation, would adversely affect [the] Government's prestige, and also because in the event a campaign was started by these hostile people it was probable that the Special Commissioner [i.e., Davis] would have to fight his way through the whole Kru section up to the point from which he had retired."[112] By April of 1933, Reverend Herman and many of his colleagues were in jail. Herman had been arrested for sedition, released, and rearrested in December of 1932 by executive order. He and the other Kru prisoners in the Sinoe jail complained "that since some of our people were killed in 1917 [sic] after the Kru Coast war, and now the Liberian Government is held responsible, they [i.e., the Sinoe authorities] will not put their hands on us but will starve us to death.[113]

During the crisis of the 1930s there were a number of "Educated

Natives," besides Didwo Twe, prominently opposed to the Americo-Liberian dominated regime: Postmaster General Momulu Massaquoi (Vai); ex-Vice-President Henry Too Wesley (Grebo); F. W. M. Morais, a member of the national legislature (Grebo); Justice F. E. Besylow (Vai); Justice Abayomi Karnga (Congo); and Montserrado County Attorney Doughba Carranda (Congo).[114] Massaquoi was one of the most prominent members of the group; he had been Liberian consul-general in Hamburg and, on Samuel Ross's death in 1929, had been appointed postmaster general. (He was later accused of malfeasance by the government and fired.) Before the scandal, the British consulate noted that Massaquoi was "related by marriage to the little group of influential Americo-Liberian families, and with great power amongst the Vai tribes, he may be the next President."[115] Edwin Barclay's intensified grip on the Liberian government after 1930 precluded any such possibility.

One of the sharpest thorns in the side of the Barclay regime was F. W. M. Morais. In August of 1931, Dr. Morais was sent to Europe to attend meetings of the League of Nations and present the case of Liberia's indigenous majority. Lord Lugard, speaking to the House of Lords, mentioned that he was in touch with "an intelligent, educated native of Liberia, who states that he has been sent as a delegate by 24 tribal chiefs to represent their case in Europe. . . ."[116] The British consulate in Monrovia, however, was less than enthusiastic about Morais's abilities and commented that "he was at one time employed in the French colonial service in the Ivory Coast, but was ejected for fraud, for which he served a term of imprisonment."[117] Morais was accompanied to Europe by N. S. Brownell, a Grebo lawyer. There Morais said the majority population (the indigenes) wanted proportional representation and "the introduction of civil service reforms, along with the development of an educational system under the supervision of the League of Nations. . . ." According to Morais, the indigenous people felt "that the country should not be mandated as foreshadowed in the foreign press, but that they should be given an opportunity to participate in the Government."[118]

In October of 1931 the American minister in Monrovia was informed that reprisals had been made against the Grebo chiefs and their people who had contributed to Morais's trip. Superintendent Harold Fredericks of Maryland supposedly remonstrated with a gathering of Grebo and arrested a number of prominent people.[119] Morais returned from Geneva in 1932 and was himself arrested for sedition. He was deprived of his seat in the legislature and imprisoned at Bella Yella. His collaborator, Brownell, on the other hand, was made attorney general in the Barclay cabinet, and abandoned opposition to the regime.

Brownell abandoned Morais, and Morais eventually abandoned the fight.[120] In August of 1934 the champion of Grebo rights wrote to the

superintendent of Maryland County offering his services as a peace negotiator: "As to the needed reforms suggested by the League growing out
of complaints from Native Chiefs, and which I sponsored and defended
at Geneva, I note with much satisfaction the introduction of such policies by the present administration calculated to render effective a complete change over from the regrettable past and that to the betterment of
my people's interest, in support of which I have willingly volunteered
my good offices toward an amicable but honourable settlement of this
outstanding feud."[121]

Late in 1934, in an article in the Monrovia *Weekly Mirror*, Morais
attempted to explain and exculpate his past conduct.

> In 1927 I was elected as Representative of the Native element for the
> County of Maryland in the National Legislature, at a moment that Native
> policy in vogue and pursued by the extant administration was causing great
> hardship to my people; at the time the situation created was pregnant with
> revolution[,] of feeling and loss of confidence in the Government to whom
> they look and are still looking for protection. I raised my voice against the
> abuses[,] publishing a Minority Report which revolutionized the conscience
> of the world but without effective realisation of my honest dreams.
>
> In consequence of findings, suggestions and recommendations to the
> International Commission of Inquiry I was selected by my people—the
> autochthons—to go to Geneva and solicit the good offices of the League of
> Nations towards amelioration of conditions particularly amongst the Inte-
> rior tribes. . . . [Later] whilst at Grand Cess I was arrested and sent to Belle
> Yallah; en route I suffered great discomfort, inconveniences and pain due to
> [a] recent surgical operation which physically incapacitated my undertaking
> such a journey. After a stay of six months, I was brought to Cape Palmas
> imprisoned and arranged [*sic*] for trial. Subsequently I sought an opportu-
> nity of settling down and studying at close range as to whether or not
> introduction of remarkable features then marked a radical change of policy
> in favour of the entire Native population. I have made the study and am
> now convinced that the sun is beginning to set on the regrettable past with
> its pensive memories; in my opinion if Mr. Barclay is maintained or contin-
> ued in office as President we might look forward to the dawn of a new era
> when this Country should witness the advent of better days.[122]

Morais's subsequent attempt to negotiate with the Sasstown Kru
was far from successful. Juah Nimley at first refused to see him. Then
the services of one Dr. Schneidenburger (described to the British consulate as "an old derelict German Jew who years ago went to South Africa
as [a] gold-digger and was there sentenced to a term of hard labour"),
were procured and Nimley was persuaded to receive Morais if Morais
came in African dress. When the meeting did take place, the paramount
chief still insisted on waiting for word from the League of Nations.[123]

Early in 1935 Morais wrote in the *Weekly Mirror* that Nimley was justifiably afraid of making peace because of memories of the events of 1916, but stated that he believed Barclay was making a sincere effort at a settlement.[124]

Abroad, even among blacks, the cause championed by men like Morais found little consistent support. To most Europeans and white Americans the indigenous people of Liberia could not be trusted to establish anything so radical as "Native Home Rule." In 1935 the American chargé made it clear that the troubles in Liberia had their origin in the nature of colonial rule: "The Liberian Government must weld this amorphous mass of indigenous natives into a homogeneous whole. . . . Hence they must exert pressure on the recalcitrant tribes."[125] Two years before, the black scholars Charles Wesley and Rayford Logan had written:

> We realize that the Liberian Government itself, like all small governments, in poor and backward areas, has been one of the causes of an internal conflict between the peoples of the interior and the Americo-Liberians in control of the government. An antagonism has developed and has been intensified recently between a small governing class and a larger class of the governed who have taken less interest through the years in the changes in the Liberian administration.

Having said this, their solution was paradoxical.

> Unless the hands of the present government are strengthened so that it may prove to be of assistance to the Liberian people in the advancement of their economic social life, this antagonism may continue. It seems imperative therefore to strengthen the Liberian government for the sake of its own maintenance.[126]

To many of the overseas black defenders of the Black Republic, Liberia represented the future toward which they believed Africa should move. Traditional Africa was loved, but only as an abstraction, and future glory was envisioned in terms of Western paradigms. Traditional Africa, that Africa subsumed under the rubric "Native," could not be allowed to stand in the way of race fulfillment (the nurturing and maturation of Progress in an African setting). In 1932 the National Association for the Advancement of Colored People issued a statement by a former educational adviser to Liberia maintaining that "the fundamental difficulty in Liberia is a clash between the new and the old—a clash between [the] so-called ideals of western civilization and jungle customs and traditions . . . the jungle man practically lives on the wild fruits and animals of the forests and knows not how to do a day's work. . . ."[127] Some defenders of Liberia did, disingenuously, attribute to it the character of a culturally synthetic state, one merging itself with indigenous Africa: "The true mission of Liberia in Africa, according to one of its executives, is not in the establishing of a Negro State, based upon Western ideas, rather it is the attainment of a Negro nationality having its foundations rooted in African cultural institutions and modified by Western thoughts."[128] Yet despite such rhetorical flourishes, the defenders of Liberia had little to say about the faceless "native" creators of "African cultural institutions." Where indigenes were mentioned, they appeared only as the spectres of "Kru militarism" or, in DuBois's words, "the warlike native tribes."[129]

According to DuBois, "the brutalities of the [Liberian] Frontier Force" were "brutalities practiced by soldiers everywhere—Americans in the Philippines, the English in Ireland, and the French everywhere. . . ."[130] In 1924 the black leader reportedly felt that "it was absolutely necessary for the [Liberian] government to take a high hand with them [the 'Natives'], in order to assure them that it really was a government; otherwise the tribal chiefs would take matters into their own hands."[131] In 1931 DuBois got around the issue of Americo-Liberian culpability in the labor traffic by arguing that Allen Yancy was not an Americo-Liberian at all, but a representative of indigenous Liberia: "Vice President Yancy was flagrantly guilty but Yancy was not an Americo-Liberian but a Native African tribesman, whose election to the Vice Presidency was especially hailed as a recognition of the native African in the political organization of the Liberians."[132] The system of pawning (using human beings as collateral for loans) was to DuBois "primarily a method by which native children are adopted into civilized Liberian families for purposes of education, and it has resulted in such widespread inter-marriage between American Negroes and native Liberians that the line between the two groups is today almost fanciful."[133]

To the "tribal" Liberian, however, the situation in the Black Republic presented a dilemma far more immediate than that confronting his brethren in the Diaspora. "I love Liberia and I think it has a right to exist as an independent Negro Republic and should never be placed under any kind of mandatory power," said the son of a Grebo chief at Fisk University in Tennessee, "but if Liberia continues to treat helpless individuals unfairly, as she does the Natives, just because they have no submarines and men-of-war or armies to defend them and battle against any unbearable power, she should be taken over by the League of Nations."[134] In the face of such sentiments the supporters of the Monrovia regime could only reply with the charge of racial treason. In the face of the imperatives of ethnic solidarity, they insisted, specific abuses paled in significance. "Native" pleas for help, either to the League or to a white power, constituted a breach of the racial front. In an attack on F.

W. M. Morais, Walter F. Walker, the Liberian consul in New York, argued that colonialists would use reports of conditions in Liberia as the opening wedge of imperialism: "This is an old trick practiced by dominant powers to break down racial solidarity and political understanding and to have people commit national hari-kari. . . . It was the orchestral accompaniment of American slavery to prevent uprisings among the slaves."[135] B. N. Azikiwe, the Nigerian, saw Morais's appeal to the League as a threat to the racial ideal embodied in Liberia:

> The cause espoused by Dr. Morais is a worthy one, but his method of approach is rather crude, and it completely destroys the sincereness [sic] of his mission. No useful purpose can be served by a direct approach to the League of Nations because it is an international organization, and only political entities are recognizable before it as members. . . . It is therefore painful to see this great son of Grebo, who was ably commended by the Chief Justice of the Republic, and who occupies an important position to strengthen the link between the Government and the aborigines by his enlightened leadership, fall into a miasma of partisan politics.[136]

The relationship between the wealth of the elite and the poverty of the indigenous masses was not perceived. Without any apparent compunctions, admiration could be expressed for the Americo-Liberian landowner—in DuBois's words a "curious blend of feudal lord and modern farmer"—or for a "mansion of five generations with a compound of endless native servants."[137] Unity of race supposedly mitigated economic exploitation.

However, one strident and divergent black response to the "native" question came from George Schuyler of the Pittsburgh *Courier*. Schuyler attacked DuBois's silence on the exploitative role of the Liberian elite. He asked the black elder statesman: "Are we not to expect the Negro colonists who are so excessively religious and shout 'The Love of Liberty Brought Us Here' will be more humane to their black native wards than would white colonists? Right is right and wrong is wrong regardless of the color of the individuals or groups involved. . . ." Du Bois was further chided, "Admiring you immensely as I do for your courage and tenacity in persistently championing the cause of colored peoples, I am sorry that you permitted your belligerent and commendable Negrophilism to warp your vision in the case of the Liberian racketeers."[138]

Schuyler began his career as the *enfant terrible* of black journalism and ended it as the black spokesman for the American ultra-right (paradoxically, DuBois died as a member of the Communist Party). At the time of the Liberian crisis, Schuyler saw himself as the Afro-American expert on Liberian labor conditions and as the scourge of the Americo-Liberian ruling group. He was the black journalist most exercised by the early phases of the scandal and the one most out of step with his fellows. Faced with what he considered the obvious fact of Liberian corruption, he persistently called for outside control—white control. Many of his articles appeared in white papers, such as the *American Mercury*, the New York *Evening Post*, the Buffalo *Express*, the Philadelphia *Public Ledger*, and the Washington *Post*.

Schuyler not only filled the popular press with stories of Liberian misdeeds, but wrote a novel, *Slaves Today*, which he prefaced with the hope that it might "help arouse enlightened world opinion against this brutalizing of the native population in a Negro republic" and "stop similar atrocities in native lands ruled by proud white nations that boast of their superior culture."[139] In 1931 he went to Liberia for the New York *Evening Post* and wrote a six-installment report.[140] His exposés won praise in certain circles and caused consternation in others.[141] The articles ran from June 27 to July 6, 1931 and brought from Edwin Barclay the comment that they were "a hodge-podge of all the legends that are told up and down the coast on Liberia and the Liberians, reinforced by the most recent 'revelations' of Christy and Johnson."[142] Missionaries were also upset by Schuyler's charge that "they have sat serene and complacent and observed the forced labor of whole tribes on the government roads" and "have never seen fit to protest to the outer world about the debauchery of native women living as concubines in the homes of many of the leading Liberians."[143]

Walter White, executive secretary of the NAACP, took exception to Schuyler's attacks on the Black Republic and tried to interest the New York *Evening Post* in an opposing article by an Episcopalian clergyman. White remarked, "It is interesting that Mr. Schuyler, a colored man, made charges against Liberia and that Mr. Hazzard [the clergyman] a white man, is coming to Liberia's defense."[144] Schuyler reacted to criticism with the same vehemence with which he attacked the Liberian elite. In the fall of 1931 he angrily wrote to White:

> Frankly I cannot see what the N.A.A.C.P. or the Urban League has to do with it. If anyone needs advancing in Liberia it is the natives who are systematically robbed and persecuted. Lastly, the only official delegate of Liberia at Geneva is a white man, Sottile, who I understand has never been to Liberia! The other two Liberians at Geneva, Morais and Brownell [indigenes], are fighting the present government and asking for foreign supervised elections.[145]

Later Schuyler wrote that "The N.A.A.C.P., the [New York] *Age* and almost all other Negroes want the U.S. government to end slavery and forced labor of Negroes in Mississippi, but they seem not so keen to end the slavery and forced labor of Negroes in Liberia."[146] The journalist argued that "in both instances local customs and prejudices are behind the atrocities, and local authorities will not or cannot alter them for the better." So in both cases outside intervention was called for. "The difference seems to be," Schuyler wrote, "that in Mississippi the whites are exploiting the blacks, while in Liberia the blacks are exploiting the blacks, just as blacks do in Haiti and Abyssinia." He charged that "the rabid 'race men' insist that black folk can do no wrong." He believed that "American supervision should last for at least 20 or 25 years until the Liberians are competent of administering the country, which clearly they are not at present. . . ."[147] Schuyler admitted that his views differed "from those of the majority of Afro-Americans." He retorted that "for that matter [so] do realistic views of almost everything. This divergence of view has never caused me to suffer from insomnia." In his view, Liberia's problems were of her own making since she had asked for the Firestone Company and the loan.[148] According to Schuyler, it was the "consensus among Americans in Liberia" that the United States undertake the "benevolent supervision" of the Black Republic.[149]

On the left, the Communist International attacked both the defenders of the Barclay regime and the idea of a League mandate. Communists urged an emphasis on the "workers' " struggle. While still a member of the American Communist Party, George Padmore had, on behalf of the International Trade Union Committee of Negro Workers, exhorted the black workers of the world to rally to the defense of Liberia. Within Liberia, he urged the creation of trade unions among seamen. He asserted in the *Negro Worker:* "The very first task which stands before the workers, especially the seamen and dockers in the coast ports of Liberia, such as Monrovia, Great Bassa, is to organize themselves into trade unions as the basis for the development of a broad mass anti-imperialist movement; for only in this way will the Liberian workers be able to defend their economic interests and carry on the struggle for improving their political and social conditions."[150] Another writer in the *Negro Worker* argued that a mandate for Liberia would solve nothing. "They [i.e., 'the native masses'] realise that the problem which misgovernment and particularly the economic system, have created, demands drastic solution—a solution to consist not in mandating their country and therefore in intensifying exploitation, oppression and poverty, but a solution which must consist in and be based upon revolutionary activity of the natives themselves."[151]

Apparently neither Juah Nimley's resistance nor Didwo Twe's call for a "Native Republic" qualified. In May of 1935 the same writer concluded: "Facts clearly indicate that objective factors are not wanting for the mobilisation of the Liberian masses for decisive struggle, but that on the other hand, and very unfortunately[,] they do emphatically show the total absence of the necessary subjective factors: that unless the exploited masses gird their loins and wage a relentless struggle against their subjugators and oppressors, freedom is not forthcoming: that unless the labouring masses are organised and taught through systematic propaganda, education and political enlightenment to realise that freedom does not come as a gift, but must be fought for and unless the opportunist and treacherous National Reform Native Intellectuals are persistently and consistently exposed—the great cause of the struggle of liberation is doomed to fail."[152]

If the "Natives" did not figure prominently in the thought of those who defended Liberia out of racial solidarity, the Communist International paid them little more attention. The International Trade Union Committee of Negro Workers had a definition of "worker" which *excluded* the masses within the boundaries of Liberia. Seeing the paid workers of a few ports and the Firestone Plantations as the vanguard of revolution, the Committee behaved as if revolt and resistance to the regime did not exist. The issue of hut taxes and forced requisitions was not dwelt upon. The committee paradoxically called for revolution where there was none and ignored it where it was ablaze for five years.

The 1930 investigation of Liberia and the subsequent international spotlighting of the Black Republic did have an impact on the "Native Policy" of the government. In addition to outlawing labor export and pawning, after 1930 the Liberian regime sought to curb other outrageous instances of abuse of the majority population. The Barclay administration prided itself on this new departure and in the mid-thirties proclaimed: "It is a common expression of the natives to say, that 'under this present administration we are not compelled to carry on our heads soldiers, messengers and other subordinate officials; we are not compelled to leave our homes and go miles away to work roads.' "[153] The regime sought, on numerous occasions, to avoid provoking open conflict with its indigenous population. When, in September of 1931, a group of "civilized" Maryland citizens petitioned the president for aid and ammunition for use against a suspected Grebo uprising, Barclay denied their petition and advised them not to take precipitate action against their neighbors.[154] In Maryland in the following year, Lieutenant-Colonel W. V. S. Tubman (later President, 1944–1971) reportedly allowed one of his men to burn a house in a Grebo town without provocation. The local representative of central authority, G. Brewer, thought this may have been an attempt to embarrass the administration and had a subordinate officer reprimanded by a special court of inquiry.[155] In the same month the county superintendent, Harold Fredericks, wrote to Barclay that "with

Brownell and Morais instigating the Greboes to passive resistance and prominent Kroos at your end fomenting open defiance against Government authority, it behooves all administrative officials, especially those coming in contact with Natives, to avoid semblance of any policy which might accelerate an already grave situation, in other words, let sleeping dogs lie protem."[156] Three years later Fredericks wrote the president that the old order was changing and that he hoped civil service reform would open careers to talent and benefit indigenous youth.[157]

But if the years 1929–1935 saw an amelioration of "Native Policy," there was no drastic change in the Liberian social structure. The "Reform Native Intellectuals"—men like Twe and Morais—and the idea of a Native Republic received little support from any quarter. Yet it was here, perhaps, that the greatest possibility for change lay. Had "Native Home Rule" been successful, the 1930s would have seen a significant shifting of elites. An indigenous, Western-educated elite with strong connections with the traditional rulers and political groupings could have come to the fore. The political structure of Liberia would have come to resemble that of many African states in the post-colonial period. It is evident that, in the thirties, the idea of a West African republic representing such a union of forces was anathema to a wide spectrum of outside opinion. Unfortunately this attitude served to perpetuate a situation which has only very recently given evidence of change.

7· Conclusion

The scandal of 1929 was a trauma in Liberian national life. It threatened to unseat the national elite and encouraged portions of the indigenous population to place their trust in outside intervention. But the elite was not unseated, nor was there a change in the relationship between the elite and the majority of Liberia's people. It may in fact seem that the Liberian crisis changed very little; yet the very maintenance of the *status quo* meant there had to be change in the internal running of the country. The Edwin Barclay administration (1930–1944) arrogated increased powers to the presidency, a tendency amplified during the subsequent tenure of William Tubman (1944–1971). Sedition laws imposed during the 1930s identified dissent with external subversion, and Barclay was able to solidify his position by pointing out the danger dissent presented to the entrenched power of the elite. (Thus in 1935 he was able to lengthen the presidential term to eight years.) The crisis of the thirties was a challenge and response situation in which the Liberian executive responded by strengthening its power. It is interesting to note that in 1955 Barclay was himself in opposition to the "dictatorial" policies of his successor, William Tubman, opposition which was crushed by the strengthened presidency which Barclay had himself helped inaugurate.[1]

The great claim of the Tubman regime was that it initiated a "Unification Policy" which finally brought the majority of Liberia's people into national life. (In 1944 the franchise was extended to all adult males who paid the hut tax.) But the "Unification Policy" was adumbrated during the 1930s when the Barclay regime sought to temper its Hinterland policies and exercise greater control over its agents there. Barclay was willing to coopt members of the opposition where possible to place prominent indigenes in high national office. This served as concrete proof of the regime's often-stated claim that the Americo-Liberian group and the indigenous population were melding. Such claims had been made before Barclay and would continue to be made afterwards. In the thirties this cooptation process proceeded apace and played a very great part in convincing would-be critics that the "Native Question" was being solved. But cooptation of indigenous and Americo-Liberian dissidents by the True Whig Party did not, and could not, alter the basic power relationships in Liberia. For those who refused to be coopted into the dominant clique the penalty increasingly was political prison or exile.

Besides bringing into stark relief the role of the Americo-Liberian elite, the Liberian crisis says something about the nature of concessions granted by small states to outside interests. It has been noted that certain indigenous African states (such as the Asante and the Ndebele polities) considered employing foreign capital and expertise in the late nineteenth century.[2] Unfortunately, the Liberian experience indicates that such investment was bound to be fraught with difficulties. Any relationship between a sovereign African polity and outside concessionaires was likely to raise questions of legal jurisdiction in the settlement of disputes. Given the disparity in power between African states and outside powers, and given the prevailing pseudo-scientific racism, it seems doubtful that any concessionaire relationship would have been smooth. Whites working on the spot tended to resent the imposition of African authority, and Africans, as in the Liberian case, resented the usurpation of authority felt to be theirs. Simply put, the question became—would Europeans, or Americans, operating under the purview of what they considered to be backward and obstructionist governments, have resisted the temptation to defy those governments? Would the concessionaires' home governments have been willing to resist the call to back up their nationals? On another level, would home governments have resisted demands by companies for the protection of their investments against the vagaries of local politics? In the late nineteenth century it would have been very difficult for a European government (or the government of the United States) to have said no. Liberia, in the 1920s raised the same questions and was saved from forcible outside intervention only by a combination of forces peculiar to the situation: internationally recognized sovereign status, membership in the League of Nations, mobilized support within the concessionaire's home territory, and the emergence in the United States of a policy of nonintervention.

Liberia was Africa's first republic and also its first "neocolonial" state. The labor investigation of 1930 did not change the condition of workers within Liberia, nor was it meant to. The crisis period of 1929–1936 was one of testing, after which the Liberian elite settled into a symbiotic relationship with Firestone and other large-scale foreign interests. Since then the Liberian political elite has not attempted to oust foreign capital. Indeed it has assiduously cultivated increased foreign investment, with iron mining, after 1945, supplanting rubber as the major field of foreign investment and profit. Christopher Clapham has noted that the "economic relationship with foreign corporations leads easily to the assumption that these corporations must play a large part in government" since "the government and the corporations have a common interest in maintaining a source of wealth from which both profit. . . ."[3] The Liberian government has not encouraged the growth of large-scale Liberian capital, but has, instead, sought to derive as much benefit from foreign investment as possible.

The *modus vivendi* established by the mid-thirties clarified the way in which the interests of the Liberian government and foreign capital would interdigitate. It did not resolve the issue of how questions of wage rates and land rights were to be arranged between foreign interests and their workers. In fact, while labor export was outlawed, the internal exploitation of labor may have increased. There was continued coercion of labor for both Firestone-owned and Liberian-owned rubber plantations. The Liberian Department of the Interior assisted the rubber company in its procurement of labor, often under circumstances involving duress.[4] It was not until 1962 that Firestone ceased its recruitment of workers through chiefs operating under the purview of this department. The payment of commissions to chiefs for workers produced for plantation work reportedly led to abuses analogous to those of the 1920s.[5] There was also the continued alienation of African land. At a conference of chiefs at Salala in 1945 complaints were made about the confiscation of lands by both the Firestone Company and individual Americo-Liberian farmers. Complaints against the individual farms were redressed; those against the vast Firestone holdings were not.[6]

As late as 1961–1962 a team of scholars from Northwestern University concluded that "with regard to taxation, land tenure, control over residence and movement, marriage and divorce, legal jurisdiction, access to educational and medical services, obligatory (no pay) labor services to local authorities, labor recruitment (forced labor with no pay) and extra-legal exactions of money, rice and services, tribal Liberians in the hinterland are subject to a socio-legal system different from that of the Americo Liberians."[7] In 1961 the International Labor Organization also noted instances of flagrant labor abuse on the part of Liberians and foreign interests and criticized Liberia for not adhering to the terms of the International Labor Convention of 1930 (which had been in force in Liberia since May of 1932). A three-man commission of the International Labor Organization met in Geneva in 1962 and concluded that certain Liberian laws continued to provide for forced labor on Hinterland road-building projects. The commission also noted the continuance of conscription for porterage and forced recruitment for private employers. Although the Liberian government maintained that such practices had been voided by Tubman-era legislation, the commission was unimpressed. By the time its report was completed in early 1963, the Liberian government had enacted legislation which rectified the most glaring abuses, although this legislation still failed to make forcible recruitment an offense for government officials other than chiefs.[8]

The Liberian crisis brings up a broader issue, one which has still not been resolved: on what pretext can an assumedly racist America intervene in black countries? In 1915 in Haiti an argument based on the need to maintain order sufficed (or, at least, it satisfied the official conscience). But it is probably not too far afield to argue that in 1933 American policy makers were aware of the contradictions which would have been exposed by armed intervention to "save" black Africans. This also fits within the larger framework of American policy, which, up until the 1960s, preferred to consider Africa a strictly European sphere of influence.

It has been seen that the Liberian crisis united a group of Afro-American spokesmen against the threat of direct American intervention in Africa. But the crisis demonstrates certain ambiguities in the relationship between Afro-Americans and their government. Some leaders, like DuBois for a time, considered that the reconstruction of Liberia should be put in non-American (and, supposedly, non-racist) hands. Other black leaders sought to encourage their own government to display an "enlightened" interest in Africa. The question of what role the American government should play vis-à-vis the external black world was brought up during the Liberian crisis but not clarified. The issue remains: should Afro-Americans encourage and serve their government in Africa or should they discourage the active participation there of a government that until recently has been clearly racist?

Afro-Americans can have a great impact on certain foreign policy decisions of the American government. Acknowledging that potential impact, we must also recognize that the type of issue confronted is of paramount importance. In issues which are clearly black and white— (that is, black versus white)—the formation of a consensus is fairly easy. In 1967 Stokely Carmichael said, "The best protection for Africa today is African-Americans inside the United States because when we start to move against South Africa, if the United States dares to come into this continent, the African-Americans will burn that country down to the ground."[9] This language may be somewhat hyperbolic, but it is certain that in the future blacks will influence African policies which have clear racial implications. It can be asked if American blacks and their allies will actually find means to neutralize the growth of pro-South African and pro-Rhodesian lobbies within the United States and encourage substantive changes in American foreign policy. The answer increasingly appears to be yes. A more difficult problem will be met in deciding what policies should be adopted toward black ruled Africa. Here, as seen in the Liberian case, race alone can provide no clear-cut guidelines. Divisions on what policies to pursue are likely to mirror the internal ideological divisions in the black community. Afro-Americans will, even in southern Africa, increasingly face the dilemma enunciated by C. L. R. James: "The race question is subsidiary to the class question in politics. . . . But to neglect the racial factor as merely incidental is an error only less grave than to make it fundamental."[10]

In Liberia today the term "Americo-Liberian" is banned from official use and is falling into desuetude. Although the term had, and has, validity in describing the settler-indigene cleavage it has also served to obscure a very salient point in Liberian development. By the early twentieth century—when large-scale emigration from the Diaspora became technologically feasible due to improved communications and effective tropical medicine—the Americo-Liberians were no longer an extension of Afro-America. They were a group native to Africa hoping to maintain their supremacy against all comers. Racial solidarity, although used as a propaganda instrument, played little part in the policy decisions of the Monrovia government. When thinkers such as DuBois, Padmore, Azikiwe, and others were led, in their defense of Liberia, to paint an image of a kind of Black Zionist state, which would serve as the focus for the emancipation of the African, they ignored the far more parochial and self-interested view of the Liberian elite.

This inability to see the contradictions in the Liberian situation was the signal failure of prewar Pan-Africanism. Simple Pan-Africanism was unable to answer the conundrum posed by the Liberian situation, and the movement's cosmopolitanism impeded its grasp of African realities. With a world-view molded by the Diaspora, Pan-Africanism "required a leadership class of Afro-Americans for whom it [Pan-Africanism] would easily be real, within their own individual social, economic and political capabilities." This called for "a black population who had some affluence, who had a vocation with international market value, who had verbal fluency, and who had a sense of themselves as world citizens, as part of an international community of color."[11] There was a fundamental difference between the world-view of the Pan-Africanist supporters of Liberia and the actual condition of the majority of Liberia's people. The former affirmed no difference in right between settler and indigene if both sprang from the "Race." If Liberia could prove to be a channel of economic achievement or a symbol of self-determination for blacks in the Diaspora, little thought was given to the economic impact of their settlements on the "Natives."

Looking at the DuBois-Garvey controversy of the twenties, it becomes obvious that Garvey, the "Black Zionist" (in Padmore's words), acknowledged, far more clearly than did DuBois, the nature and reality of the West African republic. J. A. Langley has written that "the alleged differences between the DuBois and Garvey concept of Pan-Africanism seem, on closer examination, to have been minimal."[12] In his view, "the DuBois-Garvey controversy was not so much an ideological conflict as one of personalities and divergence on short-run political tactics: the goal was the same—black political and economic freedom." It should be remembered, however, that where Garvey and DuBois directly confronted Africa—in Liberia—they showed considerable divergence. Both the representatives of the UNIA and DuBois got to see Liberia first hand. Beside Garvey's supposedly grandiose experiment in utopianism, DuBois's mythopoeic defense of Liberia appears even further removed from reality. DuBois's function as a propagandist was, no doubt, important and necessary. But the Liberian crisis shows that, in the mid-twenties and early thirties, his propaganda was highly unprogrammatic, having little to say about Africa as Africa. The charge by Imanuel Geiss that DuBois "missed his opportunity to give Pan-Africanism a rational basis" is, unfortunately, nowhere more clearly seen than in his failure to advocate more than the *status quo* in black ruled Africa.[13]

Liberia is now in her second century of existence. The problems of the first century are rapidly giving way to, or being compounded by, new dilemmas. A state that long maintained itself by its wits is now seeing if it can create change within its existing political order. In 1947, Raymond Buell, criticizing the past performance of the Liberian regime, said, "Whether the situation in Liberia will be changed, and how, depends largely on American policy."[14] But it is now obvious that the forces for change reside within the Black Republic itself, and that the efforts of outside forces to allay or divert that change will not be brooked. It will be interesting to see if Liberia, Africa's oldest republic, will be among the first to witness the withering away of its elite.

Notes

Introduction

1. League of Nations, Secretariat, *Report of the Liberian Commission of Enquiry* (C.658.M272), June, 1930, 36. Hereafter cited as League, *Report*.

2. Edwin Redkey, *Black Exodus: Black Nationalist and Back-to-Africa Movements, 1890–1910* (New Haven, 1969), 20.

3. M. B. Akpan, "Black Imperialism: Americo-Liberian Rule over the African Peoples of Liberia, 1841–1964," *The Canadian Journal of African Studies*, VII, 2 (1973), 218, citing a manuscript of the American Colonization Society, September 4, 1965, Library of Congress, Washington, D.C.; Liberia *Bulletin*, no. 15 (February, 1900), 28. It has been estimated that before the American Civil War, 18,858 Afro-Americans emigrated to Liberia. See Richard Strong, ed., *The African Republic of Liberia and the Belgian Congo* (Cambridge, Mass., 1930), I, 37.

Elsewhere, Akpan estimated that Liberia probably contained only slightly over half a million people in 1920, five thousand of whom were Americo-Liberians. The estimate is based on the fact that President C. D. B. King, probably inflatedly, received four thousand votes in the elections of 1919. See M. B. Akpan, "Liberia and the Universal Negro Improvement Association: The Background to the Abortion of Garvey's Scheme for African Colonization," *Journal of African History*, XIV, 1 (1973), 108, citing T. J. K. Faulkner, "An Appeal to Reason [to the Liberian Republic]," Monrovia, December 22, 1927, U.S. National Archives, Washington, D.C., Record Group 59, 888.00/772. The U.S. National Archives, Record Group 59, is hereafter cited as USNA, RG59.

4. Redkey, *Black Exodus*, 181, citing Turner in *Voice of Missions*, April 15, 1893 (published July, 1893).

5. On the Kru Coast, trade between settler and indigene was very well developed before the full imposition of Liberian governmental authority during the Howard administration (1912–1920). The export of palm kernels and palm oil was important in the mid-nineteenth century; in the year ending September, 1865, palm products accounted for over three-quarters of the entire value of Liberian exports. See Ronald Davis, *Ethnohistorical Studies on the Kru Coast* (Newark, Del., 1976), 42. Indeed, before the large-scale export of rubber in the 1920s palm products usually comprised more than half of the total value of exports.

The export of timber and piassava (a fiber obtained from a type of palm used in brushes and cordage) continued throughout the nineteenth and into the twentieth century.

6. Alexander Crummell, *The Future of Africa* (New York, 1969), 230.

7. John Hargreaves, "African Colonization in the Nineteenth Century: Liberia and Sierra Leone," in *Boston University Papers in African History* (Boston, 1964), I, 66.

8. Ibid., 65, quoting Gurley to Clayton, February 15, 1850 (U.S. 31st Congress, 1st session, 1850, Executive Document 75).

9. Ibid., 66.

10. Ibid., 65, quoting F. E. Smith, "Report," *Liberia*, no. 1 (November, 1892).

11. Ibid., citing G. W. Ellis, Jr., in *Liberia*, no. 26 (February, 1905). Also H. H. Johnston, *Liberia* (London, 1906), I, 602–603.

12. Elliot Berg, "The Development of a Labor Force in Sub-Saharan Africa," *Economic Development and Cultural Change*, XIII, 4, pt. 1 (July, 1965), 397.

13. Mary Jo Sullivan, "Sinoe Settler Politics in the Late Nineteenth Century" (Paper delivered at the Tenth Annual Conference of the Liberian Studies Association, Boston University, Boston, Mass., April 6–8, 1978). For a description of settler politics in Maryland County, see Penelope Campbell, *Maryland in Africa: The Maryland State Colonization Society, 1831–1857* (Chicago, 1971).

14. Merran Fraenkel, "Social Change on the Kru Coast of Liberia," *Africa*, XXVI (1966), 154.

15. Strong, *The African Republic of Liberia*, 37.

16. Hannah A. Jones, "The Struggle for Political and Cultural Unification in Liberia, 1847–1930" (Ph.D. diss., Northwestern University, 1962), 209. The extent of a commissioner's powers in the interior could not be easily delimited. An example was District Commissioner James Howard, who was appointed in 1916 to administer the region between the Sierra Leone boundary and the River Cess, almost two-thirds of the Liberian Hinterland. Howard governed this area without any supervision from Monrovia. Apart from the usual practices of overtaxation, exploitation, and intimidation, the district commissioner resorted to smuggling goods, including gin, guns, and gunpowder, from Pendembu in Sierra Leone into his district, where he sold them at high prices. He also used unpaid carrier service to transport vast quantities of rice which he bought at nominal prices or which had been supplied for the upkeep of interior officials. The rice was taken to Pendembu, where his agents sold it. When, in 1918, Howard's actions caused a major revolt among the Gola, and government commissioners found him guilty of maladministration and embezzlement of public funds, his punishment consisted of the seizure of $5,000 which he had placed in Monrovia's Bank of British West Africa. Two of his aides were fined, and Howard himself was appointed to his former position as lieutenant in the Frontier Force. See Jones, "The Struggle," 216–218; Akpan, "Black Imperialism," 232, citing "Records of the Department of State Relating to the Findings of the Council of Inquiry at Monrovia," June 21, 1918, USNA.

Chapter 1

1. Johnson was born in 1893 in Bristol, Virginia. He received his B.A. from Virginia Union University in 1917 and then entered the University of Chicago.

After serving in France during World War I, he returned to the University of Chicago, where he was a Fellow in Sociology and where he wrote *The Negro in Chicago* (1922), a book whose publication was spurred on by the race riots of 1919. In 1927 he published *Ebony and Topaz* and in 1930 *The Negro in American Civilization*. Johnson's posts as a race-relations expert were varied: director of research for the Chicago Urban League; investigator of black migration for the Carnegie Foundation Series of Economic Studies; associated executive secretary of the Chicago Commission of Race Relations, director of research for the National Urban League (New York), and editor of the League's journal, *Opportunity*. At the time of his appointment to the League of Nations commission, Johnson was director of the Department of Social Science at Fisk University in Nashville, Tennessee. In the same year (1930) he was awarded the William C. Harman Gold Award for distinguished achievement among Afro-Americans in the field of science. Johnson died in 1956. (*Who's Who in Colored America*, ed. Thomas Yenser, 6th ed. [New York, 1944]. See also Patrick J. Gilpin, "Charles S. Johnson: Scholar and Educator," *Negro History Bulletin*, XXXIX [March, 1976], 544–548.)

2. Christy had been senior medical officer in Northern Nigeria (1898–1900); special medical officer in Bombay for the plague (1900–1901); member of the Uganda Sickness Commission (1902); assistant lecturer at the Liverpool School of Tropical Medicine (1903); researcher on sleeping sickness in the Congo (1903–1904); in Ceylon (1906); in Uganda and East Africa (1906–1909); in Nigeria, the Gold Coast, and the Cameroons (1909–1910); publisher of a technical book on the African rubber industry (1911); in the Congo making a natural-history collection on behalf of the Belgian government (1911–1914); a researcher of malaria and sleeping sickness in Mesopotamia, the Sudan, the Congo (during World War I); winner of the Royal Geographical Medal for exploration in Central Africa (1919); in Tanganyika (1925–1928); in French Equatorial and West Africa collecting (1928–1929). J. P. Moffat Papers (Houghton Library, Harvard University), Diplomatic Journal, vol. 29, 1930–1931, Berne, February 12, 1930.

3. After six weeks, Christy and Johnson journeyed to Kataka and then to Cape Palmas, where they took the testimony of chiefs, subchiefs, and others. After Cape Palmas the commissioners visited villages on the Grebo coast. At Garawe the two men took separate routes in order to observe a wider area. They returned to Monrovia on July 7 and continued to take evidence until August 8. At the conclusion of their fact-finding the investigators had taken the testimony of 109 witnesses in Monrovia. In addition, they had heard 39 spokesmen for sections and towns at their Kataka meetings and 116 such spokesmen in Maryland County. Of the persons giving evidence, 20 were paramount chiefs, 82 subchiefs, 103 indigenous civilians, 3 cabinet ministers, and 26 public officials, including justices of the Supreme Court, senators, county superintendents, and district commissioners. In all, the League's investigators took 264 dispositions.

4. League, *Report*, 6.

5. Ibid., p. 17.

6. Radiogram, Ross to Barclay, c. October 6, 1927, Charles Johnson Papers, Fisk University Library, Nashville, Tennessee, box 88, file 5.

7. League, *Report*, 17. The influences were thought to include President C. D. B. King.

8. Davis, *Ethnohistorical Studies*, 37. See also p. 31, as well as George Brooks, *The Kru Mariner in the Nineteenth Century* (Newark, Del., 1972), 3.

Who were these migrants? One major problem in the ethnography of the Grain Coast (roughly the coastline of present-day Liberia) is that the labels applied to its inhabitants have shifted in the last century and a half as the result of the migration and amalgamation of disparate peoples. Today the Kru, along with the Bassa and Grebo, constitute the largest linguistic group in Liberia. Delimitation of the perimeters of the Kru language group is problematic since different authors have imposed different taxonomies on the same data. In the middle of the nineteenth century Sigismund Koelle said Kru should be called Kra and that Proper Kra was spoken only in the "Five Towns" of the Kru Coast (Nana Kru, King Williamstown, Kroba, Settra Kru, and Little Kru). More broadly, the designation Kru has been given to a collection of related languages which include Kru, Bassa, Grebo, De, and the Kran/Sapo languages of the present Grand Gedeh County. The French scholar Lavergne de Tressan defines the Kru languages even more broadly and divides them into three subgroups— the Bakwé, Géré, and Bété—which span the coastal region from central Liberia to eastern Ivory Coast. See Davis, *Ethnohistorical Studies*, 7 (citing Sigismund Koelle, *Polyglotta Africana* [London, 1854]), and p. 6 (citing M. de Lavergne Tressan, *Inventaire linguistique de l'Afrique Occidentale Française et du Togo* [Dakar, 1953], 133–143).

9. Ibid., 23. Local traditions also emphasize the need for salt as a factor impelling migration to the coast.

10. Brooks, *The Kru Mariner*, 17.

11. Ibid., 100. It has been hypothesized that the "Kru" represent the amalgamation of related but distinct peoples—shore-living "Fishmen" and inland agricultural "Bushmen." The wellsprings of Kru migration lie in fusion: "The most likely explanation for this achievement (large-scale overseas employment) is that many young men, perhaps numbering in the hundreds, were recruited by Fishmen-Kru headmen who profited from their kinship affiliations with Bushmen-Kru lineages on the relatively highly populated 'Kru Coast.' " According to this hypothesis, the Fishmen (described as "powerfully built fisherfolk living in small fishing hamlets . . . skilled and courageous canoe and boat-handlers") were related to shore-living peoples dwelling in the Ivory Coast and eastward. As a result of European trade (including the slave trade) the Fishmen spread (as pilots and interpreters) along what is now the Liberian coast as far north as Cape Mount and beyond. It is suggested that, due to a concentration of trading activity in the area of settlements known as the Five Towns (or "Tribes"), close contact and intermarriage took place between Fishmen and inland ("Bushmen") patrilineages in the seventeenth and eighteenth centuries. Gradually, out of the melding of these peoples, emerged the language (Krawi or Krawin) spoken by the inhabitants of the Five Towns (Krao) and their satellite communities. According to this hypothesis, the Krawi language speakers retained their identities as Fishmen-Kru and Bushmen-Kru; both groups kept many of their existing social and cultural traits as well as kinship linkages to related interior patrilineages. The emerging fusion witnessed among the Krao was not replicated among other littoral and interior peoples until the nineteenth century.

In the past century and a half there has been a coalescence of a "Kru" ethnic identity, in which most of the people inhabiting the region from Grand Cess to Garawe have come to identify themselves as ethnically Kru (as distinct from their neighbors to the north and south). This has been both the result of the fusion of groups on what, by the mid-nineteenth century, was called the Kru Coast, and the acceptance by Kru Coast groups of foreigners' (Europeans' and immigrant blacks') perception of them as Kru. See L. B. Breitborde, "Some Linguistic Evidence in the Study of Kru Ethnolinguistic Affiliation" (Paper delivered at the

Ninth Annual Conference of the Liberian Studies Association, Macomb, Ill., April, 1977).

Early-nineteenth-century European accounts refer to several groups living on what became the Kru Coast: Fishmen (or Fishermen), Bushmen, and Krumen. According to one authority, no significant political or linguistic characteristics separated the Fishmen and Krumen. The division was occupational; the Fishmen simply fished (Davis, *Ethnohistorical Studies*, 21). On another point the evidence (or at least the argument) is contradictory. Davis says that Fishmen, in spite of their name, were not the group selected for service on European vessels. Yet, evidence presented to a parliamentary committee in 1842 clearly stated that Fishmen were preferred aboard ship "as they are more at home with boats and more accustomed to live on the water than the Kroomen"; the "Kroomen" were preferred for domestic tasks because they were "much more capable of attachment to white people." (Brooks, *The Kru Mariner*, 89, citing the testimony of Joseph Denman in "Report from the Select Committee on the West Coast of Africa," *Parliamentary Papers*, XI [1842], no. 551.) Brooks (p. 78) comments: "It is significant to note that labor migrants to Sierra Leone came largely (almost exclusively?) from the Kru Coast rather than the 'Fishmen' hamlets scattered along the Liberian coast from Cape Mount to Cape Palmas and beyond." Davis says "oral traditions and written accounts indicate that the first towns to offer labor for ships and ports were those in the Settra Kru region" (*Ethnohistorical Studies*, 31).

12. In the past the peoples of the Kru Coast organized themselves into a large number of towns, each with its own independent head. Towns were often fissiparous, giving rise to satellite villages recognizing the authority of the parent community. Conflict between towns was frequent and political alliances ephemeral. Unity, where it existed, was, more often than not, cultural. Towns were united by sentiment, dialect, and migration traditions. Such ties bound various towns into *dako* or "subtribes"; on the Kru Coast there were six: Jloh, Kabor, Gbeta, Sasstown (or Pahn), Grand Cess (or Siklio), and the Five Towns (Nana Kru, King Williamstown, Kroba, Settra Kru, and Little Kru). Thirty to forty miles inland were the *kwia*, those *dako* referred to as "bush Kru" by the coastal Kru: Matro, Bolo, Nanke, and Bwa. These inland *dako*, in turn, referred to the Sapo and Putu living still further inland as "bush." Until recently the majority of Kru laborers were drawn from the coastal *dako*. Certain *dako* have tended to predominate in certain ports. The Five Towns people are found mostly in Freetown; Sasstown and Grand Cess people have traditionally sought employment in Sekondi—Takoradi, Accra, and Lagos. In Monrovia stevedoring is usually done by members of the Gbeta and Jloh.

The social organization of the Kru Coast both influenced, and was influenced by, the pattern of labor migration. On the Kru Coast the *panton*, an exogamus patrisib, is the basic social unit, and towns are divided into quarters inhabited by individual lineages. The *panton* is headed by the *nyefue*, its eldest capable male member, who is responsible for settling intragroup disputes and representing it in its dealings with other patrisibs. Farmland areas outside the towns are divided among the *pantons*, and a farmer's right to land for his dwelling and cultivation is derived from his father's *panton*. In the past, the *kroba* (or *krogba*, *kaloba*), or "father of the town," was selected by the group of *nyefei* (plural) after a priest (the *Kpotoa*), accompanied by a delegation, consulted an oracle (the *kroba* and the *panton nyefei* all belonged to a group of elders). A village's affairs were handled by the *kroba* and the *nyefei*. The latter acted as a check on the former's power. They could bring collective pressure to bear and retained the right to appoint members of their own *pantons* to various traditional offices. Another focus of authority, besides the *nyefei* and the *kroba*, was the *gbaubi* or "father of the army." In wartime the *gbaubi*'s authority largely replaced that of the *kroba*, and traditionally he led new young warriors into ritualized warfare on a neighboring town. Kru Coast societies contained age sets which were formed every eight to twelve years and which included members of all lineages. There were, according to one source, three age sets: *Kafa*, young men approximately 20–35 years old; *Nyemo*, middle-aged men approximately 35–55 years old; and *Nyekpla*, the elders. Initiation into the *Kafa*, from which warriors were drawn, was often accompanied by circumcision and elaborate ceremony (*gbau* or *gbo*). See Fraenkel, "Social Change on the Kru Coast," 154; and Brooks, *The Kru Mariner*, 77.

See also Thomas Hayden, "A Description of the 1970 Grand Cess Bo," *Liberian Studies Journal*, IV, 2 (1971–1972), 183–188. Great confusion surrounds the use of age-grade terms in Kru society. Brooks says the *gbaubi* was selected by the *Kafa* (*Sedibo*), an "age set composed of young men." Ronald Davis says the *Sedibo* were "soldiers, mostly men of middle age" and mentions a group of young men, the *Kedibo*, beneath them. In his view the *gbaubi* office was "essentially political, actual leadership of soldiers being left to younger men." See Brooks, *The Kru Mariner*, 75; and Davis, *Ethnohistorical Studies*, 24.

It has been argued that among the people of the Kru Coast there existed a secret society (*Bo, Gbo, Boviowah*) and that this organization has been confused with the organization of the polity itself. Davis (*Ethnohistorical Studies*, 24) says: "In 1839 [John Wilson] described the Kru 'body politic' according to what he thought was political organization but what really appears to be Bo [*Bo, Gbo, Boviowah*] society organization. He divided the men into three classes, of which the *Gnekbade*, or elders, had the greatest influence. During their meetings they functioned much like a senate, and had two officers, the *Bodio*, a sort of high priest and keeper of fetishes, and the *Worabanh*, who functioned as military leader in time of war. The second class was *Sedibo*, or soldiers, mostly men of middle age. Individuals became part of Sedibo, through payment of a fee, usually a cow. Two officers called *Ibadio* and *Tibawah* existed in Sedibo, but Wilson did not elaborate on their duties. The youngest men belonged to a class known as *Kedibo* and had little political or other influence. The *Deyabo*, or 'doctors,' formed a group apart from the rest, but Wilson apparently was unsure of their duties. Mary Kingsley would later report the Wilson account almost *verbatim* as a 'typical Kru political organization.' "

See John Leighton Wilson to the American Colonization Society, *African Repository*, XV (1839), 262–267; John Leighton Wilson, *Western Africa* (New York, 1856), 129–131; Mary Kingsley, *West African Studies* (New York, 1964), 447–449. Secret societies are also mentioned by F. W. Butt-Thompson, *West African Secret Societies* (London, 1929). Gordon Haliburton's *The Prophet Harris* (New York, 1973, 7–8) uses Kingsley's account to explain Grebo social organization in Maryland County. Several writers maintain that a secret society did not exist on the Kru Coast or that the membership grade terms used by the "secret society" were synonyms for those used for the age grades (e.g., *Kafa* = *Gnekbode*). See also Brooks, *The Kru Mariner*, 75. Brooks accepts the idea of a secret society, a position completely rejected by Mary Jo Sullivan: "Davis's main error in ethnography is his continuous reference to Kru 'secret societies' and a 'Grand Devil' . . . What Davis describes as a Bo secret society is a part of Kru social and political structure" (Mary Jo Sullivan, Review of *Ethnohistorical Studies on the Kru Coast*, by Ronald Davis, *Journal of African History*, XIX, 2 [1978], 280–282; see also Elizabeth Tonkin, Review of *Ethnohistorical Studies on the Kru Coast*, by Ronald Davis, *The International Journal of African Historical Studies*, X, 3 [1977], 533–535).

13. The Grebo, whose laborers were indiscriminately called "Kru-boys" in the late nineteenth century, had, like the Kru, a system of age sets. According to Gordon Haliburton, youths who became migrant laborers were from the *kinibo*, an age set composed of young unmarried men. The eldest age set in Grebo society provided the *bodio*, a chief religious official and the *wodaba* (or *worabanh*), the leader in time of war. The *bodio* had final authority in time of peace; under his leadership the village met to pass judgment and levy fines. See Gordon Haliburton, *The Prophet Harris*, 7–8. See also Jane Martin, "The Dual Legacy: Government Authority and Mission Influence Among the Glebo of Eastern Liberia" (Ph.D. diss., Boston University, 1968).

The migration of labor from the Kru Coast affected the resident societies in a number of ways, some of which remain to be fully understood. Most workers were paid with goods, and many of the items obtained from migratory labor were used to pay bride-wealth; some goods were apparently kept by patrilineages to go into a common stock of wealth. Early in the nineteenth century it was noted that the supply and flow of labor was regulated and organized by "headmen" from the coast. The headman system may have been a means by which Fishmen and Fishmen-Kru were able to organize and monopolize the flow of labor from interior ("Bushmen") groups. The origins of the system may lie in the extension of traditional institutions and patterns: the rights exercised by the *Nyemo* (middle-aged) age-group over the *Kafa* (young men), the exploitation of boys purchased or captured from other societies, the extension of preexisting patterns of father-son apprenticeship, the acknowledgment by the leaders of patrilineages or the heads of families of the benefits of entrusting novices to the care of those with previous experience abroad. In the early decades of the nineteenth century the preferred source of supply was probably the headman's own *panton*. Successful headmen could augment their recruitment base through the use of the children of their multiple wives (wives gotten with bride-wealth derived from trade). Many of these wives may have come from Bushmen lineages related to the headmen by marriage (it has been suggested that headmen probably initially recruited from their mothers' lineages). After the opening of the nineteenth century, another source, enslaved children, was probably of decreasing importance.

The littoral Fishmen and Fishmen-Kru doubtlessly exercised their greatest control over the recruitment of interior peoples in the early nineteenth century and saw an erosion of their control as the century progressed. At the same time, the persistence of differential earnings among migrants may have aided certain individuals to gain office and, at the same time, bolstered the authority of those offices. For example, the office of *gbaubi* does not appear to have declined significantly. It has been argued that the *gbaubi* often came from the young male adult age-group which supplied the bulk of the migrants. Wealth accruing from trade (the uses of that wealth) may have been influential in chosing the *gbaubi*. Although the office was originally military in nature, it has adapted well to changing political and economic conditions on the coast (e.g., the holder of this office at Grand Cess now serves as a public works supervisor who organizes fishing and land clearage). Overseas service also had an impact on the office *kroba*; many holders of this office in the twentieth century were highly successful migrants who had spent considerable time abroad.

14. M. B. Akpan, "The African Policy of the Liberian Settlers 1841–1932: A Study of the 'Native' Policy of a Non-Colonial Power in Africa" (Ph.D. diss., Ibadan University, 1968), 268, citing *The Lagos Weekly Record*, July 2, 1910.

15. The Liberian regime has used a variety of currencies during its history. In the nineteenth century there was a shortage of specie, and a variety of currencies circulated; prices were quoted in both English and American currency. Until the early 1930s the only bank in Monrovia was the Bank of British West Africa. When that bank withdrew, its place was taken by an American bank with connections with the Firestone interests. Since 1943, Liberia has used American currency, which is interchangeable with Liberian specie (at present there is no Liberian paper currency).

16. Akpan, "The African Policy," 268.

17. Raymond Leslie Buell, *The Native Problem in Africa* (New York, 1928), II, 775.

18. Mitchell to Stimson, November 27, 1931, enclosing Letter from the People of Sasstown Through Their Representatives to the International Commission of Enquiry into Slavery and Forced Labour in Liberia, USNA, RG59, 882.00/910.

Monrovia's attempts to profit from the flow of labor eventually presented a threat to Liberia's competitive position as an exporter of labor. In 1931 the president of Liberia was informed by a member of his cabinet that the high cost of Liberian labor deterred shipping lines from calling at Liberian ports and that the imposts paid by stevedores resulted in their losing about thirty percent of their earnings. See Grimes to Barclay, April 30, 1931, Louis B. Grimes Papers, Liberia/League of Nations Papers, Northwestern University Library, Evanston, Ill., microfilm, Pt. II, roll 3.

19. Frank Chalk, "The United States and the International Struggle for Rubber" (Ph.D. diss., University of Wisconsin, 1970), 78–79.

20. For a discussion of J. J. Ross's career, see Sullivan, "Sinoe Settler Politics."

21. "Bitter Canaan," 250, Johnson Papers, unfiled manuscript.

22. Sullivan, "Sinoe Settler Politics," 22.

23. Jones, "The Struggle," 232, citing Dispatch from the United States Legation, Monrovia, Liberia, January, 1913, USNA, RG59, 882.00/525.

24. Jones, "The Struggle," 232.

25. Davis, *Ethnohistorical Studies*, 56, citing Schofield to the U.S. Secretary of the Navy, November 30, 1915, USNA, RG59, 822.00/522.

26. Jones, "The Struggle," 239. See British Consul General to Kru of Sinoe, December 11, 1915, USNA, RG59, 822.001. The reply to the Kru was sent in care of C. D. B. King, Liberian secretary of state.

27. Memorandum from Kru on the revolt of 1915, transcribed September 12, 1930, Johnson Papers, box 88, file 5.

28. Ibid.

29. Jones, "The Struggle," 240.

30. Report on Leading Personalities in Liberia, including additions received in the Foreign Office up to January 30, 1930, Great Britain, Public Record Office, Foreign Office, 371/14658. Great Britain, Public Record Office, Foreign Office is hereafter cited as FO.

31. League, *Report*, 36ff.

32. The Wedabo and the Po River people perhaps represent a "Fishmen-Bushmen" dichotomy. The Po were Kru who had migrated down the coast probably before the Wedabo people had settled inland of them. The Wedabo are thought to be related to the Kru above Grand Cess, but their language contains many Grebo words. The Wedabo held a corridor to the sea, but their farming country, with their capital, Soloken, was one or two days journey in the interior. (League, *Report*, 19.)

33. Ibid.

34. Meanwhile, the commissioner, without asking the chiefs who was guilty, caught seven Wedabo men as probable culprits in the incident.

35. This was done, and supposedly the men were put to work on Yancy's private farm at Webbo (ibid., 21).

36. Ibid., 22.

37. During World War I, the Monrovia government imposed an annual "hut" tax on "uncivilized" peoples. By 1922 the amount collected from this source amounted to $151,213.70, or one-third of gross government revenue. (Akpan, "Black Imperialism," 230.)

38. "Home of the Free," *New Statesman*, XXXVI, 925 (January 17, 1931), 429.

39. Associated Negro Press News Release, January 28, 1931, Claude Barnett Papers, Chicago Historical Society.

40. Benjamin Nnamdi Azikiwe, *Liberia in World Politics* (London, 1934), 174–173, quoting Otto Rothfield, "Liberia and the League of Nations," *The Crisis*, CXXI (April, 1931).

41. Benjamin Nnamdi Azikiwe, "In Defense of Liberia," *Journal of Negro History*, XVIII (January, 1932), 44.

42. Henry F. Reeve, *The Black Republic* (London, 1923), 122.

43. Abelardo de Unzueta, *Geografía histórica de la Isla de Fernando Póo* (Madrid, 1947), 199.

44. League, *Report*, 36. Averaging *at least* 600 workers per year the figure should be higher; for a period of thirteen years the total should be significantly higher (c. 7,800).

45. H. Markham Cook to General Missionary Committee, June 10, 1915, Methodist Missionary Society (London), Primitive Methodist Mission, Fernando Po, box 3, Fernandian Cocoa Report file.

46. Unzueta, *Geografía*, 199.

47. Richard C. Bundy to Secretary of State, February 9, 1919, USNA, RG59, 882.504/6 (microfilm M613, location 10-14-5, roll 14).

48. Ibid.

49. A. C. Reeve to Consul-General, Loanda, July 4, 1920, FO, 371/5562.

50. Manuel Gonzalez Hontoria to Sir Esmé Howard, Madrid, January 6, 1922, FO, 371/7211.

51. A. C. Reeve to A. S. Paterson, June 6, 1922, FO, 371/8465.

52. Buell, *The Native Problem*, II, 780.

53. Akpan, "Liberia and the Universal Negro Improvement Association," 121. J. Chaudhuri notes that customs revenue in 1923–1924 was a little over $392,000; in 1913 the customs revenue had been $486,395.72. See Jyotirmoy Chaudhuri, "British Policy Towards Liberia, 1912–1939" (Ph.D. diss., University of Birmingham [England], 1975), 210.

54. Liberian Consul Coleman went to San Carlos, where there were a considerable number of Liberian farmers and workers. After visiting the subgov-

ernor of San Carlos, Coleman asked to visit J. Sharp, sometime Liberian secretary of state, and other of his countrymen during the evening; while this meeting was taking place, it was interrupted by African policemen who declared the meeting illegal and against the laws in force on Fernando Po. In spite of the protest of the consul and his friends, they were incarcerated in a small hut which was part of the jail. In the morning Coleman was brought to Santa Isabel. (Lewis May to Foreign Office, July 18, 1925, FO, 37/11100.)

55. Juan Bravo Carbonel, *Territorios españoles del Golfo de Guinea* (Madrid, 1925), 95.

56. Ibid.

57. Vice-Consul C. H. Chew, Santa Isabel, to Consul-General, Monrovia, November 9, 1928, FO, 37/12759.

58. Buell, *The Native Problem*, II, 781, citing *Agricultural World*, February, 1925.

59. Ibid., citing *Liberian News*, February, 1926.

60. Consul-General Rule, Monrovia, to Foreign Office, December 23, 1927, FO, 371/12758.

61. Barclay to George Johns, March 20, 1928, U.S. Department of State, Records Relating to the Affairs of Liberia, 1910–1929 (Washington, D.C., 1965), Political Affairs, microfilm available at Northwestern University Library, Evanston, Ill., roll 14. U.S. Department of State, Records Relating to the Affairs of Liberia, 1910–1929, are hereafter cited as DSRRAL.

62. Mr. Barleycorn was interviewed by the author in Santa Isabel (now Malabo) on March 2, 1970.

63. Barclay to Johns, March 20, 1928, DSRRAL, microfilm roll 14.

64. League, *Report*, 109.

65. Ibid., 36. The members of Ross's group included Thomas F. C. Pelham, Robert W. Draper, E. C. W. King, J. C. Johnston, M. A. Bracewell, and C. L. Cooper. Pelham and Draper were the sons-in-law of Ross. Two of the members of the group were female clerks.

66. Barclay and Barclay were attorneys for Thodomiro Avendano, president of the syndicate. Witnesses were J. A. Dougan, E. A. Monger, and J. W. Howard. (League, *Report*, 109.)

67. Ibid., 36.

68. Wharton to Department of State, October 22, 1929, DSRRAL, microfilm roll 14.

69. Davis, *Ethnohistorical Studies*, 59, citing Francis to Secretary of State, Report on the Recruitment of Labor on the Liberian Coast, USNA, RG59, 882.5048/19, 882.5048/53.

70. Ibid., citing W. T. Francis, U.S. Consul to Liberia, to Secretary of State, June 2, 1928, USNA, RG59, 882.66/1. Woermann was shipping Kru laborers to South West Africa (Walvis Bay) as stevedores with two-year contracts (Monroe Phelps to Secretary of State, April 10, 1929, USNA, RG59, 882.5048/21).

71. Wharton to Castle, November 29, 1929, DSRRAL, microfilm roll 14.

72. Diary of Charles Johnson, May 12, 1930, p. 110.

73. John Payne Mitchell, "America's Liberian Policy" (Master's thesis, University of Chicago, 1955), 241.

74. League, *Report*, 42–43.

75. "Bitter Canaan," 250, Johnson Papers, unfiled manuscript.

76. League, *Report*, 41.

77. Ibid., 36.

78. As late as 1936 two observers maintained, "Spanish ships are still calling at Liberian ports and are taking contract labourers to the Spanish colony" (Akpan, "The African Policy," 488, citing H. J. Grenwell and R. Wild, *Unknown Liberia* [London, 1936], 220).

79. League, *Report*, 41.

80. Ibid., 38.

81. George Johns to Samuel J. Grisby (Superintendent of Sinoe), October 26, 1927, DSRRAL, microfilm roll 14.

82. Ibid.

83. League, *Report*, 44.

84. Ibid., 45.

85. McBride Memorandum (Washington), October 3, 1934, Annexed Memorandum of the Government of Liberia on the Kru Situation, USNA, RG59, 882.01 FC/915.

86. George Schuyler, "Wide 'Slavery' Persisting in Liberia, Post Reveals," New York *Evening Post*, June 29, 1931, p. 1.

87. Ibid.

88. Azikiwe, "In Defense of Liberia," 43, citing C. D. B. King, *Annual Message* (Monrovia, 1929), 48–60.

89. Ernest Yancy, *Historic Lights of Liberia, Yesterday and Today*, 3d ed. (Tel Aviv, 1954), 211.

Chapter 2

1. James L. Sibley and D. Westermann, *Liberia—Old and New* (Garden City, N.Y., 1928), 303.

2. George Padmore, *American Imperialism Enslaves Liberia* (Moscow, 1931), 29, citing *African World*, October 5, 1929.

3. Azikiwe, "In Defense of Liberia," 40.

4. Padmore, *American Imperialism*, 45.

5. Joseph Brandes, *Herbert Hoover and Economic Diplomacy* (Pittsburgh, 1962), 117, citing James C. Lawrence, *The World's Struggle with Rubber* (New York, 1931), 46.

6. Padmore, *American Imperialism*, 18, citing *Firestone Non-Skid*, December, 1925.

7. Azikiwe, "In Defense of Liberia," 32.

8. For Firestone's projection of his labor needs see J. H. Mower, "The Republic of Liberia," *Journal of Negro History*, XXXII (July, 1947), 3, citing Harvey S. Firestone, Sr., "We Must Grow Our Own Rubber," *The Country Gentleman*, April, 1926, p. 123. In 1930 the company employed approximately 10,000 workers and was cutting back operations due to the falling price of rubber and its disagreements with the Liberian government.

Firestone established two plantations. One was on the Du River at Harbel, about 40 miles east of Monrovia. The other was in Maryland County on the Cavalla River. Firestone began regular tapping of its trees in 1934. By 1940 some 72,500 acres had been planted with rubber trees and 7,000 tons of latex were being produced from the 39,200 acres which were by then of tapping age. Thirty years after the granting of the Firestone concession, the annual average total of Liberian workers in all categories was approximately 25,000. Out of this number, slightly over 3,000 were classified as skilled or semiskilled. One-third of the workers were from the Kpelle ethnic group. See Wayne Taylor, *The Firestone Operations in Liberia* (New York, 1956), 58–59, 65.

9. W. E. B. DuBois, "Liberia, the League and the United States," *Foreign Affairs*, II, 4 (July, 1933), 695.

10. Wolfe Schmokel, "The United States and the Crisis of Liberian Independence," in *Boston University Papers on Africa* (Boston, 1966), II, 307.

11. Elliott Berg, "The Development of a Labor Force in Sub-Saharan Africa," *Economic Development and Cultural Change*, XIII, 4, pt. 1 (July, 1965), 407.

12. Akpan, "The African Policy," 447.

13. G. Warnet to Francis O'Meara, March 14, 1924, FO, 458/74. In 1924 the Liberian response was defiant. The Liberian secretary of state, Edwin Barclay, replied that he would "be more than obliged if my Government could be advised in detail of the basis of the interest which His Majesty's Government seem to take in the domestic labour regulations of Liberia and the ground upon which they found their unusual intimation that unless the Liberian Government close ports at which labourers may now be recruited for services in Fernando Poo, they will take the matter before the Council of the League of Nations" (Barclay to O'Meara, July 16, 1924, FO, 458/74).

14. Arnold Taylor, "The Involvement of Black Americans in the Liberian Forced Labor Controversy, 1929–1935," *Proceedings of the Conference on Afro-Americans and Africans: Historical and Political Linkages . . . Howard University, June 13–14, 1974* (Washington, D.C., 1974), 61, citing Bundy to Secretary of State, August 21, 1920, and October 20, 1920, USNA, RG59, 882.51/1169 and 882.5048/—.

15. W. T. Francis to William Castle, January 16, 1928, USNA, RG59, 882.5048/1. Francis wrote subsequent letters on the same topic: March 22, 1929, USNA, RG59, 882.5048/19; April 20, 1929, USNA, RG59, 882.5048/120.

16. Henry Carter (?) to Castle, January 17, 1928, USNA, RG59 (microfilm M613, location 10-14-5, roll 14).

17. Schmokel, "The United States and the Crisis," 307.

18. Frank Chalk, "The Anatomy of an Investment," *Canadian Journal of African Studies*, I, 1 (March, 1967), 17.

19. The first agreement provided for the lease of an old British-owned rubber plantation at Mt. Barclay (where Firestone would be able to conduct feasibility studies). The second granted the right to lease up to one million acres for a period of fifty years. Harbor improvements were included in the third draft accord; Firestone would improve the port of Monrovia with aid contributed by the Liberian government.

20. Chalk, "Anatomy of an Investment," 18. Sidney de la Rue was born in New Jersey in 1888. He worked for two years (1918–1920) for the American military government of the Dominican Republic as an accountant, supply and purchasing officer, and special agent. He was first employed in Liberia in 1921, when he was appointed auditor of the receivership. De la Rue was general receiver from 1922 to 1928, except for a hiatus in 1924 when he served as adviser to the Turkish minister of finance. After his tenure in Liberia, de la Rue wrote a largely sympathetic account of the country, *The Land of the Pepper Bird* (New York, 1930).

21. Chalk, "Anatomy of an Investment," 19–20, citing C. R. Russell to Castle, June 22, 1924, USNA, RG59, 882.616 F51/2.

22. According to a later report of the interview, de la Rue sought to impress

upon Firestone that "he should not expect to have any control over the country or over the loan." The receiver "explained that this must be a banker's loan and that the control would be exercised by an advisor nominated by the Government . . . the State Department would not approve of [Firestone] going into [Liberia] without a loan, that the Department had accepted '[his] policy as its policy' and that a loan would have to be made." (Ibid., 21, citing Tredwell to Harrison, January 15, 1925, USNA, RG59, 882.6176F.)

23. Raymond Buell, *Liberia: A Century of Survival, 1847–1947* (Philadelphia, 1947), 30.

24. Ibid.

25. This loan to repay a loan in reality increased Liberia's financial burden. The interest rate was raised from 5 to 7 percent, and the life of the loan was extended from 1952 to 1966. Only part of the loan was ever issued; in large part it paid off the loan of 1912 and the internal floating debt. Liberia could make no refunding loan without the consent of an American financial adviser; the Finance Corporation of America had an option on any new loan. In 1952, Liberia actually managed to repay its loan ahead of schedule. See Taylor, *The Firestone Operations*, 57.

26. Later this very financial bureaucracy was realized to be a burden. Advisers' salaries and service charges amounted to a fixed charge of nearly $270,000 a year. This constituted 20 percent of Liberian revenues in 1928 and approximately half of those revenues in 1931. Like previous loans, the Finance Corporation's was unproductive; more than ninety percent of the $2,500,000 advanced paid off existing debts.

27. Chalk, "Anatomy of an Investment," 22–23, citing a memorandum by Leland Harrison, July 8, 1924, U.S. Department of State, *Foreign Relations of the United States, 1925* (Washington, D.C.), II, 379–382. U.S. Department of State, *Foreign Relations of the United States*, is hereafter cited as *USFR*.

28. Chalk, "The U.S. and the International Struggle," 90.

29. Chalk, "Anatomy of an Investment," 25, citing Roger Tredwell to Leland Harrison, January 1, 1925, USNA, RG59, 882.6176 F51/70; Tredwell to Harrison, January 11, 1925, USNA, RG59, 882.6176 F51/72. Receiver de la Rue, in his eagerness to get a banker's loan, had already approached the British and the French about the project. The French chargé in Monrovia looked forward to the building of a railway across Liberia to the French Territory to the north. See Tredwell to Harrison, January 1, 1925, USNA, RG59, 882.6176 F51/70.

30. Chalk, "Anatomy of an Investment," 26, citing Tredwell to Harrison, January 1, 1925, USNA, RG59, 882.6176 F51/70. Tredwell, the foreign service inspector, greatly disapproved of the position taken by the receivership on the loan question. He described his tour of inspection in Liberia as "one of the most disagreeable experiences of my whole career and I shall be glad when it is finished." See Tredwell to Harrison, January 11, 1925, USNA, RG59, 882.6176 F51/72; Tredwell to Harrison, January 1, 1925, USNA, RG59, 882.6176 F51/70.

31. Chalk, "Anatomy of an Investment," 27, citing Castle to de la Rue, March 13, 1925, USNA, RG59, 882.6176 F51/82.

32. Buell, *Liberia*, 31. In November of 1929 the American chargé in Monrovia reported that a German trader had been approached by a Liberian in an effort to obtain laborers from Firestone's Du Plantations for transport to Fernando Po. See Chargé d'Affaires (Monrovia) to State Department, November –, 1929, Johnson Papers, box 89, file 6.

Earlier in the same year the American minister had informed the State Department of an attempt to have a British employee of Firestone procure labor for Fernando Po. David Ross, an adopted son of Samuel Ross, admitted to the League of Nations commission of inquiry that he had carried gin, tobacco, and rice to the No. 7 Firestone plantation in an effort to lure away labor. Certain workers did leave and go to Monrovia, but when they learned that they were to be sent to Fernando Po some escaped. One African policeman supposedly sent his brother to Ross for four shillings. See League, *Report*, 42. Wage rates were also an issue between Firestone and its competitors for labor. It was reported, "They, certain Americo-Liberians, solicited Mr. Firestone confidentially, it seems, not to pay wages in excess of twenty-five cents a day or the rubber work would rob their private farms of labor" (James C. Young, *Liberia Rediscovered* [Garden City, N.Y., 1934], 43).

It was also reported: "In the beginning common laborers were paid 2 to 4 shillings per day, but the government objected saying that Liberian farmers were protesting on grounds that high wages took away their labor" (George W. Brown, *Economic History of Liberia* [Washington, D.C., 1941], 206, citing George Schuyler, "Is Liberia a Slave State?" New York *Evening Post*, July 2, 1931).

33. Buell, *Liberia*, 31.

34. Chalk, "Anatomy of an Investment," 30, citing *USFR, 1926*, II, 568–570.

35. Ibid.

36. R. Earle Anderson, *Liberia: America's African Friend* (Chapel Hill, N.C., 1952), 134.

37. Long before the Firestone investment, an American minister to Liberia had spotted the potential for American use of the existing labor force. In 1912 the minister prepared a report on the subject. See Richard Bundy to Secretary of State, November 20, 1912, USNA, RG59, 882.5048 (microfilm M613, location 10-14-5, roll 14).

38. Sidney de la Rue, "Annual Report of the General Receiver of Customs and Financial Adviser to the Republic of Liberia for the Fiscal Year 1925–26," 27–28, DSRRAL, microfilm roll 30.

39. Buell, *The Native Problem*, II, 834–835.

40. Clifton R. Wharton to Castle, March 3, 1927, DSRRAL, microfilm roll 30.

41. Clipping from the *Liberian Express and Agricultural World*, November–December, 1928, enclosure in William Francis to Department of State, March 22, 1929, DSRRAL, microfilm roll 14.

42. Report on Firestone Plantations, "Bo Zieko Fahtow," DSRRAL, microfilm roll 31.

43. Wharton to Secretary of State, September 8, 1929, DSRRAL, microfilm roll 14.

44. League, *Report*, 79.

45. John Loomis to Henry Carter, May 10, 1929, DSRRAL, microfilm roll 27. It was added, "The number of laborers shipped is not the question but the demoralizing influence it has upon officials and the further effect of driving natives across the frontiers to other countries."

46. Memorandum: International Labor Conference at Geneva, May 20, 1929; American Interest Therein (State Department memorandum?), Johnson Papers, box 88, file 6.

47. Department of State Memorandum, June 13, 1929, on Preliminary

Summary of Report on Slavery by American Minister at Monrovia, DSRRAL, microfilm roll 14.

48. Chargé in Liberia (Carter) to Secretary of State, May 12, 1930, *USFR, 1930*, III (USNA, 882.51/2096).

49. Azikiwe, *Liberia in World Politics*, 206, citing U.S. Press Release No. 67, 21–22; and League Document No. CL 3.1931 VI. Azikiwe also refers to U.S. Press Release No. 68, 28.

50. Buell, *The Native Problem*, II, 831.

51. Schmokel, "The United States and the Crisis," 308.

52. Buell, *The Native Problem*, II, 831. See also Lloyd Beecher, "The State Department and Liberia, 1908–1941: A Heterogeneous Record" (Ph.D. diss., University of Georgia, 1971), 139, citing Memorandum of interview with Barclay, Washington, D.C., August 24, 1925, USNA, RG59, 882.617 F51/125.

53. Buell, *The Native Problem*, II, 833.

54. Ibid., 847. Buell may have overstated the diplomatic role of the United States in this regard. The United States had traditionally supported the integrity of Liberia in its boundary disputes with its European neighbors. During the Firestone negotiations the United States may have been doing no more than displaying its traditional solicitude for the Black Republic. William Castle of the State Department did inform Liberian Secretary of State Barclay that the French were playing a "disreputable political game" in claiming certain territory on the border between French Guinea and Liberia. For a discussion of the boundary dispute in the context of the Firestone negotiations, see Beecher, "The State Department and Liberia," 148, citing G. H. M. to Castle, Washington, D.C., August 13, 1924, USNA, RG59, 751.8215/191; Carter to Castle, Washington, D.C., August 13, 1925, USNA, RG59, 751.8215/209; Castle interview with Barclay, August 24, 1925, USNA, RG59, 882.6176 F51/125; Kellogg to American Embassy in Paris, Washington, D.C., October 28, 1925, USNA, RG59, 751.8215/212; Myron Herrick, Ambassador to France, to Secretary of State, Paris, November 13, 1925, USNA, RG59, 751.8215/219. See also Nancy Forderhase, "The Plans That Failed: The United States and Liberia, 1920–1935" (Ph D diss., University of Missouri, 1971), 61.

The King regime may have used the "French menace" to cow internal opposition to the Firestone concession, arguing that by anchoring American investment in Liberia the republic was saving itself. Thirty years after the Firestone negotiations, President William Tubman justified the granting of the concession on the grounds of national security: "One of the main reasons why the terms of the loan were accepted was political rather than economic. Border incidents and boundary disputes thereafter ceased" (Taylor, *The Firestone Operations*, x).

55. Division of Western European Affairs Memorandum to William Castle, June 6, 1927, USNA, RG59, 882.00/766 (microfilm M613, location 10-14-5, roll 14). Professor G. Wilson of the Bureau of International Research, Harvard University and Radcliffe College, sent the chapter dealing with Liberia in Buell's book, *The Native Problem in Africa*, to the State Department.

56. Raymond Buell, "Mr. Firestone's Liberia," *The Nation*, CXXVI, 3278 (May, 1928), 521–524.

57. Castle (Department of State) to William T. Francis (Monrovia), June 21, 1928, DSRRAL, microfilm roll 14.

58. Chief Clerk to President (Monroe Phelps?) to Commissioner David S. Carter, January 20, 1930, Liberian National Archives (Monrovia).

59. League, *Report*, 79.

60. Ibid. Labor discontent with Firestone also resulted from pay practices. The pay began with a shilling a day at both the Du and Cavalla plantations. On the advice of the white staff at the latter plantation, pay was changed to one pound per month and food. The laborers complained and the new pay system was abandoned.

61. Kellogg to American Consul, Geneva, July 28, 1928, DSRRAL, microfilm roll 14. An American magazine, *The Outlook*, dismissed Junod's activities and quoted Harvey Firestone, Sr., as saying, "As the Firestone Company controls only one million acres in Liberia and there are forty-two million acres of land available, it is obvious that no such scheme [peonage and land confiscation] is contemplated" ("No Rubber Peonage," *The Outlook*, CXLIX, 16 [August 8, 1928], 607).

62. Castle to American Legation, Monrovia, August 18, 1928, DSRRAL, microfilm roll 14.

63. Francis to Department of State, August 28, 1929, DSRRAL, microfilm roll 14.

64. Castle to American Legation, Monrovia, August 29, 1928, DSRRAL, microfilm roll 14.

65. Carter (Department of State) to Harvey S. Firestone, Jr., August 29, 1928, DSRRAL, microfilm roll 14.

66. C. D. B. King to Department of State, August 30, 1928, DSRRAL, microfilm roll 14.

67. Department of State Memorandum of the Press Conference, August 30, 1928, USNA, RG59, 882.5048/12 (microfilm M613, location 10-14-5, roll 14).

68. Chalk, "Anatomy of an Investment," 27, citing Castle to de la Rue, February 25, 1925, USNA, RG59, 882.6176 F51/81; Castle to de la Rue, March 13, 1925, USNA, RG59, 882.6176 F51/82.

69. Francis to Castle, March 22, 1924, DSRRAL, microfilm roll 14.

70. Castle to Undersecretary of State, April 25, 1929, USNA, RG59, 882.5048/22 (microfilm M613, location 10-14-5, roll 14).

71. Castle to Patton, May 3, 1929, USNA, RG59, 882.00/787 (microfilm M613, location 10-14-5, roll 14). Phelps-Stokes had written to Castle on April 29 informing him of Patton's report.

72. Castle to Secretary of State, May 24, 1929, USNA, RG59, 882.5048/54 (microfilm M613, location 10-14-5, roll 14).

73. Taylor, "The Involvement of Black Americans," 62, citing Stimson to Wharton, July 22, 1929.

74. Wharton to Department of State, September 21, 1929, DSRRAL, microfilm roll 14.

75. Francis to Department of State, Supplemental Memorandum, May 4, 1929, DSRRAL, microfilm roll 14. After the Liberian government expressed a willingness to appoint a commission for the investigation of the slavery allegations, the department expressed the fear "that the Liberian Government will attempt to entangle the Firestone Plantations Company in order to save its own face" (Clifton Wharton to Secretary of State, July 30, 1929, DSRRAL, microfilm roll 14).

76. Department of State, Division of West European Affairs, Memorandum to Castle, July 30, 1929, DSRRAL, microfilm roll 14.

77. Memorandum (Henry Carter), Suggestions as to Policy During My Absence on Leave, September 4, 1929, USNA, RG59, 882.5048/214.

78. Raymond Bixler, *The Foreign Policy of the United States in Liberia* (New York, 1947), 87.

79. Ibid., citing Minister at Monrovia to Department of State, March 8, 1929, USNA, RG59, 882.617 F51/272.

80. Ibid., citing Secretary of the Treasury of Liberia to Supervisor of Customs, April 4, 1929, USNA, RG59, 892.51/2005.

81. Chargé (?) (Monrovia) to Department of State, October 21, 1921, enclosing: "A Few Articles Refused Publication by the Editors of the Newspapers," Albert Porte, Crozierville, Liberia, September, 1929, Johnson Papers, box 89, file 5.

82. B. M. Robinson to Harvey Firestone, Jr., December 23, 1929, Johnson Papers, box 88, file 6.

83. Ibid.

84. Department of State (J. P. M.) to Charles S. Johnson, Mr. Marriner, and Mr. Gilbert, January 3, 1930, Johnson Papers, box 89, file 5.

85. Gabriel L. Dennis, Annual Report of the Secretary of the Treasury, R. L. for Treasury Operations . . . (Monrovia, 1933), Claude Barnett Papers, Liberia, 1925–45. The report covers the period January 1 to September 30, 1930.

Chapter 3

1. See Beecher, "The State Department and Liberia"; Chalk, "The U.S. and the International Struggle"; Jyotirmoy P. Chaudhuri, "British Policy Towards Liberia, 1912–1939" (Ph.D. diss., University of Birmingham [England], 1975); Joseph Guannu, "Liberia and the League of Nations" (Ph.D. diss., Fordham University, 1972); John Payne Mitchell, "America's Liberian Policy" (thesis, University of Chicago, 1955); Parthenia Norris, "The United States and Liberia: The Slavery Crisis, 1929–1935" (Ph.D. diss., Indiana University, 1961).

2. George Schuyler, "Wide 'Slavery' Persisting in Liberia, Post Reveals," New York *Evening Post*, June 29, 1931, p 1 In July of 1929 the King administration consisted of King (president), Edwin Barclay (secretary of state), Samuel G. Harmon (treasury secretary), Louis A. Grimes (attorney general), Samuel Ross (postmaster general), James W. Cooper (interior secretary), B. W. Payne (public instruction secretary), John L. Morris (public works secretary). Supposedly, King, Barclay, Ross, and Morris were widely known to be connected with the labor trade.

3. Monrovia Legation Report on Leading Personalities, December 21, 1930, FO, 371/1456. King was the son of a West Indian immigrant. He was educated in Sierra Leone and had been attorney general and secretary of state.

4. Akpan, "The African Policy," 464; Azikiwe, *Liberia in World Politics*, 212.

5. Akpan, "The African Policy," 464, citing Reber to Secretary of State, Monrovia, October 9, 1930, USNA, RG59, 882.00/856.

6. Grimes to King, July 31, 1930, Grimes Papers, Miscellaneous Pamphlets and Documents, Monrovia, Liberia, Pt. I, roll 2.

7. Ford to Henderson, December 12, 1930, in Great Britain, *Papers Concerning Affairs in Liberia, December, 1930–May, 1934*, Cmd. 4614 (London, 1934).

8. Chalk, "Anatomy of an Investment," 29, citing Carter to Castle, June 7, 1926, USNA, RG59, 882.6176 F51/177.

9. Clifton Wharton, Chargé d'Affaires, Monrovia, to Secretary of State, July 30, 1929, DSRRAL, microfilm roll 14.

10. Joseph Johnson to Secretary of State, September 1, 1929, DSRRAL, microfilm roll 6.

11. Division of Western European Affairs memorandum, unsigned, 1929, DSRRAL, microfilm roll 6. For an article critical of slavery in Liberia and praising Faulkner, see Caroline Singer, New York *Times*, January 19, 1930, Sect. V, 10; see also January 18, 1931.

12. Marriner, Firestone, Jr., and Briggs, Conversation, Conditions in Liberia, November 5, 1930, USNA, RG59, 882.00/857.

13. Akpan, "The African Policy," 447, citing Henry Stimson Memorandum, May 2, 1930, USNA, RG59, 882.W/882.

14. Report on Leading Personalities in Liberia, including additions received in the Foreign Office up to January 30, 1930 (Monrovia, December 21, 1930), FO, 371/14658.

15. Ibid.

16. Mitchell, "America's Liberian Policy," 258, citing *USFR, 1930,* III, 379.

17. Memorandum, Castle to Stimson, September 18, 1930, USNA, RG59, 882.00/846.

18. Memorandum (Henry Carter), Suggestions as to Policy During My Absence on Leave, September 4, 1929, USNA, RG59, 882.5048/214.

19. Carter to Stimson, May 3, 1930, *USFR, 1930,* III, 396 (USNA, RG59, 882.51/2093).

20. Stimson to Carter, May 19, 1930, *USFR, 1930,* III, 396 (USNA, RG59, 882.51/2093).

21. Carter to Stimson, May 12, 1930, *USFR, 1930,* III, 396 (USNA, RG59, 882.51/2093).

22. Moffat to P. Gilbert (Geneva), April 29, 1930, USNA, RG59, 882.00/820.

23. Castle to Stimson, September 18, 1930, USNA, RG59, 882.00/820.

24. Chalk, "The U.S. and the International Struggle," 183, citing Stimson, Memorandum of an interview with Harvey Firestone, December 10, 1930, *USFR, 1930,* III, 385–386.

25. Ibid., citing Ellis O. Briggs, Memorandum, December 27, 1930, *USFR, 1930,* III, 391–393.

26. Ibid., citing Stimson, Memorandum of an interview with President Hoover, January 3, 1931, *USFR, 1930,* III, 391. On January 26, Stimson had a meeting with Senator William E. Borah of Idaho in which he, among other things, outlined the alternatives for American policy in Liberia.

27. Raymond Buell, "The Reconstruction of Liberia," *Foreign Policy Reports,* VIII (August 3, 1932), 123.

28. Ibid., citing League of Nations, Memorandum of the Government of Liberia on the Report of the Experts, c/Liberia/13, April 29, 1932, p. 19.

29. Ibid. The British lent the Liberian government a medical expert and the Barclay government appointed a Hungarian, Dr. Fusyek, director of sanitation. In 1932 Buell reported that no authentic cases of yellow fever had been reported since 1929.

30. The bank was eventually replaced by the Bank of Monrovia, Inc., a Firestone subsidiary.

31. Brunot had been governor of the Ivory Coast and was later to be gover-

nor of the Cameroons. Jean Suret-Canale, *French Colonialism in Tropical Africa 1900–1945* (London, 1971), 315, 456, 463.

32. The League 1931 investigators also sought a revamping of the Liberian legal system. The chief legal adviser was to become president of the Liberian circuit court. The jury system was to be temporarily discontinued, in the apparent belief that this would strengthen the faith of foreign capital in Liberian justice. The eight administrators were to have wide-ranging powers in cases involving indigenous people. It was proposed that this include the power to exact summary penalties for petty offenses. Liberian juries were to continue to exercise authority in coastal areas. For the cost estimate of the total plan see Lloyd Beecher, "The State Department and Liberia," 182.

33. Buell, "The Reconstruction of Liberia," 130. See League of Nations, Minutes of the 10th Meeting of the Liberia Committee, January 29, 1931, c/Liberia/10. Reporting in May of 1932, the Liberia Committee stated that it would not recommend a new loan to a country "already so encumbered" as Liberia (ibid., 131).

34. It was left unclear whether the powers of the financial adviser were to be those set down in the 1926 loan contract or whether they were to be more wide-ranging.

35. Chalk, "The U.S. and the International Struggle," 186, citing Ellis Briggs, Memorandum, May 17, 1932, *USFR, 1932*, II, 726–727; P. Gilbert (Consul at Geneva) to H. L. Stimson, May 26, 1932, *USFR, 1932*, II, 732.

36. Chalk, "The U.S. and the International Struggle," 186, citing H. L. Stimson to P. Gilbert, January 13, 1932, *USFR, 1932*, II, 687–689.

37. Moffat Papers, Diplomatic Journal, vol. 29, 1930–1931, Berne, February 12, 1930.

38. Buell, "The Reconstruction of Liberia," 129, citing League of Nations, Minutes of the 6th and 10th Sessions, January, 1932.

39. Ibid., 130.

40. Ibid., quoting League of Nations, Memorandum of the Government of Liberia on the Report of the Experts, c/Liberia/13, April 29, 1932.

41. Ibid., quoting League of Nations, Letter of August 8, 1931, communicated to the Council, May 19, 1932, c.476.1932. VII, c/Liberia/31.

42. Ibid., quoting League of Nations, Memorandum of the Government of Liberia on the Report of the Experts, c/Liberia/13, April 29, 1932.

43. Chalk, "The U.S. and the International Struggle," 187, citing Mitchell to Stimson, May 26, 1932, *USFR, 1932*, II, 732.

44. Ibid., 188, citing Stimson to Mitchell, June 8, 1932, *USFR, 1932*, II, 738–740.

45. Ibid.

46. Ibid.

47. Ibid. Stimson instructed Minister Mitchell to keep these directives secret. The British consulate in Monrovia got wind of Stimson's move, although it thought that Liberia was being urged to completely abandon the League and opt for American assistance. According to an "informant," Barclay had been willing to follow such a course if Liberian sovereignty were protected. The consulate was told that the cabinet had refused the idea of an American adviser. (C. Graham to Secretary of State for Foreign Affairs, July 20, 1932 [with secret enclosure], Foreign Office, Consulate-General, Monrovia, microfilm available at Northwestern University Library, Evanston, Ill., roll 1.) For a chronology of the American attempts to get an American chief adviser, see Confidential

Memorandum on Mitchell-Barclay negotiation, June, 1932, Liberian National Archives.

48. Chalk, "The U.S. and the International Struggle," 189, citing Mitchell to Stimson, June 24, 1932, *USFR, 1932*, II, 742–743.

49. Ibid., 190, citing Mitchell to Stimson, June 24, 1932, *USFR, 1932*, II, 742–743; and Castle, Memorandum to British Embassy, August 27, 1932, *USFR, 1932*, II, 748–749.

50. Diary of J. P. Moffat, September 21, 1932, Moffat Papers, 1932, Vol. II.

51. Chalk, "The U.S. and the International Struggle," 190. See Ellis Briggs to Osborne (British chargé in Washington), August 31, 1932, *USFR, 1932*, II, 750–751; H. Wilson (American Minister in Switzerland) to Stimson, September 22, 1932, *USFR, 1932*, II, 756–757; Stimson to Gilbert, September 21, 1932, *USFR, 1932*, II, 754; Diary of J. P. Moffat, September 23, 1932.

52. Chalk, "The U.S. and the International Struggle," 190, quoting Diary of J. P. Moffat, September 26 and 28, 1932.

53. Ibid., 191, citing Stimson to Gibson, September 25, 1932, *USFR, 1932*, II, 750–759. The following day it was reported that a Firestone representative "was quite delighted" with a message from the secretary to the League (Diary of J. P. Moffat, September 26, 1932). The department feared that its instructions to the American member of the Liberia Committee would have the opposite effect when they became known. The American member was told to accept a formula whereby, if the chief adviser were accused by the Liberians of countervailing the constitution, the matter would be referred to the council of the League. While the issue was pending, Liberia would continue to carry out the orders of the chief adviser.

54. Buell, "The Reconstruction of Liberia," 129. Buell was dubious about this figure.

55. Great Britain, *Papers Concerning Affairs in Liberia*, Annex to Appendix I, Report of the Experts Designated by the Committee of the Council of the League of Nations Appointed to Study the Problem Raised by the Liberian Government's Request for Assistance.

56. See Great Britain, *Papers Concerning Affairs in Liberia*, Annex to Appendix I, citing League of Nations, Draft Plan of Assistance, c/Liberia/16, May 14, 1932.

57. Diary of Charles Johnson, March 27, 1930, Johnson Papers.

58. Jean Suret-Canale, *French Colonialism in Tropical Africa, 1900–1945* (London, 1971), 315.

59. Buell, "The Reconstruction of Liberia," 130, quoting from League of Nations, Minutes of the 8th Meeting, Committee of the Council, January 25, 1932, c/Liberia/6. Ligthart had already expressed these sentiments to British legations in Monrovia (Constantine Graham to Foreign Office, July 8, 1931, Foreign Office, Consulate-General, Monrovia, Northwestern University microfilm, roll 1).

60. Great Britain, *Papers Concerning Affairs in Liberia*, Annex to Appendix I, Report of the Experts Designated by the Committee of the Council of the League, p. 64.

61. Buell, "The Reconstruction of Liberia," 131, citing League of Nations, *Official Journal*, March, 1932, p. 523.

62. Ibid., 134, quoting League of Nations, *Official Journal*, March, 1932, p. 526.

63. Ibid., citing League of Nations, Minutes of the 11th Meeting, January 30, 1932.

64. Diary of J. P. Moffat, August 20, 1932, Moffat Papers. A month later the Harvey Firestones, Sr. and Jr., visited the State Department and announced that they wanted the nationality of the chief adviser to be discussed at Geneva. Stimson was forced to choose between antagonizing either "the Liberal and League elements" or Firestone. He chose not to antagonize Firestone, and the American representative to the Liberia Committee was instructed to bring the matter up. (Diary of J. P. Moffat, September 20, 1932.)

65. The company sent to Washington a representative (Walter Howe), who asked that the department delay publicity on the plan until he (Howe) had had a chance to change Firestone's refusal to negotiate (ibid., October 6, 1932). The next day, Moffat complained that "the Firestones having been given an inch [i.e., concessions in the League Plan] are now demanding an ell and want us to pull more chestnuts out of the fire for them" (ibid., October 7, 1932).

66. Chalk, "The U.S. and the International Struggle," 193, citing Diary of J. P. Moffat, October 8, 1932.

67. Ibid., quoting Castle to Firestone, October 10, 1932, USFR, 1932, II, 771–773.

68. Ibid., 194. At the end of the meeting, Firestone sent a telegram to Geneva saying he was willing to cooperate. See also Stimson to Gilbert, October 11, 1932, USFR, 1932, II, 773.

69. Ibid., 195, citing Stimson to Gilbert, October 13, 1932, USFR, 1932, II, 774–775; Finance Corporation of America to Castle, October 26, 1932, USFR, 1932, II, 776.

70. The repudiation was seen as solidifying the relations between the State Department and Firestone. "It offers the company," wrote Moffat, "the most admirable means of escape from negotiating further with the League Committee at Geneva. . . ." (Chalk, "The U.S. and the International Struggle," 197, quoting Diary of J. P. Moffat, December 19, 1932.)

71. Ibid., citing Diary of J. P. Moffat, December 28, 1932.

72. Ibid., 198, quoting Diary of Henry L. Stimson, January 17 and 21, 1933; the Stimson diary is available in the Special Collections of Sterling Library, Yale University, New Haven, Conn.

73. Ibid.

74. Ibid. He did, however, agree to support Firestone's determination not to alter his agreements with Liberia until the moratorium was lifted.

75. Memorandum, The Action of the League of Nations with Regards to Liberia, December 24, 1932, FO, 371/17039. The memorandum was drawn up to help the secretary of state for foreign affairs get an overview of the Liberian situation.

76. Minute by Wallinger on R. C. Lindsay to the Foreign Office, December 29, 1932, FO, 371/17039.

77. See War Office (H. J. Creedy) to Foreign Office, January 31, 1933, FO, 371/17039.

78. Foreign Office Memorandum (Wallinger), March 20, 1933, Record of interdepartmental meeting held at Foreign Office on March 20, 1933, FO, 371/17040. The consensus was that the mandate should be given to a small power, preferably Holland, Belgium, or Spain. J. V. Perowne of the Foreign Office noted that a small power mandate might conflict with earlier statements to Germany and Italy.

79. Ibid., Statement by M. Peterson.

80. Stimson to Lord Robert Cecil, January 23, 1933, FO, 371/17039.

81. M. Peterson to E. H. Carr (Geneva), January 24, 1933, FO, 371/17039.

82. Chalk, "The U.S. and the International Struggle," 201, quoting Cecil to Stimson, January 25, 1933, *USFR, 1933*, II, 884–885.

83. Ibid., citing J. P. Moffat, Memorandum, January 26, 1933, *USFR, 1933*, II, 886; Diary of J. P. Moffat, January 26, 1933.

84. Stimson was greatly disappointed and viewed the cable as a "discouraging example of League politics and impotency" (Chalk, "The U.S. and the International Struggle," 201, citing Stimson to Gilbert, *USFR, 1933*, II, 887–888; Diary of Henry L. Stimson, February 1, 1933).

85. Ibid., 199.

86. Ibid.

87. Diary of J. P. Moffat, January 21, 1933.

88. Chalk, "The U.S. and the International Struggle," 199, citing Diary of J. P. Moffat, January 21, 22, 23, 1933.

89. Dairy of J. P. Moffat, January 26, 1933.

90. Ibid., February 2, 1933.

91. Chalk, "The U.S. and the International Struggle," 202, citing Diary of Henry L. Stimson, February 3, 1933.

92. Ibid., 203; see Diary of J. P. Moffat, February 7, 1933; see also Diary of Henry L. Stimson, February 7, 1933.

93. Diary of J. P. Moffat, February 7, 1933.

94. Ibid., February 14, 1933.

95. Beecher, "The State Department and Liberia," 196.

96. This was a function somewhat misunderstood by Harvey Firestone, Jr., who came to Washington and expressed the wish that the general negotiate a completely new contract between his finance corporation and the Liberian government. (Diary of J. P. Moffat, April 6, 1933.)

97. Sir John Simon to Routh (Monrovia), March 18, 1933, FO, 371/17040.

98. Foreign Office Minute by Wallinger, May 31, 1933, on Report by Routh to Foreign Office, May 12, 1933, enclosing Lyle's proposals to Liberia, May 3, 1933, FO, 371/17041.

99. Ibid.

100. Buell, *Liberia*, 39.

101. C. von Renthe-Fink to Foreign Office, June 28, 1933, transmitting Report of the [Liberian] Committee to the Council adopted on June 27, 1933, FO, 371/17041.

102. In June of 1933, Winship had written the department and asked that he be allowed to state that the United States would accept a satisfactory neutral. The department quashed the suggestion in an effort "to abstain from breaking with the Firestones." (Diary of J. P. Moffat, June 19, 1933.)

103. The secretary-general would write to the American government and ask whether there were any Americans suitable for the post of chief adviser. After the nomination of one or two, the secretary-general could pick the most suitable candidate. United Kingdom Delegation (Geneva) to Foreign Office, June 2, 1933, enclosing in no. 1 Note by Cecil on conversation with Winship, FO, 371/1704.

104. Diary of J. P. Moffat, June 23, 1933.

105. Cecil to von Renthe-Fink, June 30, 1933, FO, 371/17042.

106. Telegram from Routh (Monrovia) to Foreign Office, June 6, 1933, FO, 371/17041.

107. Foreign Office Memorandum (M. Peterson), July 1, 1933, FO, 371/17042.

108. Ibid. See also Osborne (Washington) to Foreign Office, August 19, 1933, FO, 371/1703.

109. Raymond Buell to Cecil, August 4, 1933; Cecil to Buell, August 14, 1933, Papers of Viscount Cecil of Chelwood, British Museum, ADD 51168. Buell sent Cecil the proofs of an article he had written to be published in *The New Republic.*

110. Diary of J. P. Moffat, September 23 and 24, 1933.

111. Ibid., September 9, 1933.

112. Routh to Foreign Office, September 18, 1933, FO, 371/17043.

113. Ibid.

114. League of Nations, Committee of the Council appointed to examine the problem raised by the Liberian Government's request for assistance, Minutes of the thirty-first meeting, Geneva, October 9, 1933, c/Liberia/31 (1), p. 12, FO, 371/17044.

115. Diary of J. P. Moffat, October 16, 1933. Moffat wrote: "We had at once to get off a telegram ruling this out as our good faith might be seriously challenged. We got it off just in time to reach General Winship who is leaving Europe tomorrow morning and authorized him to bring the contents of the incoming and outgoing telegrams to Cecil's attention."

116. Ibid., October 30, 1933.

117. Ibid., November 1, 1933.

118. Buell, *Liberia*, 40, citing U.S. Department of State, *Liberia: Documents Relating to the Plan of Assistance Proposed by the League of Nations* (1933), p. 1.

119. Diary of J. P. Moffat, January 17, 1934.

120. Ibid., February 24, 1934.

121. Ibid., April 26, 1934.

122. Ibid., May 25, 1934. In April the French ordered a gunboat to Monrovia to protest a diplomatic incident. See Diary of J. P. Moffat, April 20, 1934.

123. MacVeagh to Secretary of State, February 5, 1934, USNA, RG59, 882.01 FC/791. A year before, Moffat had reported receiving "a memorandum from the British Embassy which Osborne, who delivered it, termed 'rather nasty.' " This was accompanied by "the gratuitous oral statement that according to their agents in Monrovia, the Americans in Liberia were deliberately endeavoring to produce a condition which would force American intervention." (Diary of J. P. Moffat, February 11 and 12, 1933.)

124. Diary of J. P. Moffat, February 14, 1934.

125. Ibid., May 8, 1934.

126. Walton to Barnett, May 10, 1934, Barnett Papers, Lester Walton File, 1925–1937.

127. D. C. Howard, "A Warning," Monrovia, May 5, 1934, Albert Porte Papers (microfilm, Northwestern University Library, Evanston, Ill., Roll 1, Personal Papers and Documents.

128. Diary of J. P. Moffat, May 9, 1934.

129. Chalk, "The U.S. and the International Struggle," 209, citing Diary of J. P. Moffat, May 8, 9, 18, 21, 25, June 14, 1934; Gilbert to Hull, *USFR, 1934,* II, 797–798. See also Diary of J. P. Moffat, July 20, 1932.

130. Clarence Simpson, *Memoirs: The Symbol of Liberia* (London, 1961), 187. Simpson was born in Royesville in 1896 and had started his political career as a customs official. Later he was acting postmaster general and speaker of the Liberian House of Representatives. He was secretary general of the True Whig Party from 1930 to 1944. He took over the office of secretary of state from Grimes in late 1933 and visited Geneva in September of 1934. In 1944 Simpson became vice-president.

Juah Nimley, the leader of the Kru people of Sasstown, described Simpson as "one of the principal men used by Ross to decoy in men to be sent to Fernando Po by misrepresenting to them their real destination. In some cases the men were really kidnapped . . . he is therefore one of the men who should have been prosecuted for slave dealing according to their [the Christy-Johnson commission's] recommendation." Juah Nimley [Sopon Nabwe, secretary] to Cecil, August 6, 1934, Papers of Viscount Cecil of Chelwood, British Museum, ADD 51101.

131. Diary of J. P. Moffat, May 10, 1934. Moffat said, "In order to block up both of those holes, we prepared a statement for the Secretary to hand to Lyon. . . ."

132. Great Britain, *Parliamentary Debates* (Lords), 5th series, XCI (1934), 753.

133. Lugard to Stanhope, April 16, 1934, FO, 371/18041.

134. Great Britain, *Parliamentary Debates* (Lords), 5th series, XCI (1934), 747–748.

135. Consul Patterson (Geneva) to Foreign Office, January 17, 1934, Minute by Peterson, January 19, 1934, FO, 371/18040.

136. See Foreign Office Minute (Sir John Simon), March 15, 1934, FO, 371/18040; Foreign Office Minute, Liberian situation, March 21, 1934, FO, 371/18040.

137. R. C. Stevenson (Geneva) to Peterson, April 11, 1934, FO, 371/18040.

138. United Kingdom Delegation to the League of Nations to the Foreign Office, May 19, 1934, FO, 371/18040.

139. Buell, *Liberia*, 41. See Great Britain, Papers Concerning Affairs in Liberia, p. 52. See also Sir R. Lindsay (Washington) to Foreign Office, June 12, 1934, FO, 371/18041.

140. Simpson, *Memoirs*, 190.

141. Clipping from *The Weekly Mirror* (Monrovia), July 6, 1934, Phelps-Stokes Fund Archives, New York, box 47, S-5.

142. MacVeagh to Secretary of State, July 24, 1934, USNA, RG52, 882.01 FC/886.

143. A British Foreign Office official saw the visit as "a temporizing move" and failed to see what new information McBride could unearth in light of all the previous missions. (Osborne [Washington] to Foreign Office, July 23, 1934, Foreign Office Minute by Wallinger, FO, 371/18042.)

144. The State Department gave Barclay a free hand, although Firestone, Jr., complained that Barclay was making political capital out of McBride's visit and that the Liberians were preparing to annul the plantations contract.

145. Buell, *Liberia*, 41.

146. McBride Memorandum, Conditions and Recommendations on Liberia, October 3, 1934, USNA, RG59, 882.01 FC/915.

147. Ibid. Firestone read McBride's report and objected to mention of Firestone's advocacy of force against Liberia. Firestone said he had only wanted a

"show of force." McBride promised to delete the offending passages. McBride Memorandum, October 19, 1934, USNA, RG59, 882.01 FC/924.

148. Chalk, "The U.S. and the International Struggle," 211, citing Diary of J. P. Moffat, October 5, 1934.

149. MacVeagh Memorandum, The Liberian Problem, June 11, 1934, USNA, RG59, 882.01 FC/851.

150. Memorandum to Secretary of State, August 23, 1934, Moffat Papers, Memoranda, 1934–1935, vol. 23.

151. Buell, *Liberia*, 42.

152. Ibid., 42–43. On December 31, 1934, the floating debt stood at $650,000.

153. Ibid., 43.

154. Franklin Roosevelt, Memorandum for the Secretary of State, May 29, 1935, USNA, RG59, 882.01/48.

155. Yapp to Foreign Office, October 22, 1934, FO, 371/18043, enclosing press clipping from *The West African* (Gold Coast), October, 1934.

Chapter 4

1. Taylor, "The Involvement of Black Americans," 88.

2. *The Negro Year Book, 1931–1932*, ed. Monroe N. Work (Tuskegee, Ala., 1931), 262.

3. Chalk, "Anatomy of an Investment," 20, citing C. R. Bussell to W. R. Castle, Jr., June 22, 1924, USNA, RG59, 882.6176 F51/2; de la Rue to Castle, December 21, 1924, USNA, RG59, 882.6176 F51/79. De la Rue was not on good terms with the American minister to Liberia, an Afro-American, Solomon Porter Hood. Of Hood, de la Rue wrote, "Hood could have gotten filled up with race hatred while he [was] back [in the United States]. . . . It took him nearly a year to forget he was black the time he first came out." (Quoted by Chalk, p. 24.)

4. McBride Memorandum, Conditions and Recommendations on Liberia, October 3, 1934, USNA, RG59, 882.01 FC/915.

5. Howard to McBride, September 11, 1934, USNA, RG59, 862.01 FC/922 1/2.

6. Hibbard to McBride, July 17, 1935, USNA, RG59, 882.01 FC/951 1/2.

7. George Padmore, "Workers Defend Liberia," *The Negro Worker*, October–November, 1931, 7.

8. Stimson to Hoover, October 24, 1929, DSRRAL, microfilm roll 14.

9. Castle to Trevor Arnett, November 26, 1929, DSRRAL, microfilm roll 14.

10. Stimson to Hoover, October 24, 1929, DSRRAL, microfilm roll 14. If a suitable "colored man" could not be found, Henry L. West of the American Colonization Society was recommended.

11. Department of State Memorandum to Castle, November 18, 1929, DSRRAL, microfilm roll 14.

12. Moffat Papers, Diplomatic Journal, vol. 29, 1930–1931, Berne, February 17, 1930.

13. Diary of Charles Johnson, April 12, 1930, p. 76, Johnson Papers.

14. Ibid. Johnson noted, "They have been trying even longer than the Liberians. Czecho-Slovakia [is] another illustration." Later Christy conceded that Liberia should be a black republic, if possible (Diary of Charles Johnson, April

25, 1930, p. 89). Johnson thought that Christy had been aided in his appraisal of black potential by Johnson's example.

15. Ibid., June 14, 1930.

16. "The Regeneration of Liberia," *Opportunity*, IX (February, 1931), 38.

17. Taylor, "The Involvement of Black Americans," citing Alain Locke, "Slavery in the Modern Manner," *Survey*, March 1, 1931, p. 590–593, 629–631. The year before, Locke had written Lady Simon in England, "I am at work on the article on Forced Labour and will be happy to receive from Mr. Harris [of the Anti-Slavery Society] the promised statement and literature" (Alain Locke to Lady Simon, July 9, 1930, Papers of Lady Kathleen Simon, Rhodes House, Oxford, K2).

18. Taylor, "The Involvement of Black Americans," 72, citing Rayford W. Logan, "The International Status of the Negro," *Journal of Negro History*, XVIII (April, 1933), 35–36.

19. Ibid., citing *The Crisis*, XXXIX (November, 1932), 362.

20. National Baptist Convention (the Revs. W. F. Graham, W. H. Jernagin, J. C. Jackson, Mrs. S. W. Layten, the Rev. J. E. East) to Stimson, March 4, 1931, Phelps-Stokes Fund Archives, box 47, S-4 (4).

21. Taylor, "The Involvement of Black Americans," 77; Memorandum by Ellis O. Briggs of a conversation between Briggs, East, and Jernagin, March 14, 1932 (USNA, RG59, 882.01 FC/226).

22. Memorandum by Briggs of a conversation with Jernagin, September 2, 1932, USNA, RG59, 882.01 FC/348. The letter delivered by Jernagin and his colleagues was from the executive secretaries of the Lott Carey Baptist Mission Society and the Foreign Mission Boards of the National Baptist Convention, the A.M.E. Church, and the A.M.E. Zion Church.

23. Stimson to E. H. Coit, September 9, 1932, Phelps-Stokes Archives, box 47, S-4 to S-8. Coit had written to Stimson on September 1, 1932.

24. The committee included the following organizations: the American Colonization Society (Washington, D.C.), the New York State Colonization Society, the Boston Trustees of Donations, the Phelps-Stokes Fund, the Trustees of the Booker Washington Agricultural and Industrial Institute, the National Council of the Protestant Episcopal Church, the Board of Foreign Missions of the Methodist Episcopal Church, the Board of Foreign Missions of the United Lutheran Church in America, the Foreign Mission Board of the National Baptist Convention.

25. Phillips to Roosevelt, August 16, 1933, USNA, RG59, 882.01 FC/620a.

26. Thomas J. Jones, Tentative Views on Liberian Affairs, August 31, 1931, Phelps-Stokes Archives, box 47, S-4 (4).

27. Diary of J. P. Moffat, August 19, 1932.

28. Ibid., January 6, 1933.

29. Henry West, *The Liberian Crisis* (Washington, D.C., 1933), 33. He also felt that Liberia would "either go along in its own way until it finally disintegrates upon the sands of national bankruptcy or else some nation will lay a heavy hand upon it."

30. Foreign Office Minute by Wallinger on A. Fletcher (British Library of Information, New York) to R. Leeper (Foreign Office), May 19, 1933, enclosing pamphlet by Henry West, *The Liberian Crisis*, FO, 371/17041. It was added that the British chargé d'affaires in Monrovia described West "as a 'voluble and self-important old gentleman,' but thought Mr. Jesse Jones less objectionable."

31. Briggs to Moffat, February 28, 1933, Moffat Papers, Vol. II, 1933, A–F Personal File.

32. Briggs (Monrovia) to Moffat, April 21, 1933, enclosing a letter from a person named Leasure at the Booker T. Washington Institute, Kakata, Liberia, to Jones, undated, Moffat Papers, Vol. II, 1933, A–F Personal File.

33. Memorandum on Liberian Situation, February 10, 1933(?), Phelps-Stokes Archives, box 47 (S4-3).

34. Ibid.

35. Diary of J. P. Moffat, March 3, 1933.

36. Jones to Moton, May 6, 1933, Phelps-Stokes Archives, box 47, S-4 (4).

37. Diary of J. P. Moffat, March 12, 1933. In July certain white and black missionary interests met with Winship. See Confidential Memorandum on Informal Conference with General Blanton Winship on July 24, 1933 (report dated August 3, 1933), Barnett Papers, Lester Walton File, 1927–1935. The report was written by L. A. Roy, assistant secretary of the Advisory Committee of the Booker T. Washington Institute (Kakata, Liberia). Also present were Ellis Briggs, A. B. Parson, and J. E. East.

38. Phillips to Roosevelt, August 16, 1933, USNA, RG59, 882.01 FC/620a.

39. White to William Steen, March 20, 1931, Records of the National Association for the Advancement of Colored People, Library of Congress, Washington, D.C., G-220. White thanked Steen, a State Department employee, for "the valuable report on slavery in Liberia." Steen had previously supplied the NAACP with information on Haiti. Records of the National Association for the Advancement of Colored People are henceforth cited as NAACP Papers.

40. Ibid. See White to Dantes Bellegrade, March 24, 1932.

41. Johnson to White, September 30, 1932, NAACP Papers, G-220.

42. Frazier to White, October 1, 1932, NAACP Papers, G-220.

43. Castle to White, October 17, 1932, NAACP Papers, G-220. On October 11, White had written to Johnson, and they agreed that at least one black should be on the Advisory Committee of Experts. White passed this information on to Stimson. (White to Johnson, October 11, 1932, NAACP Papers, G-220.)

44. White to Stimson, October 1, 1932, enclosing NAACP press release by Howard Oxley, USNA, RG59, 882.01 FC/383.

45. State Department note regarding White to Stimson, October 1, 1933, USNA, RG59, 882.01 FC/383. The opinion in the State Department was that Oxley had been "let out by the Advisory Committee last March because his political racketeering at Monrovia, while very piously meant, had altogether destroyed his usefulness as Educational Adviser."

46. White and DuBois to Stimson, September 27, 1932, USNA, RG59, 882.01 FC/377.

47. Azikiwe, *Liberia in World Politics*, 278–279, quoting from the Baltimore *Afro-American*, November 5, 1932, p. 8.

48. See Castle to White, October 17, 1932, USNA, RG59, 882.01 FC/403. Phillips to White, June 21, 1933, NAACP Papers, G-220.

49. White to Grimes, October 11, 1932, NAACP Papers, G-220.

50. Grimes to White, October 27, 1932, NAACP Papers, G-220. Grimes also opposed taking the position of financial adviser away from an American so that the chief adviser could be of that nationality.

51. White to Grimes, June 8, 1933, NAACP Papers, G-221.

52. Dorothy Detzer, *Appointment on the Hill* (New York, 1948), 124. Detzer

herself, while in Geneva, spoke with Cecil on the question of the nationality of the chief adviser.

53. Maud Miles to White, September 26, 1932, NAACP Papers, G-220. On September 27 the NAACP sent a telegram of protest to Stimson. In early 1933, Graves sent Walter White a long memorandum on the background of the Liberian scandal. White sent the document to Buell for comment. It was the political scientist's view that the memorandum was in large part accurate but too specific in its allegations to be substantiated.

54. Graves (Geneva) to White, July 19, 1933, NAACP Papers, G-221.

55. Graves to White, August 13, 1933, NAACP Papers, G-221.

56. Diary of J. P. Moffat, January 23, 1933. Graves claimed that Harvey Firestone, Jr.'s conversion to Buchmanism (Moral Rearmament) was a publicity stunt. She also supported Liberia's financial moratorium.

57. Detzer to White, June 8, 1933, NAACP Papers, G-220.

58. Memorandum of conversation between General Winship and Dorothy Detzer, July 18, 1933, USNA, RG59, 882.01 FC/599.

59. Other members of the group were Addie W. Dickerson, president of the International Council of Women of Darker Races; Addie W. Hunton, chairman of the board, Interracial Commission, WILPF; Archie Pinket, secretary of the Washington branch of the NAACP; Mrs. Daniel Partridge, Jr., secretary of the Washington branch, WILPF. Nannie Burroughs of the National Association of Colored Women and Charles H. Houston of the National Bar Association were members of the delegation but unable to attend. (White to Wilkins, August 2, 1933, NAACP Papers, G-221.) Those who declined to attend were Claude Barnett of the Associated Negro Press, Carl Murphy of the *Afro-American*, Dr. Robert Moton of Tuskegee, and John Hope.

60. Mordecai Johnson to White, July 27, 1933, NAACP Papers, G-221. There was a difference of opinion on some issues. Some members of the delegation wanted an American chief adviser, while others wanted a European (preferably a Scandinavian).

61. Forderhase, "The Plans That Failed," 140.

62. Ibid., citing Copy of speech delivered by DuBois, July 31, 1933, USNA, 882.01 FC/61 1/2.

63. Ibid.

64. Statement of DuBois at State Department, July 31, 1933, NAACP Papers, G-221.

65. Press Release, August 4, 1933, NAACP Papers, G-221.

66. Rayford Logan, "Liberia's Dilemma," *The Southern Workman*, LXII (September, 1933), 360.

67. State Department Press Release, July 31, 1933, NAACP Papers, G-221.

68. Logan, "Liberia's Dilemma," 361.

69. Detzer to White, August 3, 1933, NAACP Papers, G-221. White was out of town, so the letter was given to DuBois.

70. Diary of J. P. Moffat, August 15, 1933.

71. White to Buell, September 8, 1933, NAACP Papers, G-221.

72. Memorandum of conversation between William Phillips (Undersecretary of State) and Delegation Opposing United States Policy in Liberia, July 31, 1933, USNA, RG59, 882.01 FC/612 1/2.

73. Phillips to Franklin Roosevelt, August 16, 1933, USNA, RG59, 882.01 FC/620a.

74. Taylor, "The Involvement of Black Americans," 76. See Phillips to Winship, August 2, 1933, USNA, RG59, 882.01 FC/612A; Winship to Secretary of State, August 5, 1933, USNA, RG59, 882.01 FC/614; Winship to Secretary of State, August 8, 1933, USNA, 882.01 FC/617; Secretary of State Hull to Winship, August 7, 1933, USNA, RG59, 882.01 FC/614.

75. Chalk, "The U.S. and the International Struggle," 206.

76. Diary of J. P. Moffat, September 8, 1933, Moffat Papers. He added, "They were particularly mean to Bill Phillips."

77. Raymond Buell, "The New Deal and Liberia," *The New Republic*, LXXVI (August, 1933), 19.

78. The British information agency in New York took note of Buell's article and sent London a news comment which took cognizance of Liberia's wider significance. Buell had raised the question of "whether the State Department is at present equipped to carry out in our foreign policy the political philosophy which dominates the Roosevelt administration elsewhere. . . . In its first real test the State Department is found tenaciously supporting the Firestone concession, which violates every principle of the New Deal" (British Library of Information [New York] to News Department British Foreign Office, August 18, 1933, enclosing clipping, FO, 371/17043). See *The New Republic*, August 23, 1933.

79. Mauritz Hallgren, "Liberia in Shackles," *The Nation*, CXXXVII (August 16, 1933), 185.

80. Detzer, *Appointment on the Hill*, 136. A British foreign office telegram to the Monrovia consulate on August 23 said: "You make it clear that provided this opportunity is taken, the League plan accepted and an amnesty thereafter granted to all political prisoners now detained by the Liberian Government, His Majesty's Government will be prepared to recognize and enter into full diplomatic relations with the existing Liberian Administration." The United States adopted a similar course. Sir John Simon to Routh (Monrovia), August 23, 1933, Great Britain, *Papers Concerning Affairs in Liberia*, no. 11.

81. Detzer, *Appointment on the Hill*, 135. Morris Ernst was the man who supposedly suggested Detzer contact Frankfurter.

82. Ibid.

83. Memorandum for the Secretary of State, September 26, 1933, USNA, RG59, 882.01 FC/709.

84. Taylor, "The Involvement of Black Americans," 76. See Memorandum of conversation with Harvey Firestone, Jr., September 21, 1933, USNA, RG59, 882.01 FC/663. White of the NAACP suspected such a shift and asked a State Department messenger to attempt to obtain a copy of the document on the subject (White to Steen, October 2, 1933, NAACP Papers, G-221).

85. Grimes to White, July 18, 1933, NAACP Papers, G-221.

86. Samuel Cavert to Phillips, May 29, 1933, USNA, RG59, 882.01 A/10 1/2.

87. James Young, *Liberia Rediscovered* (Garden City, N.Y., 1934), 92.

88. Detzer to Van Kirk, June 24, 1933, NAACP Papers, G-220.

89. Ibid., September 8, 1933. Later Detzer spoke to Van Kirk, who appeared sympathetic. (Detzer to White, September 16, 1933, NAACP Papers, G-221).

90. Memorandum (Hibbard) on conversation with T. J. Jones, January 31, 1934, USNA, RG59, 882.01 FC/791 1/2.

91. Ibid. The Phelps-Stokes Archives do contain a "Proposed Statement for Liberian meeting: Tentative Resolutions." Part of the resolutions read: "We are

emphatically convinced that the sovereignty of Liberia can be saved only by the immediate and sincere acceptance of the League Plan of Assistance by the Republic of Liberia." (Phelps-Stokes Archives, box 47, S-5.)

92. Taylor, "The Involvement of Black Americans," 79, citing J. E. East and H. T. Medford to Secretary of State Hull, February 9, 1934, USNA, RG59, 882.01 FC/905. See also Baltimore *Afro-American*, February 17, 1934, p. 21, and [George A Kuyper], "Liberia," *The Southern Workman*, LXIII (April, 1934), 99–100. Present at the meeting were the foreign mission boards of the National Baptist Convention of America, the New England Baptist Missionary Convention, the Lott Carey Baptist Convention, African Methodist Episcopal Zion and African Methodist Episcopal churches, the Methodist Episcopal, Lutheran, Protestant Episcopal and Presbyterian churches, and Friends of Liberia. Also present were Lester Walton of the New York *Age*, William Jones, Henry West, Thomas J. Jones, and Harvey Firestone, Jr. Judge Frederick C. Fisher, an expert on the legal phases of the Liberian situation, was present, as well as George A. Kuyper, editor of *The Southern Workman* of Hampton Institute.

93. Taylor, "The Involvement of Black Americans," citing Baltimore *Afro-American*, February 17, 1934, p. 21; and East and Medford to Secretary of State Hull, February 9, 1934, USNA, RG59, 882.01 FC/905.

94. Ibid. See Memorandum of conversation between William Phillips and Bishop Matthews on February 6, 1934, and February 16, 1934, USNA, RG59, 882.01/33.

95. Moffatt to Phillips, February 9, 1934, Moffat Papers, Personal Correspondence, vol. 7: N-Z, 1934.

96. Diary of J. P. Moffat, February 14, 1934. See also Memorandum on Hull meeting with Organization of Foreign Missions on February 14, 1934, USNA, RG59, 882.01 FC/904.

97. J. E. East of the National Baptist Convention to the Advisory Committee on Education in Liberia and the Board of Trustees of the Booker T. Washington Institute in Liberia, May 1, 1934, Phelps-Stokes Archives, box 47, S-4 (4).

98. Jones to West, May 8, 1934, Phelps-Stokes Archives, box 47, S-4 (3).

99. Taylor, "The Involvement of Black Americans," 80. See Memorandum by Hibbard of conversation with East and attachments, May 16, 1934, USNA, RG59, 882.01 FC/825. See also Baltimore *Afro-American*, May 19, 1934, and Diary of J. P. Moffat, May 16, 1934.

100. Memorandum (Hibbard) of conversation with Foreign Mission secretaries, May 21, 1934, USNA, RG59, 882.01 FC/825. Present were East; Dr. J. Harry Randolph, treasurer; the Rev. E. L. Harrison; Dr. G. O. Bullock; the Rev. J. L. F. Holloman; and Dr. John R. Hawkins, representing the Rev. L. L. Berry. The memorandum also contains a clipping from the Baltimore *Afro-American* of May 19, 1934: "U.S. Aid Sought If Liberia and League Differ."

101. Young, *Liberia Rediscovered*, 127.

102. Taylor, "The Involvement of Black Americans," 88. See R. R. Moton to Franklin Roosevelt, June 23, 1934, USNA, RG59, 882.01 FC/841 2/3.

103. Rupert Emerson, "Race in Africa: United States Foreign Policy," in *Racial Influences on American Foreign Policy*, ed. George W. Shepherd (New York, 1970), 167.

104. Chalk, "The U.S. and the International Struggle," 213.

105. The practice of sending special emissaries to iron out disputes was more frequently resorted to, and by 1931 the United States was planning to

withdraw from Nicaragua and had refused to intervene in the Cuban revolution of 1929–1930.

106. Chalk, "The U.S. and the International Struggle," citing Briggs, Memorandum, December 27, 1930, *USFR 1930*, III, 391–393.

107. Taylor, "The Involvement of Black Americans," 84, citing Memorandum, Castle to Stimson, September 18, 1930, USNA, RG59, 882.00/846.

108. Ibid., citing Memorandum, Briggs to Marriner, n.d., USNA, RG59, 882.01 FC/908.

109. When the League withdrew its plan of assistance, a Foreign Office official spoke to a member of the American embassy staff in London and inquired whether the argument that the United States would take some responsibility in Liberia because of the American black population was valid. See Conversation between Butterworth (American embassy) and Peterson (Foreign Office), May 4, 1934, FO, 371/18041. Peterson "said that this argument [black interest] was of a nature which made it perhaps easier and more suitable to utilise in conversation rather that [*sic*] to put it down on paper. Mr. Butterworth, however, said he regarded the point as quite admissable, althought the effect it might produce would depend on the individual by whom it was considered; he himself as a Southerner paid little attention to his negro fellow citizens and therefore to any argument based upon their presence in the United States."

110. White to DuBois to Stimson, September 27, 1932, USNA, RG59, 882.01 FC/377.

111. Diary of J. P. Moffat, January 21, 1933.

112. Chalk, "The U.S. and the International Struggle," 205, citing Diary of J. P. Moffat, February 27, 1933.

113. Diary of J. P. Moffat, April 18, 1934; see also November 11, 1933.

114. Ibid., May 21, 1934.

115. Phillips, Memorandum of conversation with the Liberian Consul-General, May 24, 1934, USNA, RG59, 882.51 A/225.

116. W. E. B. DuBois, "Liberia and Rubber," *The New Republic*, XLIV, 572 (November 18, 1925).

117. Schuyler to White, June 17, 1933, NAACP Papers, G-220.

118. Moffat Papers, Diplomatic Journal, vol. 29, 1930–31, Berne.

119. Beecher, "The State Department and Liberia," 168.

120. For specific concern with black voter impact, see ibid., 120.

121. Taylor, "The Involvement of Black Americans," 73–74. See Memorandum, Department of State, October 13, 1932, USNA, RG59, 882.01 FC/410.

122. White to Frazier, October 4, 1932, NAACP Papers, G-220.

123. Chalk, "The U.S. and the International Struggle," 192.

124. Diary of J. P. Moffat, October 11, 1932.

125. Chalk, "The U.S. and the International Struggle," 192, citing Diary of J. P. Moffat, September 26 and 28, 1932.

126. Detzer to Graves, July 18, 1933, NAACP Papers, G-221.

127. Great Britain, *Parliamentary Debates* (Lords), 5th series, XCI (1934), 737.

128. Frank Church quoted by Francis A. Kornegay, "Africa and Presidential Politics," *Africa Report*, XXI, 4 (July–August 1976), 8. Church was speaking to an April, 1976, caucus of black Democrats in Charlotte, North Carolina.

129. E. Franklin Frazier, "What Can the American Negro Contribute to the

Social Development?" in *Africa from the Point of View of American Negro Scholars*, ed. John A. Davis (Paris, 1959), 268, 277.

130. Beecher, "The State Department and Liberia," 179, 181.

131. Ibid., citing Mitchell to Secretary of State, January 20, 1933, USNA, RG59, 882.01 FC/467; January 25, 1933, USNA, RG59, 882.01 FC/479.

132. Diary of J. P. Moffat, August 31, 1932.

133. Ibid., January 31, 1933.

134. Taylor, "The Involvement of Black Americans," 74. See Memorandum of conversation between Castle and Liberian Consul-General Ernest Lyon, February 11, 1933, USNA, RG59, 882.01 FC/526.

135. Taylor, "The Involvement of Black Americans." See Stimson to Mitchell, February 21, 1933, USNA, RG59, 882.01, Winship Mission/10. See also Routh (Monrovia) to Foreign Office, January 6, 1933, FO, 371/17044; Baltimore *Afro-American*, February 11, 1933.

136. McCeney Werlirch (Monrovia) to Moffat, September 17, 1933, Moffat Papers, vol. 4, 1933, 0–2.

137. Hibbard to Secretary of State (cable) June 6, 1935, USNA, RG59, 882.01 FC/951.

138. Walton to Barnett, July 1, 1933, Barnett Papers, Lester Walton File, 1927–1935. In January of 1933, Barnett had written to Barclay asking him his racial preferences in ministers (Barnett to Barclay, January 19, 1933, Barnett Papers, Associated Negro Press and World News Service, Business Dealings, Liberia). In May, Walton strongly remonstrated with Barnett for mentioning him in connection with the Liberian post (Walton to Barnett, May 20, 1933, Barnett Papers).

Walton, who had been born in St. Louis, Missouri, in 1882, had held a succession of reportorial positions: From 1902 to 1906 he worked for the St. Louis *Star Sayings* (later renamed the St. Louis *Star-Times*). Afterwards he was employed by the St. Louis *Globe Democrat* and the St. Louis *Post-Dispatch*. In New York Walton worked for the New York *Age*, 1917–1919; the New York *World*, 1922–1931; and the New York *Herald Tribune*, 1931. From 1932 to 1938 he was associate editor of the New York *Age* (of which his father-in-law, Fred Moore, was editor). In addition to his work as a journalist, he was a songwriter and the manager of the Lafayette Theatre in New York (1914–1916, 1919–1921). He was a member of the military Entertainment Service during World War I and a correspondent at the Versailles Peace Conference in 1919. From 1926 until 1935, the newspaperman was director of publicity for the National Negro Business League and prominent in Democratic politics.

139. Walton to Barnett, July 21, 1933, Barnett Papers, Lester Walton File, 1927–1935.

140. Ibid. Barnett and Walton followed the appointments being given to black Democrats with great interest in the first months of the Roosevelt administration. On July 11, 1933, Barnett wrote to Walton: "Well Bob [Robert Vann, appointed to the U.S. Attorney General's office] seems to have landed. He states the job is the biggest appointment ever given a Negro."

141. Walton to Barnett, January 9, 1934, Barnett Papers, Lester Walton File, 1927–1935.

142. Hibbard to McBride, July 17, 1935, USNA, RG59, 882.01 FC/951 1/2.

143. Yapp to Foreign Office, October 16, 1936, FO, 371/19235.

144. Walton to Drew Pearson, November 17, 1933, USNA, RG59, 882.00/966? (misfiled).

145. Will Alexander to Phelps-Stokes, November 7, 1929, Phelps-Stokes Archives, box 33, K-6.

146. L. A. Roy to Phelps-Stokes, February 7, 1931, Phelps-Stokes Archives, box 33, K-6.

147. Phelps-Stokes to Alexander, February 9, 1931, Phelps-Stokes Archives, box 33, K-6.

148. Alexander to Phelps-Stokes, February 19, 1931, Phelps-Stokes Archives, box 33, K-26.

149. Walton to Phelps-Stokes, February 14, 1931, Phelps-Stokes Archives, box 33, K-26.

150. Ibid.

151. Ibid. Walton obviously needed money. Jones and a Mr. Peabody attempted to get him work at the New York *Times*.

152. Walton to Barnett, May 17, 1933, Barnett Papers, Lester Walton File, 1927–1935.

153. Roy to Jones (Monrovia), May 17, 1933, Phelps-Stokes Archives, box 7A, A-22 (1c).

154. Walton to Jones, October 4, 1935, Phelps-Stokes Archives, box 38, K-26.

155. Walton to Barnett, November 26, 1935, Barnett Papers, Lester Walton File, 1927–1935.

156. Beecher, "The State Department and Liberia," 221; Walton to Secretary of State, Monrovia, May 28, 1941, USNA, RG59, 882.00/1151.

Chapter 5

1. Rennie Smith, "Negro Self-Government at a Crisis in Liberia," *Current History*, XXXIV (August, 1931), 736.

2. Yancy, *Historic Lights*, 218.

3. Azikiwe, *Liberia in World Politics*, 245, citing Edwin Barclay, *Annual Message*, 1931, 1–3.

4. Ibid., 395.

5. DuBois, "Liberia, the League and the United States," 682.

6. W. E. B. DuBois, "Pan-Africa and New Racial Philosophy," *The Crisis*, XL (November, 1933), 247, 262.

7. George Padmore, *Pan-Africanism or Communism* (London, 1956), 148.

8. T. Ras Makonnen for the International African Service Bureau to Edwin Barclay, April 20, 1938, Liberian National Archives. Others associated with the IASB were I. Wallace-Johnson, C. L. R. James, Jomo Kenyatta, and B. N. Azikiwe. For a discussion of the rule and impact of the organization see J. Ayodele Langley, *Pan-Africanism and Nationalism in West Africa, 1900–1945* (London, 1973), 337–346.

9. J. R. Hooker, *Black Revolutionary: George Padmore's Path from Communism to Pan Africanism* (London, 1967), 22, citing *The New Leader*, September 13, 1941.

10. "Free Liberia," *Literary Digest*, CXXII, 6 (August 8, 1936), 14.

11. *The Weekly Mirror* (Monrovia), March 6, 1936, reprinting article from *African Morning Post* (Accra), Liberian National Archives, Executive Mansion, 1936.

12. L. H. Whittall (Monrovia) to Sir Samuel Hoare, August 9, 1935, Foreign Office, Consulate-General, Monrovia, Northwestern University microfilm, roll 2.

13. Walter F. Walker (Consul, New York) to R. S. L. Bright (Executive Mansion, Monrovia), June 29, 1935, Liberian National Archives.

14. Lyon to Barclay, June 20, 1933, Liberian National Archives.

15. T. Ras Makonnen for the International African Service Bureau to Edwin Barclay, April 20, 1938, Liberian National Archives.

16. Great Britain, *Papers Concerning Affairs in Liberia*, Annex to Appendix I, Report of the Experts Designated by the Committee of the Council of the League of Nations: Final Observations, p. 80.

17. Barnett to Jones, December 19, 1934, Phelps-Stokes Archives, box 37, K-8.

18. Azikiwe, *Liberia in World Politics*, 353, citing W. E. B. DuBois, "Sensitive Liberia," *The Crisis*, May, 1924, pp. 9-11. Also see "United States Envoy," *The Crisis*, February, 1924, p. 151.

19. Clipping, "Woman Scores 'Backwardness' of Liberians," Pittsburgh *Courier*, December 9, 1933, USNA, RG59, 882.00/997. Mrs. McWillie was a hairdresser who had returned to America with her husband, Herman. She said the Liberian authorities had been afraid of her exposure of conditions and had attempted to detain her in Liberia.

20. Barnett to Walton, October 18, 1934, Barnett Papers, Lester Walton File, 1927–1935.

21. For a discussion of Garvey and Garveyism see E. David Cronon, *Black Moses: The Story of Marcus Garvey and the Universal Negro Improvement Association* (Madison, Wis., 1957); A. J. Garvey, *The Philosophy and Opinions of Marcus Garvey* (New York, 1923); A. J. Garvey, *Garvey and Garveyism* (Kingston, 1963); Elton Fax, *Garvey: The Story of a Pioneer Black Nationalist* (New York, 1972). The impact of Garvey is also dealt with in Imanuel Geiss's *The Pan-African Movement* (New York, 1974); and Langley's *Pan-Africanism and Nationalism in West Africa*. Also see M. B. Akpan, "Liberia and the Universal Negro Improvement Association: The Background to the Abortion of Garvey's Scheme for African Colonization," *Journal of African History*, XIV, 1 (1973), 105–127; and Theodore Vincent, *Black Power and the Garvey Movement* (Berkeley, Cal., n.d.).

22. Chaudhuri, "British Policy Towards Liberia," 205.

23. Akpan, "Liberia and the Universal Negro Improvement Association," 114, citing Report of the Secretary of the Treasury for the fiscal year ended October 1919 to September 1920, p. 9, Liberian National Archives.

24. Chaudhuri, "British Policy Towards Liberia," 205, citing O'Meara to Foreign Office, February 22, 1924, FO, 371/9553.

25. Ibid., citing Barclay to the Agent Elder Dempster Company (Monrovia), June 30, 1924, FO, 371/9553.

26. Ibid., citing O'Meara to Foreign Office, August 8, 1924, FO, 371/9553.

27. Akpan, "Liberia and the Universal Negro Improvement Association," 126, citing "An Act Approving the Deportation of the Emissaries of the Universal Negro Improvement Association by H. E. C. D. B. King, President of Liberia; approved January 14, 1925," Acts 1924–1925, Liberia National Archives.

28. Article, "Garveyism in Liberia," Liberian National Archives.

29. Akpan, "Liberia and the Universal Negro Improvement Association," 112, citing Cable of U.S. Department of State to J. L. Johnson, May 25, 1921, USNA, RG59, 882.00/703.

30. Ibid., 123, citing DuBois to Secretary of State, March 24, 1924, USNA, RG59, 882.00/739; U.S. Department of State, Memorandum of conver-

sation with Mr. DuBois, Special Representative of the President at the Inauguration of President King of Liberia, March 26, 1924, USNA, RG59, 882.00/742.

31. Ibid., citing A. J. Garvey, *Garvey and Garveyism*, 129.

32. Ibid., 118, citing Cyril Critchlow to M. Garvey, June 24, 1921,
USNA, RG59, 882.00/705.

33. Ibid., 119, citing C. D. B. King, Inaugural Address, January 5, 1920,
p. 18.

34. Ibid., 116, citing Critchlow to M. Garvey, June 24, 1971, USNA,
RG59, 882.00/705.

35. Article, "Marcus Garvey and Liberia," 1924(?), Liberian National
Archives.

36. Akpan, "Liberia and the Universal Negro Improvement Association,"
124–125.

37. See Wharton (Monrovia) to Secretary of State, August 1, 1929,
DSRRAL, microfilm roll 14.

38. Memorandum by John H. MacVeagh, April 25, 1934, USNA, RG59,
882.01 FC/829.

39. Lyon to Simpson, July –, 1934, Liberian National Archives.

40. West to T. J. Jones, September 27, 1934, Phelps-Stokes Archives, box
47, S-4 (3).

41. Walton (via Firestone communications) to T. J. Jones, May 6, 1936,
Phelps-Stokes Archives, box 38, K-6. The message was sent to Jones but was
addressed to the Liberian consul in New York to be passed on to the press.

42. Robert Weisbord, *Ebony Kinship* (Westport, Conn., 1973), 120. The
Peace Movement of Ethiopia was an outgrowth of the Garvey Movement,
founded in Chicago in 1932. The movement circulated a petition urging the
Roosevelt administration to take relief money destined for blacks and apply it to
Liberian emigration; concentrating its efforts in Illinois and Indiana, the organization claimed to have obtained 400,000 names in eight months. After the
White House rejected its proposal as impractical, the movement turned to the
state of Virginia for assistance. In 1936 the General Assembly of Virginia asked
the United States Congress for aid in assisting Afro-Americans to emigrate to
Liberia or elsewhere in Africa. Consult Ralph Bunche, "The Programs, Ideolo-
gies, Tactics and Achievements of Negro Betterment and Interracial Organizations—A Research Memorandum," Unpublished study conducted for the Car-
negie-Myrdal Project, II, 419.

In 1939, Senator Theodore Bilbo of Mississippi introduced an emigration
bill, "the Greater Liberia" bill, into the Senate in an effort to get federal funds
for an Afro-American exodus.

43. Ian Duffield, "Pan-Africanism, Rational and Irrational," Review of *The
Pan-African Movement*, by Imanuel Geiss, *Journal of African History*, XVIII, 4
(1977), 611.

44. William Phillips to Legation (Monrovia), December 29, 1933, USNA,
RG59, 882.01 FC/753. The State Department said it could not take any official
cognizance of such a commission.

45. Frank Chalk, "DuBois and Garvey Confront Liberia: Two Incidents of
the Coolidge Years," *Canadian Journal of African Studies*, I, 2 (November, 1967),
141, citing A. J. Garvey, *Philosophy and Opinions of Marcus Garvey*, II, 397–398.

46. DuBois to Secretary of State, March 24, 1924, USNA, RG59,
882.00/739 (microfilm M613, location 10-14-5, roll 14).

47. DuBois, "Liberia," 684. Earlier in the century DuBois had hoped the

Belgian or German colonial governments would let Afro-Americans be the economic leaders in their colonies (Elliot M. Rudwick, *W. E. B. DuBois: Propagandist of the Negro Protest* [New York, 1968], 210).

48. Chalk, "DuBois and Garvey," 141, quoting W. E. B. DuBois, "A Second Journey to Pan-Africa," *The New Republic*, XXIX (December 7, 1921), 41.

49. Ibid., 137. Lewis also noted that the visit presented "a good chance to play a little politics, which will not cost anybody anything, unless the Department of State desires to make a small contribution toward Dr. DuBois' expense account."

50. Chalk, "Anatomy of an Investment," 20, citing Castle to Harrison, July 1, 1924, USNA, RG59, 882.6176 F51/1. De la Rue is also reported to have urged that the replacement for American Consul Solomon Hood be a white man. If Hood remained in the United States (where he was visiting temporarily), it was argued that he could be very influential in creating support for Firestone among the black population.

51. Chalk, "The U.S. and the International Struggle," 139. See A. J. Garvey, *Philosophy and Opinions of Marcus Garvey*, II, 384–394.

52. Chicago *Defender*, November 7, 1925, p. 10, quoted by Charles A. Bodie, "The Images of Africa in the Black American Press, 1890–1930" (Ph.D. diss., Indiana University, 1975), 189.

53. Anonymous news clipping, 1925, Barnett Papers, Firestone Rubber Company File, 1925–1953.

54. Newport News *Star*, October 22, 1925, Barnett Papers, Firestone Rubber Company File, 1925–1953.

55. New York *News*, February 13, 1926, Barnett Papers, Firestone Rubber Company File, 1925–1953.

56. Dalvan Coger, "Black American Immigration to Liberia, 1900–1930" (Paper delivered at the Eighth Annual Conference, Liberian Studies Association, Bloomington, Indiana, March, 1976), p. 5, citing extracts from the personal journal of Thomas Jesse Jones, September 13–November 1, 1920.

57. Ford to Foreign Office, August 6, 1930, Foreign Office, Consulate-General, Monrovia Northwestern University microfilm, roll 1.

58. Memorandum of conversation with Thomas J. R. Faulkner, Washington, D.C., August 14, 1930, USNA, RG59, 882.00/841.

59. William Edgenton, "As to Liberian 'Slavery,' " *The Atlantean*, November, 1931, p. 11, Barnett Papers, Firestone Rubber Company File, 1925–1953. Edgenton had been in Liberia in 1918 and, in all, had spent five years there. Later he lived in Kansas City, Missouri.

60. J. Edmund Jones (Acting Secretary of State) to Barclay, January 6, 1934, enclosing Proclamation of Dr. S. P. Radway of the Afro-West India Round Trip Association, Liberian National Archives.

61. Richard N. Bedell to Barclay, January 2, 1934, Liberian National Archives.

62. J. T. Betts to Edwin Barclay, July 20, 1934, Liberian National Archives.

63. Lyon had been minister to Liberia during the administration of Theodore Roosevelt. The black diplomat had been a Methodist minister and was a protégé of Booker T. Washington. Lyon was a staunch Republican and, in addition to his political activities, had served in several churches in New Orleans, New York, and Baltimore. Sometime before 1903, Lyon had served as secretary of the West African Steamship Company. However there is very little evidence that the company ever functioned. In 1903, after his appointment as

minister to Liberia, Lyon opposed the immigration of indigent Afro-Americans to Liberia.

64. By the time of Jones's visit, the *Afro-American* had considerably softened its stance on Liberia. Earlier (1932) the paper had characterized the Monrovia government's treatment of the indigenes as "inhuman measures . . . directly traceable to President Barclay, who has shown his determination to repress members of those tribes not favorably disposed towards his administration." After his visit Jones could write, somewhat optimistically, that the government was "striving to cultivate and cement friendship between the natives and the Government and it is only a matter of time when the district commissioners will locally select representatives."

Colonel Davis of the Frontier Force reportedly remarked that the *"Afro-American* had always published defamatory articles about conditions in Liberia. . . . But now with this great crisis staring the world in the face Mr. Jones is out here to get the truth and take it back home with him to his people. . . ." (Report prepared by Vice-Consul William C. George, in McCeney Werlich to Cordell Hull, November 23, 1933, USNA, RG59, 882.01 FC/752.) Jones spoke at the Monrovia Methodist Church on November 19, 1933. He had addressed the Liberian legislature on November 17.

65. Werlich (Monrovia) to Hull, November 23, 1933, enclosing William Jones to Gabriel L. Dennis, Secretary of the Treasury, A Memorandum of Co-Operation Between Liberia and America, USNA, RG59, 882.01 FC/752.

66. Ibid.

67. On leaving Liberia, Jones was optimistic. Noting the relative prosperity of Freetown, he wrote of the good prospects of a certain European trader and his African wife: "Some possibilities of trade expansion in Liberia are exemplified in the successful wholesale and retail establishment conducted by H. Genet here" (News clipping, "Women in Freetown, Africa, Want Silk Hose Now," Baltimore *Afro-American*, December 9, 1933, USNA, RG59, 882.01 A/15).

68. News clipping, William Jones, "Liberian Legislature Puts Future up to U.S.," Baltimore *Afro-American*, December 2, 1933, USNA, RG59, 882.01 A15. In early 1934, Carl Murphy, president of the *Afro American*, notified Walter White of the NAACP that Jones had returned and wanted a meeting of black leaders to draw up a program for Liberia for presentation to Roosevelt (Murphy to Walter White, January 19, 1934, NAACP Papers, C-335).

69. Murphy to White, January 19, 1934, NAACP Papers, C-335. For Jones's promotion of his scheme, see Baltimore *Afro-American*, December 23, 1933, p. 1; December 30, 1933, p. 1; January 20, 1934, p. 17; February 10, 1934, p. 5; March 3, 1933, p. 5; March 10, 1934, p. 5; March 17, 1934, p. 5; April 7, 1934, p. 5; June 23, 1934, p. 4. (Cited by Taylor, "The Involvement of Black Americans," 70.)

70. Taylor, "The Involvement of Black Americans," 80. Among those listed as supporting the Jones plan were Carl Murphy, Charles S. Johnson, Oscar De Priest, C. C. Spaulding, Emmett Scott, Charles H. Wesley, Rayford Logan, W. E. B. DuBois, Mary McLeod Bethune, Carter G. Woodson, Channing H. Tobias, P. Bernard Young, Walter White, Eugenie Kincle Jones, the Rev. J. H. Jernagin, Daisy C. Lampkin, Charlotte Hawkins Brown, William L. Patterson, E. Washington Rhodes, Hellen Allen Boys, John W. Davis, and Bishop W. Sampson Brooks. White members of the proposed committee included Raymond Leslie Buell and Henry L. West.

71. For the State Department reaction see Memorandum by Phillips of

conversation with Ernest Lyon, W. W. Allen, and W. N. Jones, January 12, 1934, USNA, RG59, 882.01 FC/767. Also see Memorandum (Hibbard) on conversation with T. J. Jones, January 31, 1934, USNA, RG59, 882.01 FC/791 1/2.

72. Taylor, "The Involvement of Black Americans," 80. See Pittsburgh *Courier*, February 3, 1934, p. 10.

73. Acting Secretary of State (Monrovia) to Lyon, August 29, 1934, Liberian National Archives.

74. Walter F. Walker (Consul, New York) to R. S. L. Bright (Executive Mansion, Monrovia), June 29, 1935, enclosing William Jones's column, "Day by Day," Baltimore *Afro-American*, n.d., Liberian National Archives.

75. Taylor, "The Involvement of Black Americans," 80. See Baltimore *Afro-American*, August 4, 1934, p. 4.

76. Harry Haywood, unpublished autobiographical manuscript, Chapter 13: "Eighth Convention: Description of Eighth Convention of the Communist Party of the United States, Cleveland, Ohio, April 2–8, 1934." For an abbreviated discussion of the Jones plan see Harry Haywood, *Black Bolshevik: Autobiography of an Afro-American Communist* (Chicago, 1978), 428.

77. Haywood, unpublished autobiographical manuscript, Chapter 13.

78. "The Struggle for the Independence of Liberia," *The Negro Worker*, IV, 2 (June, 1934), 14.

79. "Expulsion of George Padmore from the Revolutionary Movement," Statement of the International Trade Union Committee of Negro Workers, Charles Woodson, Secretary, *The Negro Worker*, IV, 2 (June, 1934), 14–15.

80. "The Struggle for the Independence of Liberia," 12.

81. "A Betrayer of the Negro Liberation Struggle," *The Negro Worker*, IV, 3 (July, 1934), 9.

82. George Padmore, "An Open Letter to Earl Browder," *The Crisis*, XLII, 10 (October, 1935), 302. Padmore counterattacked by charging that the Negro Trade Union Committee had been abolished on orders from the Soviets, who were seeking to appease the British Foreign Office.

83. Earl Browder, "Earl Browder Replies," *The Crisis*, XLII, 12 (December, 1935), 372.

84. Hooker, *Black Revolutionary*, 22.

85. Padmore, "Workers Defend Liberia," *The Negro Worker*, October–November, 1931, p. 7.

86. Hooker, *Black Revolutionary*, citing Padmore to DuBois, February 17, 1934.

87. Padmore, "An Open Letter," 302.

88. Memorandum of conversation with Thomas J. R. Faulkner, August 14, 1930, USNA, RG59, 882.00/841.

89. J. K. Obatala, "Liberia: The Meaning of Dual Citizenship," *The Black Scholar*, IV, 10 (July–August, 1973), 17.

90. J. Gus Liebenow, *Liberia: The Evolution of Privilege* (Ithaca, N.Y., 1969), 92.

91. Lyon to Secretary of State (Monrovia), June 20, 1933, Liberian National Archives.

92. For a discussion of the "Syrian Problem" and capital from America, see the article by "Zephyrus" in *The Liberian Crisis*, special issue, July, 1935, "If Not an Agreement with America, Why Not a Liberian-American Agreement?" Liberian National Archives.

Chapter 6

1. "Forced Labor in Liberia," *The Nation*, CXXX, 3373 (February 26, 1930), 130.

2. Buell, "The Reconstruction of Liberia," 133, citing League of Nations, Minutes of the 7th meeting, Committee of the Council, January 26, 1932.

3. Mitchell to Secretary of State, May 3, 1932, enclosing D. D. Rydings' Report of April 15, 1932, USNA, RG59, 882.01/966. Also see Report by Mr. W. A. Travell, Chairman of the Liberian government's Special Commission to Sasstown, April 21, 1932 (Monrovia), Grimes Papers, Liberia/League of Nations Papers, Pt. II, roll 2.

4. Yapp (Monrovia) to Sir John Simon, February 20, 1935, FO, 371/19235.

5. Diary of Charles Johnson, March 30, 1930, Johnson Papers. Johnson also said that Davis had served in the Medical Department under Carranza (presumably with the Mexican army).

6. McBride Memorandum, October 3, 1934, USNA, RG59, 882.01 FC/915; see annexed Memorandum of the Government of Liberia on the Kru Situation. Davis also found that Frontier Force soldiers had made unjust demands upon the local people.

7. Davis, *Ethnological Studies*, 114. Davis says: "It is claimed that Jehiupo was on the verge of famine, whereupon the Liberian commander ordered that the inhabitants of the towns be given certain areas then being cultivated by the Gbeta settlers at Sobobo."

8. McBride Memorandum, October 3, 1934, USNA, RG59, 882.01 FC/915; see annexed Memorandum of the Government of Liberia on the Kru Situation. According to Jones ("The Struggle for Political and Cultural Unification," 258), Nimley was not present at the meeting.

9. Bolloh, Dio, and Wissepo Kru groups burned the principal towns of the Niffu and Sobo groups which had remained loyal to the government. See Rydings Report of April 15, 1932, pp. 18–20, in Mitchell to the Secretary of State, May 3, 1932, USNA, RG59, 882.01/966.

10. Nimley (Sonpon Nabwe secretary) to Cecil, February 28, 1934, Cecil Papers, ADD 51101.

11. Mitchell to Stimson, November 27, 1931, enclosing Complaint of the Sasstown Tribe Made Before the Special Delegation Sent to Kru Coast by the President of Liberia to Make Peace, USNA, RG59, 882.00/910.

12. Rydings Report, Statement made by Paramount Chief Juah Nimley of the Sasstown Tribe, USNA, RG59, 882.00/966.

13. See Buell, "The Reconstruction of Liberia," 127.

14. Mitchell to Secretary of State, December 28, 1931, enclosing copy of a complaint of Chief Yourfee; copy of a complaint from the Gola section; copy of a complaint from the Kru Coast District, USNA, RG59, 882.915. See also Mitchell to Stimson, November 5, 1931, USNA, RG59, 882.00/899.

15. Mitchell to Secretary of State, January 22, 1932, enclosing clipping from *West African Review* for January, 1932, USNA, RG59, 882.00/932.

16. Thorgues Sie, et al. to Stimson, February 8, 1932, USNA, RG59, 882.00/920.

17. Mr. Graham to Sir John Simon (telegram), January 27, 1932, Great Britain, *Papers Concerning Affairs in Liberia*, no. 6.

18. Buell, "The Reconstruction of Liberia," 127.

19. Graham to Simon (telegram), March 9, 1932, enclosing Barclay to Graham, March 8, 1932, Great Britain, *Papers Concerning Affairs in Liberia*, no. 8.

20. Castle (telegram) to Reber (Geneva), April 26, 1932, regarding telegraphed paraphrase of Travell report sent from Monrovia by Minister Mitchell, USNA, RG59, 882.00/950.

21. For the report of Barclay's commission to the Kru Coast see Mitchell to Secretary of State, March 21, 1932, USNA, RG59, 882.00/941.

22. Mitchell to Secretary of State, May 3, 1932, enclosing Rydings Report, April 15, 1932, p. 23, USNA, RG59, 882.00/966. Rydings had an unauthorized meeting with Nimley.

23. Ibid.

24. Samuel Reber (Geneva) to Stimson, April 20, 1932, USNA, RG59, 882.00/949.

25. Grimes to Graham, June 16, 1932, Cecil Papers, ADD 51100.

26. Great Britain, *Papers Concerning Affairs in Liberia*, Chronological Survey, p. 4.

27. Werlich to Secretary of State, September 18, 1935, USNA, RG59, 882.00/991.

28. Extract from the Annual Message of President Barclay delivered before the Liberian Legislature on October 25, 1933, FO, 371/18041.

29. Walton to Phillips, September 14, 1934, enclosing Grimes to Walton, August 21, 1934, USNA, RG59, 882.00/1024.

30. McBride Memorandum (Washington), October 3, 1934, Annexed letter: Barclay (Sasstown) to Secretary of State (Monrovia), May 5, 1934, USNA, RG59, 882.01 FC/915.

31. Ibid.

32. Ibid.

33. Frank Walter (League of Nations) to William Stang, December 3, 1934, transmitting letter from Mackenzie, November 9, 1934, FO, 371/18043.

34. Yapp (Monrovia) to Foreign Office, October 23, 1934, FO, 371/18043. It was also reported that the Mano people had been driven back from the Bassa country and flogged by troops.

35. MacVeagh to Hull, April 30, 1934, USNA, RG59, 882.00/1018. The situation on the Kru Coast was only part of the problem. MacVeagh reported that "two Dutchmen employed by the Holland Syndicate, who have been prospecting for the past few months in the bush back of Bassa, have told their chief that they were horrified at the way the natives were treated by the District Commissioners who took from them of their rice and left them barely enough to live on."

36. MacVeagh, Chargé d'affaires ad interim, to Secretary of State, March 5, 1934, USNA, RG59, 882.00/1006. Cooper took twenty-six prisoners from the Wissepo tribe and fifty-three from the Geoh tribe.

37. MacVeagh to Hull, April 17, 1934, USNA, RG59, 882.00/1010.

38. Foreign Office Minute (Sir John Simon), March 15, 1934, FO, 371/18040. Simon wanted much stronger action than most of the functionaries in the Foreign Office had hitherto envisaged. An anonymous minute spoke of Simon's "sending eventually one of H. M. ships to Liberia—after the May [1934] meeting."

39. Sir John Simon to Routh (Monrovia), telegram, March 16, 1934, Great Britain, *Papers Concerning Affairs in Liberia*, no. 16.

40. Great Britain, *Parliamentary Debates* (Lords), 5th series, XCI (1934), 754–755.

41. Great Britain, *Papers Concerning Affairs in Liberia*, no. 19, Seventy-ninth Session of the Council of the League of Nations, Extract from Final Minutes of the 4th Meeting, Public, held on May 18 [1934], Geneva.

42. Simpson, *Memoirs*, 87.

43. Sir John Simon to Lindsay, May 29, 1934, Great Britain, *Papers Concerning Affairs in Liberia*, no. 20.

44. MacVeagh to Hull, April 17, 1934, USNA, RG59, 882.00/1010.

45. Memorandum of conversation between Butterworth (third secretary of the U.S. embassy) and Peterson, May 4, 1934, FO, 371/1804. The American chargé in Monrovia was suspicious of British intentions and mentioned the fact that his opposite number had alluded to the sending of a naval vessel. (MacVeagh to Secretary of State, March 5, 1934, USNA, RG59, 882.00/1007.) See also Routh to Foreign Office, April 19, 1934, FO, 371/18041.

46. Yapp to Foreign Office, October 23, 1934 (Minute by Wallinger), FO, 371/18043.

47. Fitzsimmons to Thompson, November–, 1934 (Minute of meeting between Wallinger, Thompson, and Fitzsimmons, November 28, 1934), FO, 371/18043.

48. Sir John Simon to Lindsay, December 18, 1934, FO, 371/18043.

49. Yapp to Foreign Office, April 3, 1935, FO, 371/19232.

50. Lindsay (Washington) to Foreign Office, April 4, 1935, FO, 371/19232.

51. Hibbard to McBride, April 19, 1935, USNA, RG59, 882.01 FC/945 1/2.

52. Ibid., May 4, 1935, enclosing Yapp to Paramount Chief Nimley of Old Sasstown, April 20, 1935, USNA, RG59, 882.00/1030 1/2.

53. Ibid., enclosing Yapp to Simpson (Liberian Department of State), April 20, 1935, and Simpson to Yapp, May 1, 1935, USNA, RG59, 882.00/1030 1/2.

54. Ibid.

55. Yapp to Foreign Office, October 22, 1934, press clipping from *West African Review*, October, 1934, FO, 371/18043.

56. De Long to Lady Simon, May 18, 1936, enclosing Chieftains Council of Assembly (Sasstown hinterland), An Appeal, March 15, 1936, British Anti-Slavery and Aborigines Protection Society Papers, London.

57. Hibbard to McBride, April 19, 1935, USNA, RG59 882.01 FC/945 1/2.

58. Ibid. Hibbard added that these grievances were "often more fancied than real, but the vivid African imagination makes them into a horrible and terrifying picture."

59. Ibid.

60. Hibbard to Harry (McBride?), April 19, 1935, USNA, RG59, 882.01 FC/945 1/2.

61. G. H. Thompson (Foreign Office) to A. H. Wiggin (Washington embassy), December 31, 1934, Foreign Office, Consulate-General, Monrovia, Northwestern University microfilm, roll 2.

62. Lindsay (British embassy, Washington) to Hull, January 17, 1935, USNA, RG59, 882.01 FC/937. See Moffat Papers, Memoranda, 1934–35, vol. 23, January 25, 1935.

63. Yapp to Foreign Office, May 13, 1935, Situation in Liberia, Minute by Thompson, May 14, 1935, FO, 371/19233.

64. Hibbard to McBride, May 4, 1935, USNA, , 882.00/1030 1/2.

65. Ibid. Liberian politician Louis Grimes took note of British interest in Liberian mineral resources and wrote: "You may have read that recently gold, platinum and diamonds have been discovered in the Sierra Leone protectorate. Their geologists have still more recently advised that the central lode is in Galahun [Liberia] . . . [as] the branches of a tree . . . to its parent trunk. The Consolidated African Selection Trust Co., a British mining concern, has, in the meantime offered to give the Sierra Leone Government £100,000 per annum for permission to work Galahun which they voluntarily transferred to us for a valuable consideration in 1909." (Walton to Phillips, September 14, 1934, enclosing L. A. Grimes to Emily S. Balch, July 23, 1934, USNA, RG59, 882.00/1024. See also Hibbard to Secretary of State, September 16, 1935, USNA, RG59 711.82/47 and 841.6367.)

66. Minute by Thompson of Foreign Office on Yapp (Monrovia) to Foreign Office, April 30, 1935, FO, 371/19233.

67. Minute (August 23, 1935) by Thompson on Yapp (on leave in England) to Thompson, August 16, 1935, FO, 371/19233.

68. Yapp to R. I Campbell (Foreign Office), March 3, 1936, FO, 371/20213.

69. Lindsay (Washington) to Foreign Office, n.d., Minute by W. R. Rich, FO, 371/19233.

70. Hibbard to McBride, April 19, 1935, FO, 882.01 FC/945 1/2.

71. John H. Harris, "Liberian Slavery: The Essentials," reprinted from *The Contemporary Review*, March, 1931, Anti-Slavery and Aborigines Protection Society Papers, London.

72. Sir John Harris (Anti-Slavery and Aborigines Protection Society) to Ronald (Foreign Office), June 15, 1934, FO, 371/18041.

73. Harris to A. Cartwright to Harris, February 8, 1935; Harris to Eppstein (League of Nations Union), February 13, 1935, Anti-Slavery Papers, Rhodes House, Oxford, no. 6490.

74. *Anti-Slavery Reporter and Aborigines Friend*, Series 5, XXV, 4 (January, 1936).

75. Cecil to Anthony Eden, August 31, 1936, FO, 377/2013.

76. S. Reber (Geneva) to Secretary of State, April 13, 1934, USNA, RG59, 882.00/1011.

77. "In Re the Petition of the Kroo Community of Accra on Behalf of Their Chiefs . . . and Kinsfolk of the Republic of Liberia . . . to the Secretary-General of the Council of the League of Nations, June 23, 1934," Cecil Papers, ADD 51130.

78. J. Royal(?) to Sir John Simon, July 13, 1934, FO, 371/18042.

79. F. O. Hefty (Bureau International pour la Defense des Indigène) to Simon, July 3, 1934, FO, 371/18041. Yapp to Foreign Office, September 3, 1934, FO, 371/18042; Frank Walters (League of Nations) to William Strong, Foreign Office, n.d., FO, 371/18043.

80. Juah Nimley (Sonpon Nabwe, secretary) to Cecil, February 28, 1934, Cecil Papers, ADD 51101.

81. Ibid., August 6, 1934.

82. Yapp to Foreign Office, transmitting copy of letter from Nimley, February 13, 1935, FO, 371/19232.

83. W. E. De Lang (Paris) to Lady Simon, May 13, 1936, Anti-Slavery and Aborigines Protection Society Papers, London.

84. Private Secretary Colonial Office to Foreign Office, transmitting a copy

of Mrs. F. M. Morgan to the Archbishop of Canterbury, containing a copy of C. J. Julius to D. Twe, June 13, 1936, FO, 371/20213.

85. Minute by I. M. Pink on C. J. Julius to A. Eden (received August 25, 1936), FO, 371/2013. A similar petition was received from J. T. Nelson on September 7.

86. Yapp to Foreign Office, July 12, 1936, FO, 371/2012.

87. Minute by I. M. Pink on Private Secretary Colonial Office to Foreign Office, August 11, 1936, FO, 371/2013.

88. Yapp to Eden, October 29, 1936, FO, 371/20213.

89. Ibid.

90. Wharton (telegram) to Secretary of State, October 29, 1936, USNA, RG59, 882.00/1044.

91. Yapp to Foreign Office, November 6, 1936 (transmits copies of the Annual Message of the President of Liberia delivered before the legislature on October 28, 1936), FO, 371/2013.

92. McBride Memorandum (Washington), October 3, 1934, USNA, RG59, 882.01 FC/915.

93. Twe to Johnson, December 1, 1930, Johnson Papers, box 88, file 13.

94. Mitchell to Stimson, April 28, 1932, enclosing Twe to Mitchell, April 22, 1932, USNA, RG59, 882.00/965. See also Yapp to Simon, February 20, 1935, FO, 371/19235.

95. Mitchell to Stimson, April 28, 1932, enclosing Twe to Mitchell, April 22, 1932, USNA, RG59, 882.00/965.

96. Yapp to Foreign Office, February 20, 1935, Liberian Personalities, FO, 371/19235. The consulate also indicated that he had once been charged with murder.

97. Clifton R. Wharton, Chargé d'Affaires ad interim, to Secretary of State, January 28, 1927, USNA, RG59, 882.00/762 (microfilm M613, location 10-14-5).

98. MacVeagh, Chargé d'Affaires ad interim, to Secretary of State, March 5, 1934, and Faulkner to MacVeagh, February 28, 1934, USNA, RG59, 882.00/1006.

99. Eppstein (League of Nations Union) to Wallinger, October 4, 1934, enclosing two letters from Twe to Mrs. Florence Morgan in England, FO, 371/18042. The letter of September 10, 1934 advocated an uprising.

100. Yapp to Thompson, January 8, 1935, FO, 371/19232.

101. Twe to Cecil, October 8, 1934, Cecil Papers, ADD 51101.

102. Cecil to Twe, October 22, 1934, Cecil Papers, ADD 51101.

103. Twe to Harris, February 6, 1935, British Anti-Slavery and Aborigines Protection Society Papers, Rhodes House, Oxford, no. 6490.

104. See Graham Greene, *Journey Without Maps* (London, 1936).

105. Yapp to Foreign Office, January 26, 1936, FO, 371/20213. In May of 1936 it was reported that since his return, Twe had continued to give aid and encouragement to rebels (I. Whisant to E. Barclay, August 29, 1936, Liberian National Archives).

106. Stephen Hlophe, "The Significance of Barth and Geertz' Model of Ethnicity in the Analysis of Nationalism in Liberia," *Canadian Journal of African Studies*, VII, 2 (1973), 251.

107. Fraenkel, "Social Change on the Kru Coast," 155.

108. Akpan, "The African Policy," 106.

109. Ibid.

110. Al-Haj Massaquoi to Lady Simon, October 3, 1931, British Anti-Slavery and Aborigines Protection Society Papers, London. Al-Haj was at University College in Dublin and requested financial assistance from Lady Simon to continue his studies.

111. Mitchell to Stimson, November 27, 1931, enclosing D. W. Herman, Chairman, Special Delegation (to Kru Coast), to Barclay, October 26, 1931, USNA, RG59, 882.00/910.

112. McBride Memorandum, October 3, 1934, Annexed Memorandum of the Government of Liberia on the Kru Situation, USNA, RG59, 882.01 FC/915.

113. Kru Prisoners in Sinoe Jail to J. R. Sorbor (Sierra Leone), April 19, 1933, Phelps-Stokes Archives, box 47, S-5. Sorbor had escaped from Monrovia.

114. Akpan, "The African Policy," 469. P. G. Wolo was another prominent indigenous dissident.

115. Report on Leading Personalities in Liberia, including additions received in the Foreign Office up to January 30, 1930, G. Rule (Monrovia) to Foreign Office, December 21, 1930, FO, 371/14658. The consulate further noted of Massaquoi: "About 45 years of age (1927). An educated Vai Chief of considerable intelligence, but unscrupulous and thoroughly dishonest, as several English firms have reason to know. Unfavorably known to the authorities in Sierra Leone. An intriguer with political aspirations. Believed to have been concerned in the abortive attempt to overthrow the Government in January 1927."

116. Great Britain, *Parliamentary Debates* (Lords), 5th series, XCI (1934), 926.

117. Yapp to Foreign Office, February 20, 1935, FO, 371/19235.

118. Azikiwe, *Liberia in World Politics*, 337.

119. Mitchell to Stimpson, November 5, 1931, enclosing Faulkner to Mitchell, October 22, 1931, USNA, RG59, 822.00/899. The men arrested included "Dr. Sie, a Graduate of Chicago, of Grebo tribe, influential among his people. W. T. Sancea, a Liberian influential among the natives, strong supporter of Dr. Morais, influential among the natives and was elected by them for representative in the recent election. . . ."

120. In the spring of 1934, Morais appeared to be still championing those rights. See F. O. Hefty (International Office for the Protection of Native Races, Geneva) to Department of State, July 17, 1934, enclosing letter from Morais to Henri A. Junod, May 9, 1934, USNA, RG59, 822.01 FC/870. In Liberia, Morais said the letter was not written by him (Harold Fredericks to Morais, July 7, 1934, Liberian National Archives).

121. League of Nations (C.460.M197.1934 VII), October 12, 1934, Annex: Morais to Fredericks, Superintendent, Maryland County, August 21, 1934, FO, 371/18043.

122. Yapp to Wallinger, February 4, 1935, enclsoing F. W. M. Morais, "My Role to the Life" [sic], *The Weekly Mirror* (Monrovia), December 21, 1934, p. 5, FO, 371/19232.

123. Yapp to Foreign Office, October 23, 1934, FO, 371/18043.

124. Yapp to Wallinger, February 4, 1935, enclosing copy of *The Weekly Mirror* (Monrovia), January 4, 1934, p. 4, FO, 371/19232.

125. Hibbard to McBride, April 19, 1935, USNA, RG59, 882.01 FC/945 1/2.

126. Mordecai Johnson to W. White, July 27, 1933, enclosing statement on Liberia by Charles Wesley and Rayford Logan, NAACP Papers, G-221.

127. White to Stimson, October 1, 1932, enclosing NAACP press release by Howard Oxley, USNA, RG59, 882.01 FC/383.

128. Azikiwe, *Liberia in World Politics*, 398.

129. Chalk, "DuBois and Garvey," 2.

130. W. E. B. DuBois, "Postscript from a Traveller," *The Crisis*, XXXIX (December, 1932), 387–388.

131. Taylor, "The Involvement of Black Americans," 62, citing Memorandum by Castle of conversation with DuBois, March 26, 1924, USNA, RG59, 882.000/742.

132. W. E. B. DuBois, "Postscript—Liberia," *The Crisis*, XXXIX (March, 1931), 102.

133. Ibid. Liberian Secretary of State Grimes made the same point in Geneva and maintained that the distinction between "civilized" and "uncivilized" was a specious one. Only one hundred settlers had initially arrived from America and now there were 12,000 Americo-Liberians. Assimilation was, in Grimes's eyes, the obvious reason for this growth. See Committee of the Council Appointed to Study the Problem Raised by the Liberian Government's Request for Assistance. . . . January 26, 1932, Grimes Papers, Liberia/League of Nations Papers, Pt. II, roll 1, c/Liberia/ 7C.

134. Azikiwe, *Liberia in World Politics*, 338n., citing the Baltimore *Afro-American*, August 20, 1932, p. 15.

135. Walter F. Walker, "Did the Liberian Natives Speak?" *The Crisis*, XLI (November, 1934), 340. See W. F. N. [*sic*] Morais, "Liberia Natives Tell Their Story," *The Crisis*, XLI (September, 1934), 272–273.

136. Azikiwe, *Liberia in World Politics*, 337.

137. Chalk, "DuBois and Garvey," quoting W. E. B. DuBois, *The Crisis*, XXVII (April, 1924), 248–251.

138. Ibid., citing George Schuyler, *The Crisis*, XXXVIII (March, 1931), 101–102.

139. George Schuyler, *Slaves Today* (New York, 1931), Preface.

140. George Schuyler, "Schuyler Exposes Liberia," New York *Amsterdam News*, July 15, 1931, NAACP Papers, C-335.

141. Henry L. West of the American Colonization Society praised them, as did Senator Henry F. Ashurst of Arizona. See "Liberian Series in Post Praised" (reference to the New York *Evening Post* of July 1, 1931), NAACP Papers, C-335.

142. Azikiwe, "In Defense of Liberia," 45. Answers to Schuyler's criticisms may be found in New York *Evening Post*, July 1, 1931; *Negro World*, July 18, 25, August 1, 8, 1931; also New York *News* and *Harlem Home Journal*, July 18, 1931.

143. Schuyler, "Slaves Today—Missionaries 'Wink' at Conditions in Liberia," Pittsburgh *Courier*, October 17, 1931, reprinted in *Apropos of Africa: Sentiments of Negro American Leaders on Africa from the 1800's to the 1950's*, ed. Adelaide Hill and Martin Kilson (London, 1969), 345.

144. Memorandum from White to Royal Davis, July 14, 1931, NAACP Papers, C-335.

145. Schuyler to White, October 20, 1931, NAACP Papers, C-335. Schuyler was very annoyed about the letter of one Roger Baldwin, who disagreed with Schuyler on the whole Liberian matter.

146. George Schuyler, "Views and Reviews," Pittsburgh *Courier*, October 8, 1932 (enclosure), USNA, RG59, 882.01 FC/407.

147. Ibid.

148. [George Schuyler], Pittsburgh *Courier*, October 12, 1932, NAACP Papers, G-220.

149. William Koren, "Liberia, the League and the United States," *Foreign Policy Reports* X, 1 (November 21, 1934), 247, citing George Schuyler, "Uncle Sam's Black Step-Child," Baltimore *Afro-American*, March 11, 1933.

150. Padmore, "Workers Defend Liberia," *The Negro Worker*, October–November, 1931, p. 10, Barnett Papers, Liberian News Releases, Miscellaneous, 1925–1950. To Padmore the struggle among Liberian politicians was a useless game in which rival imperialisms moved politicians back and forth at will. The competition between Faulkner and King had been nothing more than an epiphenomenon of the clash of British and American imperialism:

"The chief source [the British Bank of West Africa] from which King and his party got their funds to control the Government having been removed King was unable to put up any struggle against the opposition. The pro-American black politicians having ousted King immediately elected a provisional president to office in the person of Arthur Barkeley [sic], the very same faker who had served on the slavery commission on behalf of Liberia. The very first act of Barkeley [sic] in reward for the spoils of office was to issue permission to the Firestone Rubber Company to establish a bank in Monrovia in place of the defunct British establishment.

"Thus, within a period of a few weeks a 'bloodless revolution' took place in Liberia, in which the pro-American forces defeated their British opponents."

151. M. Nelson, "Liberia and Imperialism," *The Negro Worker*, IV, 3 (July, 1934), 19.

152. M. Nelson, "The Situation in Liberia," *The Negro Worker*, V, 5 (May, 1935), 24. See Isaac Wallace-Johnson, "Liberia Ahoy," *The Liberian Patriot* (Monrovia), VI, 12 (August 10, 1935), enclosed in Whittall (Monrovia) to Pink (Foreign Office), August 23, 1935, FO, 371/19234.

153. True Whig Party Memorandum, "The Significance of the Last Presidential Election," 1935(?), Liberian National Archives.

154. Special Committee of Citizens, Maryland County, to Barclay, September 8, 1931, Liberian National Archives.

155. G. Brewer (Harper) to Barclay, April 10, 1932, Liberian National Archives.

156. Fredericks to Barclay, April 26, 1932, Liberian National Archives.

157. Fredericks to Barclay, May 20, 1935, Liberian National Archives.

Conclusion

1. See Tuan Wreh, *The Love of Liberty: The Rule of President William V. S. Tubman in Liberia 1944–1971* (London, 1976), chap. 8.

2. See Ivor Wilks, *Asante in the Nineteenth Century* (New York, 1975), 650, 656, 722.

3. Christopher Clapham, *Liberia and Sierra Leone: An Essay in Comparative Politics* (New York, 1975), 105.

4. Johnetta Cole, "Traditional and Wage-Earning Labor Among Tribal Liberians" (Ph.D. diss., Northwestern University, 1967), 211, 215.

5. Jonathan Derrick, *Africa's Slaves Today* (London, 1975), 200.

6. Akpan, "The African Policy," 109, citing Department of the Interior, Monrovia, Decisions Rendered by the President of Liberia on Administrative and Other Matters, September, 1945.

7. Robert W. Clower, George Dalton, Michael Harwitz and A. A. Walters, *Growth Without Development* (Evanston, Illinois, 1966), 5.

8. Ibid., citing International Labor Organization Commission, *Report*, 222, 417. For a discussion of the present condition of Liberian labor, see Dew Tuan-Wleh Mayson and Amos Sawyer, "Capitalism and the Struggle of the Working Class in Liberia" (Paper delivered at the meeting of the Liberian Research Association, Buchanan, Liberia, June 24, 1978).

9. Stokely Carmichael, Interview in the *Sunday News* (Dar es Salaam), November 5, 1967, quoted by Locksley G. Edmundson, "Africa and the African Diaspora: The Years Ahead," in Ali Mazrui and Hasu Patel, eds., *Africa in World Affairs* (New York, 1973), 11.

10. C. L. R. James, quoted in Walter Rodney, *How Europeans Underdeveloped Africa* (London, 1972), 100.

11. Robert Chrisman, "Aspects of Pan-Africanism," *The Black Scholar*, IV (July–August, 1973), 10.

12. Langley, *Pan-Africanism and Nationalism*, 369.

13. Geiss, *The Pan-African Movement*, 260.

14. Buell, *Liberia*, 19.

Select Bibliography

I. Primary Sources

GOVERNMENTAL ARCHIVAL AND MANUSCRIPT SOURCES

Public Record Office, London
  Foreign Office, 72/1626
  Foreign Office, 367/16, 17, 61
  Foreign Office, 47/36 Liberia
  Foreign Office, 371
  Foreign Office, 368/1632
  Foreign Office, 458 (Correspondence between the Foreign Office and the British Consulate-General in Monrovia)
  Foreign Office, 458/104–458/127 (Correspondence from the Consulate-General, Monrovia, Liberia), available on microfilm, Northwestern University Library, Evanston, Illinois
Liberian National Archives, Ashmun St., Monrovia, Liberia
U.S. National Archives, Washington, D.C. Department of State. Record Group 59: General Records of the Department of State
  Records of the Department of State Relating to the Internal Affairs of Liberia, 1910–1941
  Records of the Department of State Relating to the Political Relations of Liberia with the United States, 1910–1941
  Records of the Department of State Relating to the Affairs of Liberia, 1910–1929. Political Affairs. Washington, D.C., 1965. Available on microfilm, Northwestern University Library, Evanston, Illinois

OTHER ARCHIVAL AND MANUSCRIPT SOURCES

Barnett, Claude. Papers. Chicago Historical Society. Chicago, Illinois.
British Anti-Slavery and Aborigines Protection Society Archives. London, England. (The vast majority of the society's papers are at Rhodes House, Oxford University.)
British Anti-Slavery and Aborigines Protection Society Papers. Rhodes House, Oxford University, Oxford, England.

Cassell, C. Abayomi. Papers. Microfilm (filmed by African Imprint Library Services, Bedford, N.Y.). Northwestern University Library, Evanston, Illinois.

Cecil, Viscount. The Papers of Viscount Cecil of Chelwood. British Museum (ADD 51071–204). London, England.

Grimes, Louis B. Papers. Microfilm (filmed by African Imprint Library Services, Bedford, N.Y.). Northwestern University Library, Evanston, Illinois; Part I, roll 1; Part I, roll 2: Liberia/League of Nations Papers; Part II, roll 3: Liberia/League of Nations Papers; Part III: Newspapers.

Johnson, Charles S. Papers. Fisk University Library, Nashville, Tennessee.

Methodist Missionary Society Archives. London, England.

Moffat, J. Pierrepont. Papers. Houghton Library, Harvard University, Cambridge, Massachusetts.

National Association for the Advancement of Colored People. Records. Library of Congress, Washington, D.C.

Phelps-Stokes Fund Archives. New York, New York.

Phillips, William. Papers. Houghton Library, Harvard University, Cambridge, Massachusetts.

Porte, Albert. Papers. Microfilm (filmed by African Imprint Library Services, Bedford, N.Y.). Northwestern University Library, Evanston, Illinois. Roll 1, Personal Papers and Documents.

Simon, Lady Kathleen. Papers. Manuscripts. British Empire S25. Rhodes House, Oxford, England.

PUBLIC DOCUMENTS

Great Britain. *Papers Concerning Affairs in Liberia, December, 1930–May, 1934.* Cmd. 4614 (1934). London: His Majesty's Stationery Office, 1934.

Great Britain. *Parliamentary Debates* (Lords). 5th series. Vols. LXXXI, LXXXIII, XCI.

League of Nations. Secretariat. *Report of the Liberian Commission of Enquiry,* C.658.M272, June, 1930.

U.S. Department of State. *Foreign Relations of the United States,* 1910–1941. Washington: U.S. Government Printing Office. Published annually.

II. Secondary Sources

BOOKS AND PAMPHLETS

Allen, William, and Thompson, Thomas. *Narratives of the Expedition Sent by Her Majesty's Government to the River Niger . . . .* 2 vols. New York: Johnson Reprint Corp., 1967.

Anderson, R. Earle. *Liberia: America's African Friend.* Chapel Hill, N.C.: University of North Carolina Press, 1952.

Arija, Julio. *La Guinea española y sus riquezas.* Madrid: España Colpe, 1930.

Azikiwe, Benjamin Nnamdi. *Liberia in World Politics.* London: A. W. Stockwell, 1935.

Behrens, Christine. *Les Kroumen de la côte occidentale d'Afrique.* Travaux et documents de geographie tropicales, no. 18, Centre d'Études de Geographie Tropicale (CNRS). Talence, France: Domaine Universaire de Bordeaux, 1974.

Brandes, Jospeh. *Herbert Hoover and Economic Diplomacy*. Pittsburgh: University of Pittsburgh Press, 1962.

Bravo Carbonel, Juan. *Fernando Po y el Muni, sus misterios y riquezas* . . . . Madrid: Imprenta de "Alrededor del Mundo," 1917.

Brooks, George E. *The Kru Mariner in the Nineteenth Century*. Newark, Del.: Liberian Studies Association, 1972.

Brown, George W. *Economic History of Liberia*. Washington, D.C.: Associated Publishers, 1941.

Buell, Raymond Leslie. *Liberia: A Century of Survival, 1847–1947*. Philadelphia: University of Pennsylvania Press, 1947.

————. *The Native Problem in Africa*. 2 vols. New York: Macmillan Co., 1928.

Campbell, Penelope. *Maryland in Africa: The Maryland State Colonization Society, 1831–1857*. Chicago: University of Illinois Press, 1971.

Church, R. J. Harrison. *Africa and the Islands*. New York: John Wiley and Sons, 1964.

Clapham, Christopher. *Liberia and Sierra Leone: An Essay in Comparative Politics*. New York: Cambridge University Press, 1975.

Clower, Robert W., Dalton, George, Harwitz, Mitchell, and Walters, A. A. *Growth Without Development*. Evanston: Northwestern University Press, 1966.

Cookey, S. J. S. *Britain and the Congo Question*. New York: Humanities Press, 1968.

Cronon, E. David. *Black Moses: The Story of Marcus Garvey and the Universal Negro Improvement Association*. Madison, Wis.: University of Wisconsin Press, 1957.

Davis, Ronald. *Ethnohistorical Studies on the Kru Coast*. Newark, Del.: Liberian Studies Association, 1976.

de la Rue, Sidney. *Land of the Pepper Bird: Liberia*. New York: G. P. Putnam's Sons, 1930.

Derrick, Jonathan. *Africa's Slaves Today*. London: George Allen and Unwin, 1975.

Detzer, Dorothy. *Appointment on the Hill*. New York: Henry Holt and Co., 1948.

Fax, Elton. *Garvey: The Story of a Pioneer Black Nationalist*. New York: Dodd, Mead and Co., 1972.

Fleming, G. James, and Burckel, Christian, eds. *Who's Who in Colored America*. 7th edition. Yonkers on Hudson, N.Y.: Christian E. Burckel and Assoc., 1950.

Fraenkel, Merran. *Tribe and Class in Monrovia*. Oxford: Oxford University Press for the International African Institute, 1964.

Geiss, Imanuel. *The Pan-African Movement*. New York: Africana Publishing Co., 1974.

Greenwall, Harry James, and Wild, Roland. *Unknown Liberia*. London: Hutchinson and Co., 1936.

Haliburton, Gordon. *The Prophet Harris*. New York: Oxford University Press, 1973.

Haywood, Harry. *Black Bolshevik: Autobiography of an Afro-American Communist*. Chicago: Liberator Press, 1978.

Hill, Adelaide Cromwell, and Kilson, Martin. *Apropos of Africa: Sentiments of Negro American Leaders on Africa from the 1800's to the 1950's*. London: Frank Cass and Co., 1969.

Hill, Polly. *Migrant Cocoa Farmers of Southern Ghana*. Cambridge: Cambridge University Press, 1963.

Hooker, J. R. *Black Revolutionary: George Padmore's Path from Communism to Pan-Africanism*. London: Pall Mall, 1967.

Hopkins, A. G. *An Economic History of West Africa*. New York: Cambridge University Press, 1973.

Langley, J. Ayodele. *Pan-Africanism and Nationalism in West Africa, 1900–1945*. London: Oxford University Press, 1973.

Liebenow, J. Gus. *Liberia: The Evolution of Privilege*. Ithaca, N.Y.: Cornell University Press, 1969.

Lief, Alfred. *The Firestone Story*. New York: McGraw-Hill, 1951.

Louis, William R., and Stengers, Jean. *E. D. Morel's History of the Congo Reform Movement*. Oxford: Clarendon Press, 1968.

Lowenkopf, Martin. *Politics in Liberia*. Stanford, Calif.: Hoover Institution, 1976.

Madariaga, Salvador de. *Americans*. London: Oxford University Press, 1930.

Mantero, Francisco. *Portuguese Planters and British Humanitarians: The Case for S. Thome*. Lisbon: Redaccão de Reforma, 1911.

Mecklenburg, Adolf Friederich, Duke of. *From the Congo to the Niger and the Nile*. London: Duckworth and Co., 1913.

Moreno-Moreno, José A. *Reseña histórica de la presencia de España en el Golfo de Guinea*. Madrid: Consejo Superior de Investigaciones Cientificas, Instituto de Estudios Africanos, 1952.

Nevinson, H. W. *A Modern Slavery*. London & New York: Harper and Bros., 1906.

Padmore, George. *American Imperialism Enslaves Liberia*. Moscow: Centirzdat, 1931.

———. *Pan-Africanism or Communism*. London: Dennis Dobson, 1956.

Ramos-Izquierdo y Vivar, Luis. *Descripción geográfica y gobierno, administración y colonización de las colonias españolas del Golfo de Guniea*. Madrid: Impenta de Felipe Peña Cruz, 1912.

Redkey, Edwin. *Black Exodus: Black Nationalist and Back-to-Africa Movements, 1890–1910*. New Haven: Yale University Press, 1969.

Reeve, Henry F. *The Black Republic*. London: H. F. & G. Witherby, 1923.

Rodney, Walter. *How Europe Underdeveloped Africa*. London: Bogle l'Overture Publications, 1972.

Rudwick, Elliot M. *W. E. B. DuBois: Propagandist of the Negro Protest*. New York: Atheneum, 1968.

Schuyler, George. *Slaves Today*. New York: Brewer, Warren and Putnum, 1931.

Shepherd, George W., Jr., ed. *Racial Influences on American Foreign Policy*. New York: Basic Books, 1970.

Sibley, James L., and Westermann, D. *Liberia—Old and New*. Garden City, N.Y.: Doubleday, 1928.

Simon, Kathleen. *Slavery*. New York: Negro Universities Press, 1969.

Simpson, Clarence. *Memoirs: The Symbol of Liberia*. London: Diplomatic Press and Publishing Co., 1961.

Smith, Robert A. *The American Foreign Policy in Liberia*. Monrovia: Providence Publications, 1972.

Strong, Richard, ed. *The African Republic of Liberia and the Belgian Congo*. 2 vols. Cambridge: Harvard University Press, 1930.

Suret-Canale, Jean. *French Colonialism in Tropical Africa, 1900–1945*. London: C. Hurst and Co., 1971.

Taylor, Wayne Chatfield. *The Firestone Operations in Liberia*. Washington, D.C.: National Planning Association, 1956.

Teran, Manuel de. *Síntesis geográfica de Fernando Póo*. Madrid: Instituto de Estudios Africanos, 1962.

Unzueta, Abelardo de. *Geografía histórica de la Isla de Fernando Póo*. Madrid: Consejo Superior de Investigaciones Científicas, Instituto de Estudios Africanos, 1947.

Vincent, Theodore. *Black Power and the Garvey Movement*. Berkeley, Calif.: Ramparts Press, n.d.

Von Gnielinski, Stefan. *Liberia in Maps*. London: University of London Press, 1972.

Weisbord, Robert. *Ebony Kinship*. Westport, Conn.: Greenwood Press, 1973.

West, Henry. *The Liberian Crisis*. Washington, D.C.: American Colonization Society, 1933.

Wilks, Ivor. *Asante in the Nineteenth Century*. New York: Cambridge University Press, 1975.

Williams, Walter B. and Maude W. *Adventures with the Krus in West Africa*. New York: Vantage Press, 1955.

Woodson, Carter G. *The African Background Outlined: Or, Handbook for the Study of the Negro*. Washington, D.C.: Association for the Study of Negro Life and History, 1936.

Work, Monroe N., ed. *The Negro Year Book, 1931–1932*.Tuskegee, Ala.: Alabama Negro Yearbook Publishing Co.. 1931.

Wreh, Tuan. *The Love of Liberty: The Rule of President William V. S. Tubman in Liberia 1944–1971*. London: C. Hurst and Co., 1976.

Yancy, Ernest Jerome. *Historic Lights of Liberia Yesterday and Today*. 3d ed. Tel-Aviv, Israel: Around the World Publishing House, c. 1967.

————. *The Recent Liberian Crisis and Its Causes*. Buffalo, N.Y.: Buffalo Liberian Research Society, 1934.

Yenser, Thomas, ed. *Who's Who in Colored America*. 6th ed. New York: Thomas Yenser, 1944.

Young, James Capers. *Liberia Rediscovered*. Garden City, N.Y.: Doubleday, Doran and Co., 1934.

JOURNAL AND NEWSPAPER ARTICLES

Akpan, M. B. "Black Imperialism: Americo-Liberian Rule over the African Peoples of Liberia, 1841–1964." *The Canadian Journal of African Studies*, VII, 2 (1973), 217–236.

————. "Liberia and the Universal Negro Improvement Association: The Background to the Abortion of Garvey's Scheme for African Colonization." *Journal of African History*, XIV, 1 (1973), 105–127.

Azikiwe, Benjamin Nnamdi. "In Defense of Liberia." *Journal of Negro History*, XVII, 1 (January, 1932), 30–50.

————."Liberia and World Diplomacy." *The Southern Workman*, LXI (May, 1932), 229–232.

————. "Liberia Declares a Moratorium." *The Southern Workman*, LXII (June, 1933), 276–280.

Barclay, Edwin. "The Case of Liberia." *The Crisis*, XLI (February, 1934), 40–42.

Benson, W. "After Liberia." *Political Quarterly*, II, 2 (April, 1931), 257–266.

Berg, Elliot. "The Development of a Labor Force in Sub-Saharan Africa." *Economic Development and Cultural Change*, XIII, 4, pt. 1 (July, 1965), 394–412.

Bravo Carbonel, Juan. "Possibilidades económicas de la Guinea Española." *Boletín de la Sociedad Geográfica Nacional*, LXXIII, 8 (August, 1933), 524–547.

Browder, Earl. "Earl Browder Replies," *The Crisis*, XL, 12 (December, 1935), 372.

Buell, Raymond Leslie. "The Liberian Paradox." *The Virginia Quarterly Review*, VII (April, 1931), 161–175.

———. "Mr. Firestone's Liberia." *The Nation*, CXXVI, 3278 (May 2, 1928), 521–524.

———. "The New Deal and Liberia." *The New Republic*, LXXVI (August 16, 1933), 17–19.

———. "The Reconstruction of Liberia." *Foreign Policy Reports*, VIII (August 3, 1932), 120–124.

Buxton, Charles R. "Improvement in Liberia." *The Crisis*, XLII, 2 (March, 1935), 92.

Cassell, Nathaniel H. B. "Liberia Defended by a Liberian." *Current History*, XXXIV (September, 1931), 880–882.

Chalk, Frank. "The Anatomy of an Investment: Firestone's 1927 Loan to Liberia." *Canadian Journal of African Studies*, I, 1 (March, 1967), 12–32.

———. "Du Bois and Garvey Confront Liberia: Two Incidents of the Coolidge Years." *Canadian Journal of African Studies*, I, 2 (November, 1967), 135–142.

Chrisman, Robert. "Aspects of Pan-Africanism." *The Black Scholar*, IV, 10 (July–August, 1973), 2–8.

Christy, Cuthbert. "Liberia in 1930, with Discussion." *The Geographical Journal*, LXXVII (1931).

"Clearing up the Liberian Mess." *The Christian Century*, XLVIII, 5 (February 4, 1931), 156.

DuBois, W. E. B. "Liberia and Rubber." *The New Republic*, XLIV, 572 (November 18, 1925), 326–329.

———. "Liberia, the League and the United States." *Foreign Affairs*, XI, 4 (July, 1933), 682–695.

———. "Pan-Africa and New Racial Philosophy." *The Crisis*, XL (November, 1933), 247–262.

———"Postscript—From a Traveller." *The Crisis*, XXXIX (December, 1932), 387–388.

———. "Postscript—Liberia." *The Crisis*, XXXIX (March, 1931), 102.

[DuBois, W. E. B.] "Again, Liberia." *The Crisis*, XL (October, 1933), 236.

———. "Stand Fast, Liberia." *The Crisis*, XL (November, 1933), 260–261.

Duffield, Ian. "Pan-Africanism, Rational and Irrational." Review of *The Pan-African Movement*, by Imanuel Geiss. *Journal of African History*, XVIII, 4 (1977), 597–620.

"Forced Labor in Liberia." *The Nation*, CXXX, 3373 (February, 26, 1930), 256.

Fraenkel, Merran. "Social Change on the Kru Coast of Liberia." *Africa*, XXVI (1966), 154–172.

Gilpin, Patrick J. "Charles S. Johnson: Scholar and Educator." *Negro History Bulletin*, XXXIX, 3 (March, 1976), 544–548.

Gutherey-Sobral, José. "The Outlook at Fernando Po." *West Africa*, XI, 1 (March 2, 1901), 334–336.

Hallgren, Mauritz A. "Liberia in Shackles." *The Nation*, CXXXVII (August 16, 1933), 185–188.

Hayden, Thomas. "A Description of the 1970 Grand Cess Bo." *Liberian Studies Journal*, IV, 2 (1971–1972), 183–188.

Hlophe, Stephen. "The Significance of Barth and Geertz' Model of Ethnicity in the Analysis of Nationalism in Liberia." *Canadian Journal of African Studies*, VII, 2 (1973), 237–256.

Hooker, J. R. "The Negro American Press and Africa in the Nineteen Thirties." *Canadian Journal of African Studies*, I (March, 1967), 43–50.

Ivy, James W. "A Negro's View of Liberia." Letter to the editor, *The Nation*, CXXXVII (December 6, 1933), 653.

Koren, William. "Liberia, the League and the United States." *Foreign Policy Reports*, X, 1 (November 21, 1934), 239–248.

Kornegay, Francis. "Africa and Presidential Politics." *Africa Report*, XXI, 4 (July–August, 1976), 7–20.

Kuyper, George Adrian. "Liberia and the League of Nations." *The Southern Workman*, LXIII (April, 1934), 112–117.

"Liberia," Editorial in *The Southern Workman*, LXIII (April, 1934), 99–100.

"The Liberian Commission." *Opportunity*, XI, 1 (January, 1931), 6.

"Liberian Slavery." *The Spectator*, V, 349 (Janaury 3, 1931), 68–69.

Logan, Rayford. "Liberia's Dilemma." *The Southern Workman*, LXII (September, 1933), 357–363.

Morais, W. M. "Liberian Natives Tell Their Story." *The Crisis*, XLI (September, 1934), 272–273.

Mower, J. H. "The Republic of Liberia." *Journal of Negro History*, XXXII, 3 (July, 1947), 265–306.

"No Rubber Peonage." *The Outlook*, CXLIX, 16 (August 8, 1928), 607.

Obatala, J. K. "Liberia: The Meaning of Dual Citizenship." *The Black Scholar*, IV, 10 (July–August, 1973), 16–19.

Padgett, J. A. "American Ministers to Liberia and Their Diplomacy." *Journal of Negro History*, XXII (January, 1937), 50–92.

Padmore, George. "Forced Labor in Africa." *Labor Monthly*, XIII, 4 (April, 1937), 237–247.

———. "Hands Off Liberia." *The Negro Worker*, October–November, 1931, p. 10.

———. "An Open Letter to Earl Browder." *The Crisis*, XLII, 10 (October, 1935), 302, 315.

———. "Workers Defend Liberia." *The Negro Worker*, October–November, 1931, p. 10.

"Proceedings of the Annual Meeting of the Association for the Study of Negro Life and History Held in New York City, November 8–12, 1931." *Journal of Negro History*, XVII, 1 (January, 1932), 1–7.

"The Regeneration of Liberia." *Opportunity*, IX (February, 1931), 38.

Renner, G. T. "Liberia Where America Meets Africa." *Home Geographic Monthly*, I (April, 1932), 31–36.

Schuyler, George. "More About Liberia." Letter to the editor, *The Crisis*, XLI (December, 1934), 375–376.

———"Wide 'Slavery' Persisting in Liberia, *Post* Reveals." New York *Evening Post*, June 29, 1931, p. 1.

"Slavery and Forced Labor in Liberia." *International Labor Review*, XXIII (April, 1931), 533–547.

"Slavery in Liberia." *The Economist*, CXII, 4, 560 (January 17, 1931), 105–106.

Smith, Rennie. "Negro Self-Government at a Crisis in Liberia." *Current History*, XXXIV (August, 1931), 732–736.

Sullivan, Mary Jo. Review of *Ethnohistorical Studies on the Kru Coast*, by Ronald Davis. *Journal of African History*, XIX, 2 (1978), 280–282.

Taylor, R. R. "Looking Over Liberia." *The Southern Workman*, LIX (March, 1930), 122–131.

Tonkin, Elizabeth. Review of *Ethnohistorical Studies on the Kru Coast*, by Ronald Davis. *The International Journal of African Historical Studies*, X, 3 (1977), 533–535.

Walker, Walter F. "Did the Liberian Natives Speak?" *The Crisis*, XLI (November, 1934), 340.

Walton, Lester. "Liberia's New Industrial Development." *Current History*, XXX, 1 (April, 1929), 108–114.

"War in Liberia: Kru King Captured as Beaten Tribesmen Die in Jungle." *Literary Digest*, CXXII (November 7, 1936), 15–16.

ESSAYS, PAPERS, AND UNPUBLISHED MANUSCRIPTS

Breitborde, L. B. "Some Linguistic Evidence in the Study of Kru Ethnolinguistic Affiliation." Paper delivered at the Ninth Annual Conference, Liberian Studies Association, Macomb, Illinois, April, 1977.

Coger, Dalvan. "Black American Immigration to Liberia, 1900–1930." Paper delivered at the Eighth Annual Conference, Liberian Studies Association, Bloomington, Indiana, March, 1976.

Edmundson, Locksley. "Africa and the African Diaspora: The Years Ahead." In *Africa in World Affairs: The Next Thirty Years*, edited by Ali A. Mazrui and H. S. H. Petel. New York: The Third Press, 1973.

Emerson, Rupert. "Race in Africa: United States Foreign Policy." In *Racial Influences on American Foreign Policy*, edited by George W. Shepherd, Jr. New York: Basic Books, 1970.

Frazier, E. Franklin. "Potential American Negro Contributions to African Social Development." In *Africa from the Point of View of American Negro Scholars*, edited by John A. Davis. Paris: Présence Africaine, 1959.

Hargreaves, J. D. "African Colonization in the Nineteenth Century: Liberia and Sierra Leone." *Boston University Papers in African History*, Vol. I. Boston: Boston University Press, 1964.

Haywood, Harry. Unpublished autobiographical manuscript draft, Chapter 13: "Eighth Convention, Description of Eighth Convention of the Communist Party of the United States, Cleveland, Ohio, April 2–8, 1934."

Johnson, Charles. "Bitter Canaan: The Story of Liberia." Nashville, Tenn.: Department of Social Science, 1930.

Mayson, Dew Tuan-Wleh, and Amos Sawyer. "Capitalism and the Struggle of the Working Class in Liberia." Paper delivered at the meeting of the Liberian Research Association, Buchanan, Liberia, June 23, 1978.

Schmokel, Wolfe. "The United States and the Crisis of Liberian Independence." *Boston University Papers on Africa*, Vol. II. Boston: Boston University Press, 1966.

Sullivan, Mary Jo. "Sinoe Settler Politics in the Late Nineteenth Century." Paper delivered at the Tenth Annual Conference, Liberian Studies Association, Boston University, Boston, Massachusetts, April 6–8, 1978.

Taylor, Arnold. "The Involvement of Black Americans in the [Liberian] Forced Labor Controversy, 1929–1935." *Proceedings of the Conference on Afro-Americans and Africans: Historical and Political Linkages, June 13–14, 1974.* Washington, D.C.: Howard University, 1974.

Tonkin, Elizabeth. "Producers in Jlao [Sasstown]." Paper delivered in absentia at the Ninth Annual Conference, Liberian Studies Association, Macomb, Illinois, April, 1977.

UNPUBLISHED DISSERTATIONS AND THESES

Akpan, M. B. "The African Policy of the Liberian Settlers 1841–1932: A Study of the 'Native' Policy of a Non-Colonial Power in Africa." Ph.D. dissertation, Ibadan University, 1968.

Beecher, Lloyd N. "The State Department and Liberia, 1908–1941: A Heterogeneous Record." Ph.D. dissertation, University of Georgia, 1971.

Bodie, Charles A. "The Images of Africa in the Black American Press, 1890–1930." Ph.D. dissertation, Indiana University, 1975.

Chalk, Frank. "The United States and the International Struggle for Rubber, 1914–1941." Ph.D. dissertation, University of Wisconsin, 1970.

Chaudhuri, Jyotirmoy P. "British Policy Towards Liberia, 1912–1939." Ph.D. dissertation, University of Birmingham, 1975.

Cole, Johnetta Betsch. "Traditional and Wage-Earning Labor Among Tribal Liberians." Ph.D. dissertation, Northwestern University, 1967.

Cole, Robert Eugene. "The Liberian Elite as a Barrier to Economic Development." Ph.D. dissertation, Northwestern University, 1967.

Forderhase, Nancy. "The Plans That Failed: The United States and Liberia, 1920–1935." Ph.D. dissertation, University of Missouri, 1971.

Guannu, Joseph. "Liberia and the League of Nations." Ph.D. dissertation, Fordham University, 1972.

Jones, Hanna Abeodu Bowen. "The Struggle for Political and Cultural Unification in Liberia, 1847–1930." Ph.D. dissertation, Northwestern University, 1962.

Martin, Jane Jackson. "The Dual Legacy: Government Authority and Mission Influence Among the Glebo of Eastern Liberia 1834–1910." Ph.D. dissertation, Boston University, 1968.

Mitchell, John Payne. "America's Liberian Policy." Thesis, University of Chicago, 1955.

Norris, Parthenia. "The United States and Liberia: The Slavery Crisis, 1929–1935." Ph.D. dissertation, Indiana University, 1961.

INTERVIEW

Interview with Edward Barleycorn, negotiator of the 1928 labor agreement, Santa Isabel (now Malabo), Republic of Equatorial Guinea, March 2, 1970.

Index

About the Author

I. K. Sundiata is an Assistant Professor of History at the University of Illinois at Chicago Circle. He has also taught at Rutgers University and Northwestern University, where he received his Ph.D. in 1972.

In 1965 he served as a summer intern in the Foreign Affairs Scholars Program of the State Department, a program designed to recruit young blacks into the foreign service. Since then he has done research in both Equatorial Guinea and Liberia, and has received Woodrow Wilson and Fulbright-Hays awards. His articles have appeared in *Présence Africaine, Liberator, Africa Report, Journal of Negro History, Journal of African History,* and *Journal of Ethnic Studies.*